FREE AND FULFILLED

FREE AND FULFILLED

Victorious Christian Living in the Twenty-first Century

ROBERTSON MCQUILKIN

General Editor

THOMAS NELSON PUBLISHERS

Nashville • Atlanta • London • Vancouver

Published in Nashville, Tennessee, by Thomas Nelson, Inc., Publishers, and distributed in Canada by Word Communications, Ltd., Richmond, British Columbia, and in the United Kingdom by Word (UK), Ltd., Milton Keynes, England.

Unless otherwise noted, all Scripture quotations are from the NEW KING JAMES VERSION of the Bible, © 1979, 1980, 1982 by Thomas Nelson, Inc., Publishers.

Scripture quotations noted NASB are taken from THE NEW AMERICAN STANDARD BIBLE ®. Copyright © The Lockman Foundation 1960, 1962, 1963, 1968, 1971, 1972, 1973, 1975, 1977. Used by permission.

Scripture quotations noted NIV are taken from the HOLY BIBLE, NEW INTERNATIONAL VERSION ®. Copyright © 1973, 1978, 1984 by International Bible Society. Used by permission of Zondervan Bible Publishing House. All rights reserved.

The "NIV" and "New International Version" trademarks are registered in the United States Patent and Trademark Office by International Bible Society. Use of either trademark requires the permission of International Bible Society.

Scripture quotations noted J. B. PHILLIPS are from J. B. Phillips: THE NEW TESTAMENT IN MODERN ENGLISH, Revised Edition. Copyright © J. B. Phillips 1958, 1960, 1972. Used by permission of Macmillan Publishing Co., Inc.

Scripture Quotations noted KJV are from the KING JAMES VERSION.

Library of Congress Cataloging-in-Publication Data

Free and fulfilled : victorious Christians living in the twenty-first century / compiled by Robertson McQuilkin.
    p. cm.
  Inclides bibliographical references.
  ISBN 0-7825-7556-8 (hc)
  1. Christian life.   2. Self-realization—Religious aspects—Christianity.
I. McQuilkin, J. Robertson, 1927- .
BV4598.2.74   1997
248.4—dc21
                                    96-50234
                                        CIP

Printed in the United States of America

1 2 3 4 5 6 BVG 02 01 00 99 98 97

Dedication

Published in celebration
of the 75th anniversary of the founding of
Columbia International University.
This volume is dedicated
to the thousands of Alumni
serving around the world
and to the faculty and staff
who helped prepare them to
"know Him and to make Him known."

Contents

Introduction

Victory is a grand old *word* that has fallen on bad times. To late twentieth-century ears, "victory," when used of the spiritual life, may sound triumphalistic, even militaristic—not something we should promote as an ideal Christian experience, especially since hope of sustained holiness has grown dim anyway. It's not possible anymore, if it ever was, especially not for adult children of a dysfunctional family heritage. And even if it were possible, we're not so sure we want it. Better to be honest and admit we're just ordinary mortals with our daily quota of disappointments and failures.

So if we want to hold out hope for something more than ordinary, perhaps we should speak of freedom and fulfillment. There's something to aim for in the twenty-first century! And, in a way, that's what this book is all about. But we have to get biblical definitions first. Freedom is not license to do what I please, but power to do what I ought. Can I really get enough power to win out over the world of stuff, the fun of the flesh, and the pride of the devil? This book answers the question with a resounding yes! The new me, with all my new potentialities, has the power, not to be perfect, but to consistently overcome temptation and to grow toward greater and greater similarity to Jesus (2 Peter 1:3–8). And as if that were not enough, I have Almighty God in residence to empower me (Eph. 3:16–20).

Freedom—power to be all I was meant to be. This book describes such a freedom, not the absolute freedom to pursue personal self-fulfillment, which twentieth-century worldlings hold to be an inalienable right. Jesus says that's a sure formula for self-destruction. We have a better hope! Free at last—from the dark cloud of guilt for sins past, from the dominating control of a sinful disposition, and from apprehension or fear about the future. Free!

And then there's fulfillment. Of course, there's nothing wrong with things, fun, and recognition—God designed us to have, to enjoy, and to be of significance. Actually, these are a part of His own being. The problem is that we try to *fill up* on one or more of them, to find happiness and fulfillment primarily in successful work that people recognize, cordial relationships with "significant others," a fine home or automobile, financial security, sex, food, a hobby. To try to fill up on one of these is inherently destructive for two reasons. One, you can't fill up on those—they will never fill you more than partially or momentarily. Second, it displaces the One we were designed to fill up on. God's design was to have us fill up on Him as the grand possession, the ultimate pleasure, our true identity. Only then will we be filled full. And then no matter what things, enjoyment, or approval we feel is lacking, we can still be full! This book maps out the way to fulfillment.

If freedom and fulfillment are what we're after, why is this book so full of the old-fashioned word *victory*? For two reasons:

- the Bible uses it, which would be reason enough, and
- this book celebrates the 75th anniversary of Columbia International University, which has become the principal heir of a movement called the "Victorious Life Testimony."

We aim to trace the history, define the term *victory,* and excite God's people with the glorious resources available to live a Spirit-filled life of victory. Not perfection, not some sort of super-sainthood, but not a life of resignation to defeat and failure, either. In fact, I've called it the "normal Christian life," because it's available to every believer and, indeed, is God's intention for every child of His. Here's the way I once described this life of victory, the normal Christian life:

> Average is not necessarily normal. For example, the average temperature of patients in a hospital may be 100 degrees, but such a temperature is not normal. So it is with the Christian life. The average experience of church members is far different from New Testament norms for the Christian life.
>
> The normal Christian is characterized by loving responses to ingratitude and indifference, even hostility, and is filled with joy in the midst of unhappy circumstances and with peace when everything goes wrong. The normal Christian overcomes in the battle with temptation, consistently obeys the laws of God, and grows in self-control, contentment, humility, and courage. Thought processes are so under the control of the Holy Spirit and instructed by Scripture that the normal Christian authentically reflects the attitudes and behavior of Jesus Christ. God has first place in life, and the welfare of others takes precedence over personal desires. The normal Christian has power not only for godly living but for effective service in the church. Above all, he or she has the joy of constant companionship with the Lord.
>
> But what is the average Christian experience? Many church members typically think and behave very much like morally upright non-Christians. They are decent enough, but there is nothing supernatural about them. Their behavior is quite explainable in terms of heredity, early environment, and pres-ent circumstances. They yield to temptation more often than not, lusting when their body demands it, coveting what they do not have, and taking credit for their accomplishments. The touchstone for their choices is self-interest, and

though they have a love for God and others, it does not control their life. There is little change for the better; in fact,
most church members do not expect much improvement and
are little concerned by that prospect. Scripture is not exciting, prayer is perfunctory, and service in the church demonstrates little touch of the supernatural. Above all, their life
seems to have an empty core, for it does not center around a
constant, personal companionship with the Lord.[1]

This book is filled with powerful expositions of what a
normal victorious life of freedom and fulfillment is, and it
describes how it can be one's daily experience. It also contains
contrasting viewpoints on the Christian life that irenically
probe areas of difference. Some of the essays, like Joni
Eareckson Tada's and John Perkins's, are powerful personal
testimonies; others, like Carl Henry's and Kenneth Kantzer's,
are profound theological discourses. Still others probe the
exciting history of a dynamic movement. You'll find solid biblical studies of the issues involved, but you'll also discover
practical application. Contrast and controversy are here, but
always in a context of positive pursuit of God's highest and
best for Christian living.

Many of these essays are unique contributions to the
ongoing development of a biblical view of sanctification.
Together they are designed to outfit God's people for freedom and fulfillment, victorious Christian living in the twenty-
first century.

---

1. Robertson McQuilkin et al., *Five Views of Sanctification* (Grand Rapids:
Zondervan, 1987), 151–52.

PART ONE

Foundations

In this first section of *Free and Fulfilled: Victorious Christian Living in the Twenty-first Century,* we lay a foundation, historically and theologically, for the rest of the book. Leading church historian Bruce Shelley traces the origins of the movement and two of the chief spokesmen for the movement articulate the basic teaching. Stephen Olford brings the Keswick message, leading us step-by-step in the time-honored approach of helping God's people find "victory." Then, at the end of this section, Stuart Briscoe draws the same message out of the Bible text, providing a contemporary and exciting biblical exposition as a foundation for what is to come. In between, Robertson McQuilkin and Brad Mullen squarely address the two major criticisms of the movement, perfectionism and legalism. There are surprises in store in those chapters for both the accusers and the accused!

It is necessary, in laying the foundation, to be sure of what we do not affirm as well as what we do affirm. You will discover the foundation, laid by different men from different perspectives, to be solid, worthy of the implications and applications that follow in subsequent sections.

1

About the Author

Bruce Shelley is senior professor of Church History, Denver Seminary. He often wonders, he says, how Paul, Augustine, and Luther made it through life without an overhead projector! Though recognized by colleagues and the academic community as a premier church historian, the general public appreciates Shelley as a scholar who writes spritely prose that is readily understood. He has authored or edited more than twenty books and scores of articles in magazines and encyclopedias. His books include *Church History in Plain Language* (Word), and *All the Saints Adore Thee* (Baker). Shelley began his academic studies, following military service, at Columbia Bible College, so he had opportunity to view the Victorious Life from the inside and to learn it under the first president of the institution and leading spokesman for the movement, Robert C. McQuilkin. He and his wife, Mary, have three adult children, two of them in Christian ministry.

About This Chapter

A storyteller who has the special knack of bringing historic figures and musty theological debates to life, Bruce Shelley has provided a masterful story of the origins of the Victorious Life Movement in nineteenth-century Wesleyan and Keswick movements. I know of no summary statement that is at once so comprehensive and authoritative. A couple of things this chapter does not do: though Shelley clearly distinguishes the theology of the movement from Wesleyan teaching, he does not emphasize the more subtle distinctions between the Keswick movement and the Victorious Life Testimony. This is altogether appropriate to his broad-brush review of the historical roots of the movement. The details will become more apparent in chapter 3, "Imperfections." Shelley traces the roots of the movement through 1952. A number of other chapters in the book will bring us to the present.

Roots: Victorious Life Teaching in Historical Perspective

by Bruce L. Shelley

I n a discussion of Christian spirituality I often find my mind drifting to a striking picture of Will Sangster's little book, *The Pure in Heart*. Sangster, let me explain, was a highly respected Methodist pastor in London during the 1940s and 1950s. In his student days he had written an impressive work on holiness in the Wesleyan tradition. So he was both an experienced shepherd and a dedicated scholar.

"Just as man knows the surface of the sea," Sangster writes, "and perhaps a few hundred feet beneath it, but is aware that the ocean is over six miles deep in places, . . . so the devout believer knows that beneath the area of ordered thought there is a vast ocean. He cannot speak . . . with detailed understanding about this subterranean world but he feels its pull, and knows its effect, and enjoys experiences from it that he cannot put into plain words."[1]

What a helpful picture! Whatever else it may have been, the Victorious Life Movement was about the vast unexplored realm of Christian experience. In this sense, any Christian's "victory" is beyond history. The human mind is simply unable to fathom the hidden depth of soul and spirit. We are left to tracing its effect and feeling its pull.

Fortunately its effects can be easily traced, and in that tracing we can feel its pull. But the Victorious Life Movement is no small or aberrant teaching. In tracing the history of the movement, we will soon discover that it was in the evangelical mainstream, shaped by modern revivals in Great Britain and North America. Dwight L. Moody's influence in the 1880s and 1890s is the most obvious symbol of this identity. But Victorious Life Conferences, unlike most revivals, were not directly evangelistic. "Victory" was all about personal holiness, so the Victorious Life Movement fits more appropriately in the evangelical holiness tradition. Over the years, both Wesleyans and Calvinists first approved, then disapproved, the "victory" message. The movement is also centrally evangelical in this sense.

Looking back over a century and a half of its history, we can find a rather typical experience of "victory" in 1920 at Columbia, South Carolina. A weeklong Victorious Life Conference, under the leadership of Robert C. McQuilkin from Philadelphia, was in progress at the old six-storied YMCA building.

On the third day of the meetings, McQuilkin was scheduled to speak at Chicora College for Women. Alleene, a young student at the school that day, later described her experience: "When I awoke on the morning of February third, 1920, I did not know that this was to be the greatest day of my life—the day I would begin to live!"

When the chapel bell rang, Alleene assumed she was on her way to another ordinary morning. But this day proved extraordinary. As she sauntered into the auditorium where about two hundred other young women were seated, the atmosphere seemed charged with something new.

As McQuilkin told the young women how radically their lives could change if they "surrendered completely" to Jesus, Alleene had her own experience of "victory." During McQuilkin's talk she reasoned: "If what he says is true, then

I've been wrong for years—why did no one tell me this before? I have been worried ever since I can remember . . . If this man is right, then I *must* have what *he* has at any cost!"

During a free hour after chapel, Alleene, soon to be known in the movement as Alleene Spivey Hehl, went to her room, dropped to her knees by her bed, and prayed: "Dear Lord, I know that if what this man said is true, then I have sinned—for I worry and fret over everything. I thought every Christian had to worry and had to try hard to be good. I want what that person has—the life of Christ. He said to surrender and trust the Savior, and whatever that means, I want to do it right now, and thank Thee, Jesus."

According to her testimony, an indescribable peace instantly flooded into Alleene's soul. "Now for the first time in my life, I knew beyond a shadow of a doubt that I was a child of God. I had felt assurance that I belonged to my Savior. I couldn't wait to write my family and tell them of my experience."[2]

In his masterful history, *Fundamentalism and American Culture,* George Marsden suggests that the Victorious Life Movement—or the Keswick Conventions, as they were called in Great Britain—reflected a middle-class clientele from the established denominations, especially those in the Reformed tradition, led by Baptists, Presbyterians, and Congregationalists. Unlike earlier, more social-minded Wesleyan holiness leaders, Keswick speakers tended to emphasize *personal* joy, peace, and "victory," which resulted in a deeper devotional life and zeal for foreign missions.

Marsden's description is not intended to dismiss all questions of theology. But his "middle-class clientele" insight helps to explain what the movement meant by "victory." Consider the fact that Alleene and her close friends came from southern Presbyterian circles and that her troubling sin was "worry."

Today, seventy-five years after the Columbia meetings, we also know that the Victorious Life Movement was a tributary to a much wider stream of Christian holiness movements. Before the "victory" message spread throughout North America and the world's mission fields, there were Keswick Conventions in Great Britain. And before Keswick there was John Wesley with his "perfection" message.

Wesleyan Holiness

The passion for holiness in Protestant Christianity can be traced back at least as far as Oxford University and the little giant of Methodism, John Wesley. During his student days in the 1720s, Wesley had a conversion experience that set the course of his life in the pursuit of holiness. Years later, in "The Scripture Way of Salvation," Great Britain's greatest revivalist explained to thousands of Methodists that salvation consists of two stages in the Christian life, which we call justification and sanctification. At the same time that we are justified, he wrote, sanctification begins. And in that instant we are "born of the Spirit" or inwardly renewed by the power of God and we feel "the love of God shed abroad in our heart by the Holy Ghost."

At first, said Wesley, Christian believers tend to imagine that all sin is gone, but we soon realize that sin is only suspended, not destroyed. Before long we discover two basic tendencies within us. As our sanctification gradually develops we are enabled by the Spirit to become "more and more dead to sin," and "more and more alive to God"; thus we wait for entire sanctification, "for a full salvation from all our sins . . . or perfect love."

It is clear that Wesley sees sanctification as a process through which the believer is progressively delivered from sin. He also teaches, however, that this process culminates in a second "work of grace" identified as "entire sanctification." He defines this as "pure and disinterested love." He apparently believed that a believer could progress in love until self-interest virtually vanishes. This too is extremely important for a believer, because if one is not perfected in love, one is not "ripe for glory."

By 1763 the great revivalist was ready to affirm, on the basis of the testimony of many witnesses, that Christian perfection was a second, definite, and instantaneous work of grace that a believer could receive in this life by faith. While he continued to teach that the gift was both preceded and followed by growth in holiness, *perfection* itself also made it possible for Christians to live above all *known* sin.

This perfection, however, is limited. It is not a finished state, but a moment-by-moment reliance on God's grace so that love fills the heart and life. It does not exclude ignorance, error, infirmities, or temptation. It is "sinless" only in Wesley's sense of sin as a voluntary transgression of a *known* law of God. In other words, it is holiness of intention and motive. It is the fulfillment of faith's desire to love God through the believer's conscious will and deliberate acts.

In nineteenth-century America, Wesleyan holiness movements became a part of the general frenzy for revivals and tended to stress the instantaneous experience more than the gradual process. Many American Wesleyans fell under the influence of the "new measures" revivalism of Charles Grandison Finney. They were often impelled too by the widespread conviction that the main bodies of institutional Methodism were tragically departing from Wesley's holiness doctrine. As a result, camp meetings and new denominations by the scores arose after the Civil War to reaffirm Wesley's message and re-create the "second blessing" experience.

There were shades of perfectionism in scores of Wesleyan movements and denominations, but those that strove to follow Wesley's doctrine faithfully stressed three main points: (1) Sanctification or holiness is a work of grace that liberates the believers from inbred or original sin. The popular label for this doctrine was *eradication*. (2) Holiness is a distinct experience separate from and subsequent to justification or conversion, hence a *second blessing*. (3) This blessing is *instantaneous*, though there may be growth prior to and subsequent to the experience. Revivalists used a variety of terms to identify the "deeper work" beyond conversion, including *entire sanctification, Christian perfection, the higher Christian life,* and *full salvation*.

The Birth of Keswick

"Victorious Life" speakers first appeared during the exciting 1860s and 1870s, when the holiness message spread like a prairie wildfire. This fire for God often brought Wesleyan and something-other-than Wesleyan speakers together on the same platform. As a result the "victory" speakers were forced to explain what they meant by "surrender."

In Great Britain the victory message came to be called "Keswick" after a town about twenty-five miles from Carlisle in the beautiful Lakes Region of northwest England. It became the home for inspirational summer conferences—held to this day—and center for the new holiness message stressing surrender and faith. The early traces of Keswick-style holiness seem to lie in the writing and speaking ministries of two American couples who sounded at times like Wesleyans: Mr. and Mrs. William E. Boardman and Mr. and Mrs. Robert Pearsall Smith.

Boardman and his wife found "rest of heart in Jesus for sanctification" after reading testimonies by Charles Finney and Asa Mahan, the influential holiness teacher at Oberlin College. Boardman published his *The Higher Christian Life* in 1859 and immediately established his reputation as a holiness speaker. In only a few years the Smiths also entered the holy life. Hanna Whitall Smith testified that before she discovered "victory" over sin, she had known herself to be a child of God but was unable to act like one. She found her "second blessing" through a Methodist dressmaker. When she published her widely popular *The Christian's Secret to the Happy Life* in 1875, she was already a well-known holiness speaker.

The most significant meetings for Boardman and the Smiths came on the heels of Dwight L. Moody's 1873 campaign in England. First, they spoke for a series of breakfasts in London designed to promote holiness. In the sunshine of Moody's reputation, twenty-four hundred preachers heard the Americans witness to "the higher Christian life." Second, in July 1874, at a country estate called Broadlands, about one hundred clergy and Cambridge University students heard them describe their experiences of "victory." And, finally, later that summer an Oxford meeting devoted to "Scriptural Holiness" drew about a thousand. Asa Mahan, the influential American Wesleyan, preached the first sermon, but Pearsall Smith and Boardman were also prominent participants.[3]

This Oxford gathering proved to be the cradle of Keswick. Among those attending was Canon T. D. Harford-Battersby, vicar of Keswick. The inspiration of the Oxford meetings compelled the vicar to arrange for an open-air conference in his parish the next year. This 1875 convention proved to be the first of thousands of Keswick-style gatherings that soon circled the earth.

In some respects the early Keswick Conventions were British cousins to American camp meetings. They provided a platform for effective speakers to open their Bibles and call attendees to "the higher Christian life." But in other respects Keswick was different. The speakers were mostly Calvinist or Church of England ministers who provided the inspiration. In this "middle-class clientele" the shirtsleeve enthusiasm of the camp meeting gave way to a more thoughtful atmosphere focused on the Bible lesson.

And what about "the Keswick message"? Some thought it a sedate version of Wesleyan holiness, while others accepted it as a personalized version of traditional sanctification in the Reformed tradition. The vital issue was not so much the *aim* of sanctification as the *means*. H. W. Webb-Peploe, one of the early Keswick leaders, once contrasted the Keswick message with the traditional Evangelical-Reformed teaching. The old Evangelical teaching, he said, went something like this: "I was perfectly justified in a moment and had at that moment a standing before God. But the moment that sanctification commenced, I had to go on, struggle and strive and call in the aid of the Holy Ghost—which too often I forgot to do."[4]

Against this common evangelical experience Keswick set a doctrine of Christ the Victor. "It does not depend on wearisome struggle," said Bishop Handley Moule of Durham, "but on God's power to take the consecrated soul and to keep him . . . Keswick stands distinctively for this: Christ our righteousness, upon Calvary, received by faith, is also Christ our holiness, in the heart that submits to Him and relies upon Him."

The entrance into the experience of "victory" was a profound, personal surrender to Christ. Keswick speakers often urged their listeners to yield and trust in an instant. The convention's course was directed to that end. And many, like Alleene, testified to practical deliverance from the power of some besetting sin. Some even described their experience as a "second conversion," which sounded, to be sure, like the entire sanctification doctrine of Wesleyan teachers.

The call to "total surrender" became so common that Bishop Moule, the theologian of the movement, warned against limiting "victory" to a crisis. A crisis, he said, might be the beginning of a deeper life for many, but not for all. Sanctification is not complete in an instant but should be a progress cultivated by prayer, Scripture, and worship.

Keswick teachers also tried to guard against the suggestion that the act of surrender meant the creation of a "clean heart" spiritually different from the new life received the moment a believer receives "life from above." Victory, they said, did *not* mean the disappearance of what Paul called the "flesh" or "the old man."

Still, Keswick speakers only slowly made clear that what they called "surrender" was something quite different from the Wesleyan doctrines of "second blessing" and "entire sanctification." The problem persisted, sometimes in vivid shades, in the United States at D. L. Moody's Northfield Conferences.

Moody and Northfield

Northfield, Massachusetts, was Moody's home, so it was a natural choice for the summer conferences he started in 1880. He had dreams of providing laypersons inspirational Bible teaching and opportunities for spiritual renewal. While Moody apparently intended to provide a variety of speakers, certain themes came to dominate the meetings. Three of these were extremely significant for the Victorious Life Movement in America: First, Moody's close contact with Keswick speakers in England guaranteed a regular emphasis on the power of the Holy Spirit in the sanctified life. Second, his association with premillennial speakers who participated in Niagara, and other Bible conferences like it, meant premillennialism appeared rather often at the conferences. And, finally, in an 1886 conference approximately one hundred students surrendered their lives for Christian service on some foreign mission field. This event gave birth in a few years to the widely influential Student Volunteer Movement. Thus, the subsequent alliance of the Victorious Life Movement, the student foreign missions movement, and the premillennial movement in Bible schools was forecast by the Northfield platform.

This merging of traditions was not always smooth. In 1891, for example, when a Keswick-style speaker, British Baptist pastor F. B. Meyer, was invited to Northfield, his message provoked quite a reaction from several American premillennialists. This "Old Guard," as Moody called them, caucused and sent a representative to Moody to protest against the new heresy. A. T. Pierson, W. J. Erdman, C. I. Scofield, George C. Needham, and others at first regarded the

Keswick emphasis as "the fancied perfection taught through fancied interpretations" of the Bible.[5]

Gradually, however, the antagonism subsided as the suggestions of eradication faded from Keswick teaching and the emphasis upon the power of the Spirit for witness and world missions emerged. Meyer returned to Northfield five times and Andrew Murray, H. W. Webb-Peploe, and G. Campbell Morgan—all Keswick speakers—appeared after 1894. In addition, the influence of such premillennialists as R. A. Torrey and A. J. Gordon spread the idea of a second work of the Spirit in the believer.

By the 1890s the "life of faith" taught at Keswick and the various Victorious Life Conferences in America had become the very heartbeat of the growing faith-missions movement. The "total surrender" of one's life to God became basic to the "victory" message and offered "faith" missionaries the courage they needed to undertake the risks of entering some "pioneer" mission field. "Surrendering" all claims to one's life emerged as a major recruiting theme in the growing, premillennial missionary societies, and responding to the missionary call became for many the supreme sign of entrance into victory over sin.

After "giving her life to Jesus" at the Keswick, New Jersey, summer conference in 1925 and entering into "victory," collegian Betty Scott wrote her parents that she was "willing to be an old-maid missionary, . . . all my life, if God wants me to." Her spirit was rather typical.[6]

Trumbull and McQuilkin

Another source of the Victorious Life experience came from Charles G. Trumbull, the editor of the widely circulated *Sunday School Times*. Trumbull was converted to Keswick sanctification in 1910 and threw himself immediately into the "victory" cause. He was a prize example of Marsden's "middle-class clientele" characterization of the movement. He had graduated from Yale in 1893 and went to work for his father, Henry Clay Trumbull, a widely recognized leader in the Sunday school movement as editor of the *Sunday School Times.*

After his father's death in 1903, Charles assumed the editorship and soon turned his editorial energies to promoting the Victorious Life message. When the subscription list of the *Times* passed the 100,000 figure in the 1920s, it was obvious that "victory" had become a major element in the conservative-evangelical message.

Trumbull also organized the Victorious Life Testimony, which conducted summer conferences at a variety of locations to promote the "victory" message, and enlisted a young assistant, Robert C. McQuilkin. Under McQuilkin's leadership the first American Keswick Conference met in 1913 at the United Presbyterian Church in Oxford, Pennsylvania, with about seventy-five attending. Henry W. Frost, the home director of the China Inland Mission, and W. H. Griffith-Thomas, an Anglican who had come to North America in 1910 to teach at Wycliffe College, Toronto, were the main speakers.

The next year the assembly drew 150 delegates to Princeton, New Jersey, where the conferences continued to be held through 1918. In 1919 they moved to Stonybrook, Long Island, and remained there until making Keswick Grove, New Jersey, their permanent home in 1923.

Within the major Protestant denominations, the 1920s were marked by the fundamentalist-modernist conflict. As more and more fundamentalists separated from the traditionally evangelical denominations, they tended to create "faith-missions" and Bible schools as functional substitutes for the denominational agencies they left behind when they turned their backs on theological liberalism. The Victorious Life message came to shape the doctrine and personal holiness of many students in these schools. Moody Bible Institute, Nyack College, and Prairie Bible Institute were leaders of scores of smaller schools in the United States and Canada.

Robert McQuilkin, however, who made such an impression on Alleene Spivey Hehl at the Columbia meetings in 1920, is probably the best personification of this spread of the "victory" message in these schools. He was a zealous advocate of "victory" in the pages of the *Times* and a frequent speaker at Victorious Life Conferences. When Trumbull was unable to accept an invitation to hold the Bible conference at Columbia in 1920, he sent McQuilkin instead.

The young speaker returned to the southern city again and again until, in 1923, he resigned from the *Times* and announced the opening of Columbia Bible School. Six years later he inaugurated a four-year Bible college program and changed the name to Columbia Bible College. Today it is known as Columbia International University.[7]

From 1923 until 1952 when he died, McQuilkin preached Victorious Living to successive generations of students and conference delegates at the college. In addition, while maintaining a heavy schedule of classes and administrative responsibilities, he found time each summer for twenty-five years to speak to two conferences each season at America's Keswick Conference in New Jersey, where speakers over the years have tried to speak of the pull they felt from that "vast ocean beneath all our ordered thoughts."

Notes

1. W. E. Sangster, *The Pure in Heart* (New York: Abington, N.D.), p. 4.
2. The story is from Alleene Spivey Hehl, *This Is the Victory* (Columbia, S.C., Wentworth Printing Co., 1973), 31–35.
3. For most of the facts about Keswick, see Stephen Barabas, *So Great Salvation* (London: Marshall, Morgan, & Scott, 1952).
4. For these quotations see John C. Pollock, *The Keswick Story* (Chicago: Moody Press, 1964), 74–76.
5. See William M. Runyan, *Dr. Gray at Moody Bible Institute* (New York: Oxford University Press, 1935), 5–6.
6. See Joel A. Carpenter and Wilbert R. Shenk, eds., *Earthen Vessels: American Evangelicals and Foreign Missions*, 1880–1980 (Grand Rapids: Eerdmans, 1990), 118–20.
7. The best available biography of McQuilkin is by Marguerite McQuilkin, *Always in Triumph* (Westwood, N.J.: Revell, 1956).

About the Author

The name Steven Olford is almost synonymous with "Keswick" in the United States. During the last half of the twentieth century Olford has been a leading spokesman for the message of victorious Christian living, appearing in major conventions across the land. Africa-born son of missionaries, the Britisher gained worldwide renown as a preacher when pastor of Duke Street Baptist Church in Richmond, Surrey, England (1953–59). Later moving to America to pastor Calvary Baptist Church in New York City, Olford has not only preached on Keswick platforms and evangelistic crusades around the world, he has written twenty-two books on the victorious life, revival, preaching, and Bible exposition. Today Olford is senior lecturer of the Stephen Olford Center for Biblical Preaching in Memphis, Tennessee. And there is a strong Columbia connection: Olford served for many years on the board of trustees of Columbia International University and for a time as codirector of Columbia's conference center, Ben Lippen.

About This Chapter

Keswick does not have a doctrinal statement because it is more a movement, a method, an approach to the Christian life. Noted for a set order of proclaiming the message of "practical holiness," Keswick preachers speak to each of five specific themes on the five consecutive days of the convention. In this chapter Olford proclaims the five-step path to victory. This chapter is a masterful statement of the message of Keswick, and that message is the chief overlap with the Victorious Life Testimony, the American movement from which the themes of *Free and Fulfilled* have come. Though there are differences between the two movements, as we shall see in subsequent chapters, on this core message they are identical. Don't try to fast-forward this chapter. Olford has condensed the message of victory in Christ so skillfully that every line is significant for understanding the whole. Read it slowly, absorbing what will be the biblical foundation for the rest of the book.

2

The Message of Keswick: Preaching the Victorious Life

by Stephen F. Olford

My first exposure to the message of the victorious life was at the Keswick Convention, which is held each year in the beautiful lakeland district of England. For more than 120 years "scriptural holiness" has been proclaimed to thousands of Christians from all over the world. What initially impressed me was the high level of biblical exposition in what was called "The Bible Readings" (usually the exposition of an epistle or a comparable passage of Scripture each morning of the week), as well as the individual messages that followed a specific sequence of progressive teaching on God's "so great salvation."

Some of the distinguished expositors who ministered at Keswick over the years were Evan H. Hopkins, H. W. Webb-Peploe, J. Elder Cumming, Andrew Murray, H. C. G. Moule, F. B. Meyer, J. Hudson Taylor, A. T. Pierson, G. Campbell Morgan, W. H. Griffith Thomas, J. Stuart Holden, W. Y. Fullerton, R. A. Torrey, W. Graham Scroggie, Donald G. Barnhouse, Paul S. Rees, E. M. Blaiklock, George B. Duncan, John R. W. Stott, and others.

This preamble is intended to make an important point. The Victorious Life Movement is based on sound biblical teaching. It is not the alleged "text out of context" approach to truth that many of our uninformed critics and opponents would have us believe. As Robert B. Laurin rightly observes:

> *Victory is above all a religiously conditioned concept in Scripture*. This is rooted in the basic biblical principle that God is just, punishing sin and rewarding righteousness (cf. Deut. 11:26–28). . . . In the OT victory is almost exclusively over external foes and issues in physical peace and security (cf. Josh. 1:15; Jer. 23:6; Ps. 69:14). But in the NT victory is expressed mainly in terms of spiritual forces and blessings. It is not triumph over social or economic difficulties that is the concern of the NT; it is mastery over temptation and the powers of evil. To be sure, the ultimate issue of this age will be Christ's victory over physical forces (Rev. 5:5; 6:2) and over Satan himself (Rev. 19:11–20:3). In this the Christian will share (Rev. 3:21). But the NT gives greater emphasis to a victory that the Christian can enjoy in his present daily life, a victory over the enticements and assaults of the world. This is made possible when one appropriates by faith the power of Christ's victory on the cross (1 John 5:4–5; John 16:33; Rom. 8:37; Eph. 6:10), which is made manifest through Christ's indwelling presence (1 John 4:4), and when the word of God rules in one's life (1 John 2:14). Thus victory is both present and eschatological. It is now that a Christian enters into the power and blessings of a triumph yet to find its complete realization in the future (cf. 1 Cor. 15:24–28, 54–57).[1]

If it be asked: "What are the salient truths that best define the message on victorious living in Christ?" the answer is simple. It is a sequence of teaching that can be traced in any one of Paul's epistles on normal Christian living. Those who have attended the Keswick Conventions around the world, or have read the books and literature on the Victorious Life Movement in the U.S.A., will be familiar with the five main emphases:

Sin

"My little children, these things I write to you,
so that you may not sin." (Read 1 John 1:5–2:2.)

Right from the start it is imperative that we tell believers in Christ that it is possible for a Christian to sin. Confusion and disappointment would be obviated, to a large extent, if we expounded clearly what John tells us in these verses. He urges us to recognize sin in our lives—"I write to you, so that you may not sin" (1 John 2:1). The apostle would never make that statement if there were such a state as sinless perfection this side of heaven. Study carefully verses 6, 8, and 10, and observe that failure to walk in the light of openness and obedience to God leads to disobedience—"If we say that we have fellowship with Him, and walk in darkness, we lie and do not practice the truth" (1 John 1:6). That, in turn, leads to deceitfulness—"If we say that we have no sin, we deceive ourselves, and the truth is not in us" (1 John 1:8). Tragically and inexorably, there follows defiance—"If we say that we have not sinned, we make Him a liar, and His word is not in us" (1 John 1:10). These three stages in moral breakdown are possible in your heart and mine. So it is important to recognize sin in our lives.

But then we are to redress sin in our lives—"If we confess our sins, He is faithful and just to forgive us our sins and to cleanse us from all unrighteousness" (1 John 1:9). Redressing sin in our lives is not an excuse to sin; it is rather God's way of providing forgiveness and cleansing, if and when we do sin. When an ocean liner launches out on her voyage, she takes lifeboats with her—not in order that the ship might sink, but in case she does sink! Confession means that we tell God. Name your sins and nail them to the cross, in the presence of God; then trust God, for "He is faithful and just to forgive us our sins and to cleanse us from all unrighteousness" (1 John 1:9); and, most important, thank God. You will never know "the smile of God's forgiveness" until you say "thank you." There is no better evidence of forgiveness and victory than a thankful heart.

Of course, every day we are to resist sin in our lives—"My little children, these things I write to you, so that you may not sin. And if anyone sins, we have an Advocate with the Father, Jesus Christ the righteous. And He Himself is the propitiation for our sins, and not for ours only but also for the whole world" (1 John 2:1–2). With the possibility of sinning there is the power of enabling. Christ is not only the Propitiation (or Sacrifice) for our sins, but He is also our Advocate (or Enabler) who represents us before God. He is also our perfect Pattern—"Jesus Christ the righteous" (1 John 2:1). To experience Christ as our Sacrifice, our Strength, and our Standard, we must "walk in the light as He is in the light" (1 John 1:7). Then—and only then—can we have fellowship with God and with one another. Then—and only then—will we prove the cleansing and conquering blood of Jesus Christ, God's Son (1 John 1:7).

It has been rightly said: "Every heresy . . . has [had] its roots in defective views of sin. What we think of the Atonement depends greatly upon what we think of the evil which made that Atonement necessary. . . . If we would rise towards a full appreciation of the value of the infinite sacrifice [of our wonderful Savior], we must seek to understand, as perfectly as possible, the true nature of sin."[2]

Sanctification

"You are in Christ Jesus, who became for us wisdom from God—and . . . sanctification." (Read 1 Cor. 1:30; 2 Cor. 7:1.)

If we have truly learned how to recognize, redress, and resist sin in our lives, there is no other path to tread than that of progressive sanctification. In both Old and New Testaments, the basic idea of sanctification is to set apart someone or something for God's purpose alone. It is separation from all that is unholy.

First of all, we must acknowledge that sanctification is a gift—"You are in Christ Jesus, who became for us . . . sanctification" (1 Cor. 1:30). Those words, "You are in Christ Jesus" mean a saving union with Christ (John 15:1–7; Rom. 5:12–21; 1 Cor. 1:2). We cannot be "in Christ" without Christ being in us (Gal. 2:20). So sanctification is the gift of Christ to us and in us by the Holy Spirit. Paul links sanctification with the gift of the Holy Spirit—"This is the will of God, your sanctification . . . who has also given us His Holy Spirit" (1 Thess. 4:3–8). So to become holy we must possess the "Holy One." This incoming of the "Holy One" takes place at conversion.

But sanctification is more than a gift. Sanctification is a growth—"Let us cleanse ourselves from all filthiness of the flesh and spirit, perfecting holiness in the fear of God" (2 Cor. 7:1); and again: "Pursue . . . holiness, without which no one will see the Lord" (Heb. 12:14). "This work of sanctification is progressive, and admits of degrees. One may be more sanctified and more holy than another, [whose heart is] truly sanctified and truly holy. It is begun at once, and carried on gradually."[3]

In simple terms, this process of sanctification comes through a daily openness to the Lord—"We all, with unveiled face, beholding as in a mirror the glory of the Lord, are being transformed into the same image from glory to glory, just as by the Spirit of the Lord" (2 Cor. 3:18). Anything that dims our vision of the glory of the Lord, as mirrored in the Scriptures, we must redress and reject. As we gaze into that mirror, we are conformed into the image of Christ by the power of the Spirit. With that openness there must be a daily obedience to the Word. Jesus prayed, "Sanctify them by Your truth. Your word is truth" (John 17:17). After speaking to His disciples in the Upper Room, Jesus could declare, "You are already clean because of the word which I have spoken to you" (John 15:3). For the Word of God to have a similar impact on our lives, we must develop a daily habit to read, learn, and inwardly digest the Word. It is a devotional discipline that cannot be substituted by anything else or anything less.

Ultimately, sanctification is a goal—"By that will we have been sanctified through the offering of the body of Jesus Christ once for all. . . . By one offering He [the Lord Jesus] has perfected forever those who are being sanctified" (Heb. 10:10, 14). Sanctification is both positional and conditional. First, it is positional: "We have been sanctified through the offering of the body of Jesus Christ once for all" (Heb. 10:10). It matters immensely that this offering, once made, availed for all people, for all time. As Dr. Leon Morris observes, "This is the distinctive doctrine of Christianity."[4] What is positional is also conditional. By that same "one offering [Christ] has perfected forever those who are being sanctified" (Heb. 10:14). In that statement are the twin ideas of progressive sanctification and "perfected" sanctification (see 1 John 3:2–3).

With this truth on sanctification before us, let us "pursue [like a hunter bearing down on his prey] . . . holiness, without which no one will see the Lord" (Heb. 12:14).

Surrender

"Present your bodies a living sacrifice, holy, acceptable to God." (Read Rom. 12:1–2.)

In the previous chapters of this epistle (Romans), Paul has defined, declared, and defended his gospel. In the light of this, he now urges his readers to surrender their all to the God of all mercies. This directive is clearly detailed: First, there is the obligation to surrender—"I beseech you therefore, brethren, by the mercies of God" (Rom. 12:1). True gratitude requires expression. Love, truly appreciated, must be reciprocated. There is no more serious sin than unrequited love. With Isaac Watts we need to say: "Love so amazing, so divine, / Demands my soul, my life, my all."

Second, there is the order of surrender—"Present your bodies a living sacrifice, holy, acceptable to God" (Rom. 12:1). We are to "present" our bodies as "a living sacrifice, holy, acceptable to God," and there is nothing superficial about this. The sacrifice is to be "living" (spiritually alive, Rom. 6:13), in complete contrast to the animal sacrifices of the Old Testament. The sacrifice is to be "living," in the sense that it is "constant" (W. E. Vine).[5] Like the priest of old, we are to maintain the sacrifice on the altar with the fleshhooks of "determination and discipline" until it is wholly consumed; that is, until Jesus comes or calls. If and when we are tempted to "climb down" from that altar we must apply the fleshhooks (Ex. 27:3). Then the body is to be "a . . . holy [sacrifice]" (Rom. 12:1). When God says "a . . . holy [sacrifice]," He asks for a sacrifice that has been initially cleansed by the blood of Christ and is being cleansed by the daily application of the Word of God in the power of the Spirit (see Mal. 1:8). Again, the body has to be a pleasing sacrifice—"acceptable to God." All we do "in the body" must be pleasing to God. This calls for a life of unbroken fellowship with the Lord.

Third, there is the object in surrender. "Do not be conformed to this world, but be transformed by the renewing of your mind, that you may prove what is that good and acceptable and perfect will of God" (Rom. 12:2). The object is twofold, namely, the transformation and maturation of our lives. The transformation takes place while we maintain the attitude of yieldedness. Instead of being "conformed to this world" or "age" (controlled by the powers of darkness), we are changed by the Spirit of the Lord (2 Cor. 3:18) until Christ is revealed in all we say and do.

The maturation takes place by proving and approving the "good and acceptable and perfect will of God" (Rom. 12:2). The will of God is good because it is "beneficial in its effect. It is acceptable [because it is] well-pleasing in God's sight. It is perfect [because it is] conditioned by maturity in

Divine things."[6] This maturation means reaching "the measure of the stature of the fullness of Christ" (Eph. 4:13). What a glorious objective this is!

A young man came to the Lord Jesus one day and asked how he might have eternal life. Jesus answered, "If you want to be perfect, go, sell what you have and give to the poor" (Matt. 19:21). The Lord's desire for him was not only the good and acceptable will of God, but the perfect will of God. The one condition, however, was unreserved surrender: he must give all. The young man weighed the issues, decided that he preferred gold to God, and then turned away into the darkness and gloom of a never-ending night. He denied himself the pleasure of the eternal for the temporary enjoyment of the earthly. How tragic! God forbid that we should forfeit the blessing of a yielded life. May the language of your heart and mine be the words of Frances Ridley Havergal: "In full and glad surrender / I give myself to Thee, / Thine utterly and only / And evermore to be."

Spirit-Fullness
"Be filled with the Spirit." (Read Eph. 5:15–21.)

Every Christian is indwelt by the Holy Spirit. This miracle happens at new birth (Acts 2:38–39; Rom. 8:9). To be indwelt by the Holy Spirit, however, does not necessarily mean being filled with the Spirit. Only as we daily affirm our surrender to the lordship of Christ and yield to the Spirit's control can we experience what is Spirit-fullness.

This brings us to our text. First, Spirit-fullness is commanded—"Be filled" (Eph. 5:18). This is not an option; it is an obligation. Not to be filled is to live in disobedience, and disobedience is sin (see James 4:17). Spirit-fullness is not a higher life or a deeper life, it is the normal Christian life—in dependence on the Lord and obedience to the Word.

Second, Spirit-fullness is continuous. "Be filled." The verb is in the present tense. It could be rendered "Go on being filled with the Spirit." Dr. Handley Moule, in his *Ephesian Studies* (p. 274), renders it, "Be filled, with a fullness habitual, normal, . . . in the Spirit."

Paul tells us that there are two things that can affect the enjoyment of a Spirit-filled life. One is sin. He warns, "Do not grieve the Holy Spirit of God" (Eph. 4:30). As we have seen already in the unfolding truths of this chapter, broken fellowship can be restored by claiming that great cleansing promise: "If we confess our sins, He is faithful and just to forgive us our sins and to cleanse us from all unrighteousness" (1 John 1:9). The other hindrance to a Spirit-filled life is self. Paul exhorts, "Do not quench the Spirit" (1 Thess. 5:19). We quench the Spirit when we despise God's Word or disobey it by enthroning self instead of enthroning the Spirit. Self must be brought to the cross (see Rom. 8:13). We can't mortify the self-life, but we can cooperate with the Holy Spirit to put to death the deeds of the body that the resurrection life of the Lord Jesus might come through our human personalities in all the power of an ungrieved, unquenched Holy Spirit.

Third, Spirit-fullness is conspicuous. When we are Spirit-filled certain things follow. The first mentioned is fellowship—"speaking to one another" (Eph. 5:19). The fullness of the Holy Spirit will find manifestation in fellowship whenever Christians are found together. This is one of the most precious aspects of our Christian heritage. Next is worship—"singing and making melody" (Eph. 5:19). Worship is man's highest and holiest activity. All eternity will be filled with worship! In perfect sequence is gratitude—"giving thanks always for all things" (Eph. 5:20). This is more than an act of thanksgiving; it is an attitude of thanksgiving—a lifestyle under *all* circumstances. Then we come to discipleship—"submitting to one another in the fear of God" (Eph. 5:21). Paul knew that the secret of maintaining joyful and thankful fellowship in the Christian community is the discipline of submission to one another "with all lowliness and gentleness, with longsuffering, bearing with one another in love, endeavoring to keep the unity of the Spirit in the bond of peace" (Eph. 4:2–3). All this leads to relationships—"Wives, . . . husbands, . . . children, . . . bondservants, . . . masters" (Eph. 5:22–6:9). Only the Spirit-filled life can "oil the wheels" of human relationships. He is the supreme answer to broken homes and employment problems. Then, for the dark and demonic world, there is swordsmanship—"Take . . . the sword of the Spirit, which is the word of God" (Eph. 6:17). The weapons against the devil and all his "spiritual hosts of wickedness" are the Word of God and the Spirit of God. Best of all, Spirit-fullness brings partnership—"Praying . . . with all prayer. . . . and for me" (Eph. 6:18, 19). There is no partnership so personal and powerful as partnership in prayer. Even the mighty apostle would not face his ministry without the undergirding of prayer.

This, then, is the challenge of Spirit-fullness—not only in its importance and implications, but in its indications. So, obey the command "Be filled" (Eph. 5:18) and experience the glorious consequences of a Spirit-filled life.

Service

"His own special people, zealous for good works." (Read Titus 2:12–15.)

A footnote in *The New Scofield Reference Bible* reads: "[This] passage is one of the most concise summations in the entire N.T. of the relation of Gospel truth to life."[7]

We have here salvation, sanctification, and service. The grace of God brings salvation with its strong call to repudiate the old life of ungodliness and worldliness, and to appropriate the new life of inward self-control, outward righteousness, and upward godliness (Titus 2:11–12). The grace of God also brings sanctification through the power of the Cross to "redeem us" (Titus 2:14; 1 Peter 1:18–21), the power of the blood to "purify" us (Titus 2:14; 1 John 1:7), and the power of the "blessed hope" to motivate us (Titus 2:13; 1 John 1:1–3). The grace of God eventuates in "good works" (Titus 2:14). So we are saved and sanctified to *serve*.

These "good works" show the glory of God in our daily service. Jesus said, "Let your light so shine before men, that they may see your good works and glorify your Father in heaven" (Matt. 5:16). "Good works" here means "all right- eousness, everything [believers] are and do that [reflect] the mind and will of God. . . . Men must see this light. It may pro- voke persecution (vv. 10–12), but that is no reason for hiding the light others may see and by which they may come to glo- rify the Father (cf. 2 Cor. 4:6; 1 Peter 2:12)."[8]

These "good works" share the gospel of God in our daily service. In that matchless "hymn to Christ" in Philippians 2 we see a perfect picture of true Servanthood—"even [to] the death of the cross," and then God's exaltation of the same perfect *servant* to the throne of glory (Phil. 2:8–11). With this example before us, Paul commands: "Work out your own sal- vation with fear and trembling; for it is God who works in you . . . for [God's] good pleasure. . . . holding fast the word of life" (Phil. 2:12–13, 16). The outworking of "good works" involves "holding [fast or] forth the word of life," which, of course, is the gospel. No one can experience God's saving and sanctifying grace without a burden for a lost world.

"Good works" seal the guidance of God in our daily ser- vice—"For we are His workmanship, created in Christ Jesus for good works, which God prepared beforehand that we should walk in them" (Eph. 2:10). What is so exciting about this verse is that God has His plan of service for each one of us. As Dr. A. Skevington Wood informs us: "The road is already built." It only remains for you and me to walk the path already laid out. That route may differ with each one of us and may change from time to time, under God's sovereign guidance; but the way is there, and we fail in our duty if we do not step it out until our journey in God's service is done!

So there we have it—sin, sanctification, surrender, Spirit-fullness, and service. Like David's "five smooth stones from the brook" (1 Sam. 17:40), we are equipped by the doctrines of grace to face the Goliaths of our day.

To celebrate this "victory in Jesus," I wrote a hymn that the Keswick Convention has now published in their official hymnbook. It sums up the essence of what this chapter is all about:

> Lord, SEARCH my life in ev'ry part,
> Reveal the sins that make me fail,
> Till with a broken, contrite heart—
> I kneel to conquer and prevail.
>
> Lord, CLEANSE my life from every stain,
> As I confess my sins to Thee;
> Let no unholy thought remain,
> For Thy Name's sake, oh, set me free!
>
> Lord, TAKE my life, whate'er the price—
> My self, my gifts, my body, too;
> And through this "living sacrifice,"
> "Unite my heart" Thy will to do.
>
> Lord, FILL my life with heav'nly grace,
> That I may witness to Thy love,
> I ask in faith and seek Thy face—
> For Thy Free Spirit from above.
>
> Lord, USE my life to reach the lost,
> On friendly shore or foreign soil;
> And may I never count the cost—
> To win Thy smile for faithful toil.
>
> Chorus: Lord, hear my pray'r,
>   I humbly plead,
>   And in Thy mercy meet my need.[9]

Notes

1. Robert B. Laurin, "Victory," *Baker's Dictionary of Theology* (Grand Rapids: Baker, 1960), 542.
2. Evan H. Hopkins, *The Law of Liberty in the Spiritual Life* (Fort Washington, Pa.: Christian Literature Crusade, 1952), 15.
3. John Owen, *The Holy Spirit* (Grand Rapids: Kregel, 1960), 231.
4. Frank E. Gaebelein, ed., *The Expositor's Bible Commentary*, vol. 12 (Grand Rapids: Zondervan, 1981), 100.
5. Ibid., vol. 2, 463.
6. W. E. Vine, *The Epistle to the Romans* (Grand Rapids: Zondervan, 1957), 178.
7. *The New Scofield Reference Bible*, King James Version (New York: Oxford University Press, 1967), 1307.
8. Gaebelein, *Expositor's Bible Commentary*, vol. 8, 140.
9. Words and music copyright 1970 by Stephen F. Olford and Paul F. Liljestrand. All rights reserved.

3

About the Author

Robertson McQuilkin is a homemaker, writer, and conference speaker. In 1990 McQuilkin resigned from his twenty-two-year presidency of Columbia International University to care for his wife of forty years, Muriel, who was reaching advanced stages of Alzheimer's disease. Prior to his tenure at Columbia he served for twelve years as a church-starting missionary in Japan with The Evangelical Alliance Mission (TEAM). McQuilkin has written many magazine and journal articles and several books, including *Understanding and Applying the Bible* (Moody) and *An Introduction to Biblical Ethics* (Tyndale). Three of his five living children serve in Christian ministry, including Amy in Japan and Kent in Calcutta, India.

About This Chapter

The chief accusation leveled at Victorious Life teaching has been that it is a form of perfectionism. McQuilkin's examination of the historical data, reported in this chapter, reveals that the accusations against present-day Victorious Life teaching are ill-founded, but that the earlier accusations indeed had a basis.

But this chapter is much more than historical and doctrinal analysis. In the last half it provides a clear-cut statement of "Victorious Life" teaching, which McQuilkin calls "a mediating view of sanctification." Furthermore, it fills in some of the details omitted in chapters 1 and 2 because of space considerations.

Imperfections: How Perfectionist Is "Victorious Life" Teaching?

by Robertson McQuilkin

After the Civil War, people were desperately thirsty for a quality of spiritual life that went beyond the typical Christian experience. Thus, the half century from 1865 to 1915 became a time of unprecedented spiritual ferment, spawning the holiness movement, the Keswick movement, the pentecostal movement, the Christian Missionary Alliance—and the Victorious Life Testimony. It was an American phenomenon. Even the English Keswick movement was sparked by Americans. Historians look for root systems, and some hold that these American movements branched back to Europe through Wesley to his Anglican heritage in England and to the influence of German pietism. But the only connection, at least on the part of what the participants viewed of themselves, is one of a common concern for holiness. In achieving holiness, each movement went its own way.

Critics have seen other commonalities such as an emphasis on an encounter with God subsequent to conversion that initiates a life of some level of perfection. The movement, called at first the "Victorious Life Testimony," certainly emphasized a crisis experience needed by many, if not most,

Christians. But is the charge of perfectionism true of the founders or of the movement in subsequent generations?

Origins

The Victorious Life Movement was born in 1910 through Charles Trumbull's life-changing experience. Trumbull, editor of the influential *Sunday School Times,* then sought to help others experience a higher quality of Christian life while avoiding what he considered error in some of the other movements.

In defining their teaching broadly enough to incorporate varying theological viewpoints, the leaders of the Victorious Life Movement took their cue from English Keswick. Speakers on the Keswick platform came from a broad theological spectrum and participated in a particular conference strategy that was designed to help people experience the fullness of life in Christ.[1] It was more a strategy than a doctrine. "Keswick doctrine" is something of a misnomer since that movement was never theologically defined. In this the Victorious Life Testimony (VLT) differed, hammering out a doctrinal position from the start. In fact, it was doctrine, not method or objective, that was soon to bring painful division.

A Second Work of Grace?

Trumbull and his young protégé, Robert C. McQuilkin, were Reformed in theology, not Armenian, and McQuilkin became the theologian of the movement in the early days. He came from generations of Irish Presbyterians and remained in that theological tradition all his life. Salvation was by grace alone and sanctification also by grace alone. For McQuilkin there was never an autonomous free will that could secure salvation or maintain the Christian life. Furthermore, the Victorious Life Testimony held that a second crisis experience beyond initial salvation, though desperately needed by many Christians, was not theologically necessary. That is, the normal experience would be for a person to experience the full blessings of life in Christ from the moment of salvation. But most Christians through ignorance, drift, or rebellion forfeit that close relationship and need another encounter of surrender and faith to restore what had been theirs by right all along. That theological foundation is clear and sets VLT apart from the Wesleyan holiness and pentecostal teachings. But the question of perfectionism—that's another story. That's what split the movement. Or so it is said.

Defining Perfection: Wesley

"Sinless perfection" sounds rather absolute, but often those who adhere to the teaching define either sin or perfection in relative terms. The Westminster Catechism defines sin as "any lack of conformity to or transgression of the law of God." Pretty absolute. But, for example, Wesley would define "lack of conformity," the falling short of God's moral perfection, as part of our finite humanity, for which we are not morally culpable. Human imperfection, not sin. And "entire sanctification," sometimes defined as "perfect love," seemed restricted to the motivational. But still, to have my "sin nature" "eradicated" so that my motives, at least, were pure, would be no small blessing, first or second! Of course, John Wesley never claimed to have attained this level of perfection himself, only that it was possible and should be sought after.

Defining Perfection: The Victorious Life Testimony

What did the Victorious Life Testimony teach about sinless perfection? From the beginning, the teachers vehemently denied that a state of sinless perfection was possible in this life. But, also from the beginning, they were accused of teaching perfectionism. How could this be? Then, as if to reinforce the critics, less than a decade after the first conference in 1913, there was a major split in the movement, with Trumbull and W. H. Griffith Thomas holding that McQuilkin and his better known conference platform partner, William Ramsey, were teaching perfectionism.

The question is important far beyond the bounds of a fledgling conference movement. The *Sunday School Times* was the most influential journal among mainline Protestants, since it published weekly helps on the International Sunday School Lesson (a biblical passage that was chosen for each week of the year and used almost universally). Since the editor of the *Times* initiated the Victorious Life Movement, it was only natural that the magazine should become its leading advocate. Furthermore, Victorious Life Testimony Conferences were held nationwide and drew large audiences. One of the early leaders was C. I. Scofield, who spread the word through his widely used reference Bible. In fact, Victorious Life teaching had a molding influence on two other movements that emerged with strength during the same period: the Bible school movement and the Bible conference movement. How the controversy would end was, therefore, of great significance for the whole movement of what was later to become the evangelical renaissance.[2]

Both sides of the controversy sounded perfectionist to an outsider. The following quotes are not isolated aberrations. They are representative of the basic teaching, repeated often. Trumbull:

> Remember God's Word concerning the absoluteness of the victory that is ours in Christ. That victory is not a relative thing, not a comparative thing, not a matter of degree at all: it is the freedom with which the Son sets men free (John 8:36), so complete that God himself cannot add to it in time or eternity. Not that we are given "sinless perfection." We always have our sinful nature, which can sin and will sin any moment that we fail to trust Christ for his victory in us. But as we trust him, his victory in us is absolute.[3]

> I have learned that, as I trust Christ in surrender, there need be no fighting against sin, but complete freedom from the power and even the desire of sin. I have learned that this freedom, this more than conquering, is sustained in unbroken

continuance as I simply recognize that Christ is my cleansing, reigning life.[4]

McQuilkin:

. . . if there is not *complete victory* over sin—which includes such things as worry, discouragement, lack of love, irritation, pride, jealousy, impatience, covetousness, worldliness, lust— then you do not have the Victorious Life.[5]

This is not speaking of the impossibility of sinning, for then would the Christian be a machine, but of the impossibility while the Christian maintains his attitude of abiding Christ, walking in the Spirit.[6]

If perfectionism is held to mean a condition achieved through a postconversion experience that renders a person unable to sin in any manner, the Victorious Life Testimony is not perfectionist. It taught, rather, that the postconversion experience is not theologically necessary, only practically necessary for many. That experience, resulting from a response of surrender and faith, enables a person not to sin ("able not to sin") rather than what many perfectionists hold, that a second work of grace makes one "not able to sin."[7] But if "perfectionism" includes the idea that humans can live without conscious sin, then the movement can justly be called "perfectionist." Though only at the beginning, as we shall see.

Root of the Controversy: The Two Natures

After studying the books, magazine articles, board minutes, and personal letters of the participants, I have concluded that the controversy among the leaders was rooted in another doctrine more than in the question of perfectionism, that is, the teaching of two natures. McQuilkin, reeling from the withering attack on Victorious Life teaching in 1918 by the famed Princeton professor B. B. Warfield,[8] concluded that people are whole persons and that the two-nature theory is not biblically defensible.[9] Trumbull and Thomas affirmed the two-nature theory as the basis for teaching the Victorious Life, and McQuilkin resigned rather than cause further divisiveness within the leadership team.

McQuilkin was charged with teaching "perfectionism," but I can find no statement of his that is more perfectionist than those of Trumbull. So how could the attack on Victorious Life Testimony's perfectionism focus on Ramsey and McQuilkin rather than on Trumbull, the father of the movement? There must have been some element in McQuilkin's brand of "perfectionism" that was unacceptable. And since the only documented difference is over the two-nature theory, I have concluded that the central concern was *that* doctrine, not perfection. It is easy to see, however, how differing views of human nature could lead to differing views of its perfectibility, as we shall see.

According to the teaching that prevailed in the movement, every Christian has an old nature that is unimprovable, will be as evil after fifty years of Christian walk as it was originally, so they rightly claimed not to be perfectionist. But each Christian also has a new nature that is defined either as the indwelling Christ or as the perfected nature received at regeneration, either of which is incapable of sin. Perhaps critics may be forgiven for seeing this as one form of perfectionism.

With two natures within, constantly at war, so to speak, the gravitational pull of the old nature is counteracted by the upward power of the Holy Spirit, it was said. The prevailing force in a life is determined by the "vote" of the person. If a person fully yields and truly trusts the indwelling Christ, he can live constantly without conscious sin. But, at the same time, he can fail at any moment, as completely as before he ever believed, should he not continue in surrender and faith. Critics point out that this is confusing because of uncertainty as to which of the two natures surrenders and trusts. The old nature surely can't and the new nature never could do otherwise. McQuilkin became convinced that the doctrine is untenable biblically and psychologically. Human personhood is a unity and cannot be divided into two entities within. Of course, if this united person can live without conscious sin by trusting the indwelling Christ to live out His life, the teaching could be viewed as even more perfectionist! There is no imperfect "old nature" to blame things on. So perhaps, from that viewpoint, McQuilkin became more perfectionist than his colleagues, as they said. In any event, the controversy raged on.

Another problem with the two-nature theory is the question of growth—the old nature can't and the new nature, especially if viewed as the substituted life of Christ, can't either—Christ is already perfect. For whatever reason, both sides in the controversy, though affirming a "process" of growth following the "crisis" of surrender and faith, were very fuzzy on what such a growth might consist of. And the emphasis was clearly on the crisis, not the process of growing. In any event, the split, though very painful at the time, was short-lived and McQuilkin returned to the fellowship a few years later. Though he had moved south to become the first president of Columbia Bible School in 1923, he wrote the Sunday school lessons for the *Sunday School Times* for some years, and though he was not on the official VLT platform, his own conference ministry continued in full strength.

Did McQuilkin Remain "Perfectionist"?

Clarence Melvin Loucks has written the most thorough analysis available of the Victorious Life Movement. In his unpublished doctoral dissertation, "The Theological Foundations of the Victorious Life: An Evaluation of the Theology of the Victorious Christian Life in the Light of the Present," Loucks documents McQuilkin's change on the doctrine of the two natures but concludes, "For the rest of his life his [other] doctrine remained essentially the same as it was in 1921."[10] I'm not so sure.

In fact, I'm convinced McQuilkin did change his thinking and teaching on the entire scope of sanctification, not merely the two-nature theory, though apart from his declared change on the two-nature theory, I can find no documentation in which he said that he was changing, either in a published or unpublished statement. Of course, McQuilkin never changed his core beliefs: (1) many Christians need a "crisis" encounter of "surrender and faith" to begin living a "normal Christian life," and (2) it is possible to live life victoriously, not yielding to temptation, by the power of the indwelling Spirit.

He preached these things with vigor till his death. And he lived them out consistently. But I have been unable to discover any language used by him from the mid-twenties till his death in 1952 that was similar to his early perfectionist statements, and he consistently denied the possibility of perfection in what he did write. A typical statement:

> "Be filled with the Spirit" is a command. Christians are to live their Christian lives in the fullness of the Spirit. What does this mean? The Lord Jesus is the only one who has ever lived a perfect, sinless life. In this life no Christian attains sinlessness. Does this mean that there is merely a difference in degree between Christians, some having grown in grace more fully than others? Or are some living in the fullness of the Spirit, and others, not?
>
> There are as many differences in Christian attainment and in Christian growth as there are individual Christians. But also there is a great difference between a defeated Christian's life and a life of victory in Christ.[11]

McQuilkin taught his children the Westminster Shorter Catechism, used B. B. Warfield's *The Plan of Salvation* and Horatious Bonar's *God's Way of Holiness* as the texts for his classes, wrote a commentary on Romans[12] in which there is no trace of perfectionism, even in the chapters dealing with Romans 6—8, the Magna Carta of the Victorious Life teaching. No wonder I, as his son, sitting under his pulpit ministry and formal classroom lectures throughout the thirties and forties, was startled to learn, in doing research for this essay, of the early perfectionist tendencies. No, his branch of the Victorious Life Movement cannot be charged with perfectionism beyond the early days. But what of the other, what some call the dispensationalist branch?

Did the "Two-Nature" Branch Remain Perfectionist?

Even a cursory acquaintance with the heirs of the movement, conference centers like America's Keswick and schools like Moody Bible Institute (where the original controversy erupted) or Dallas Theological Seminary, assures us that the dispensational branch of "victory in Christ" moved even farther away from any hint of perfectionism.

On the other hand, some advocates of the two-nature view of Christian personhood hold that the second "nature" is Jesus Christ—and He is certainly perfect! So there is the danger of teaching a form of perfectionism if the "substituted life of Christ" is the focus. This is a passive view of the "life of victory," in which I am exhorted to "let go and let God" do His thing in my place. But those who hold this position of a perfect life lived out by Christ in me also hold that my old nature can fall to the depths of sinful behavior at any moment. That could hardly be called a full-fledged perfectionism.

Thus, the mainstream of the movement, both in its reformed and dispensational branches, moved deliberately away from its earlier perfectionist heritage, beginning in the early twenties. In 1985 and 1986, when the faculty of Columbia Bible College and Seminary (now Columbia International University) collaborated with me in producing a definitive statement on Keswick as published in *Five Views on Sanctifi-cation,*[13] and when John F. Walvoord, then president of Dallas Theological Seminary, responded affirmatively to that statement, we were simply reaffirming the teaching of the movement since the early twenties: though it is not possible to live a sinless life, it is possible in the power of the Spirit to live a life of glorious victory over temptation and of growth toward ever greater likeness to Jesus.[14]

The Perfectionist Flaw: Redefining Sin

How can our human imperfectability and the biblical assurances of a life of triumph both be true? The basic biblical flaw in perfectionist teaching is a redefinition of sin. One is capable of sinlessness (perfection) only because sin is defined in relative terms, the standard of God-likeness is lowered to some level achievable by fallen humans. If the error is in sin's definition, perhaps the solution could be found in looking more closely at the Bible's own view of sin.

The standard is clear: "Therefore you shall be perfect, just as your Father in heaven is perfect" (Matt. 5:48). God's plan is to fully restore the original image. Any attitude or action falling short of that standard is sin. Note, however, that Scripture differentiates among sins. It speaks of deliberate sin and unintentional sin (e.g., Num. 15:27–31; Ps. 19:12–13; Ezek. 45:20). So serious was deliberate sin that the Old Testament provided no atoning sacrifice for the guilty party, though that law seemed not to have been implemented. People like David were consistently forgiven for very intentional sins. But the principle is clear: God makes a great distinction between intentional and unintentional sin. It does not, as did early Victorious Life Testimony teaching, distinguish between known and unknown sin as the two differentiating categories. Of course, "unintentional" often stems from "unknown," and indeed the two are often synonymous. But there is also unintentional sin that is not unknown. "Unknown" and "unintentional" are not coextensive.

Perhaps the early VLT's great theological and practical fault line was in its insistence on offering hope of absolute victory for "known" sin while not offering that hope for "unknown" sin. "All known sin" surely includes my acute awareness of failing to love as fully as God expects, failing to be as contented and strong as Jesus. Yet Trumbull constantly assures us that we can live wholly free of all known sin and specifically lists sins of disposition, certainly not deliberately chosen, sins like worry, irritation, fear, dissatisfaction, pride. And since they are clearly in the "known" category of sin, we are promised complete victory. If he had said "free of all presumptuous (intentional) sin," he might have found himself on firm biblical ground. Also, the hope for total deliverance might have been more realistic.

To promise a life totally free of deliberate choices to cheat on my income tax, watch sexy movies, or spread vicious gossip is one thing. To live totally free of ever having the shadow of worry, a momentary flush of irritation, a flash of desire for something or someone not mine—that is something else entirely. Yet the early VLT promised complete freedom from these sins too. Or consider sins of omission—failing to truly love someone who has hurt me deeply or some obnoxious person, for example. I never for a moment measure up to that standard and I know it well—it is not "unknown sin." But I don't deliberately choose it, I don't plan it, it is not intentional. I don't get up in the morning and say, "Today I will lust twice, get irritated once, go on two brief ego trips, and fail to love my impossible boss as I should." From unintentional "falling short of the glorious character of God" Scripture nowhere assures I will be wholly delivered in this life.

Biblical Victory: Two Varieties

So the promise of victory in the Christian life celebrated in this volume must be described differently for those two categories of sin. Do we speak of deliberate sin, intentional choices to violate the known will of God? Because of the new power of a regenerated nature and the energizing presence of the Holy Spirit, we may promise consistent victory over temptation. On the other hand, what of the unintentional sins of disposition? The promise of Scripture is consistent growth toward ever-greater likeness to Jesus Christ (Rom. 12:2; 2 Cor. 3:18; Eph. 4:11–16; Phil. 3:12–14; Col. 3:10; 2 Peter 1:1–11). That too can be called "victory."

This approach to defining sin, clearly enunciated in the Old Testament, seems to provide the key to unlocking the mystifying teaching of 1 John. John assures us that to claim sinless perfection is gross self-deception. And it makes God a liar too! (1 John 1:8–10). How then can the same author a few verses later assure us that anyone who sins doesn't even know God? In fact, belongs to the devil! (1 John 3:6–10). I'm convinced that the solution lies in the fact that John's thinking was from the context of his Scripture, the Old Testament. Based on the Old Testament distinction among sins, he assures us that anyone who claims to be free of any and all sin is badly deceived, because even if we have not chosen to violate some command, still we fall far short of God's moral likeness (1 John 1). But, if I take that awareness of sinful failure as license to choose sin, again I am badly deceived. My choices have proved I don't belong to God at all. That this is the teaching of John in chapter 3 seems clear from the verb tense he chose, a tense that is not clear in most English translations. "If anyone is sinning . . ." says John, if anyone continues in deliberately choosing to violate God's known will, that person does not know God. At least any assurance of belonging to God does not come from Bible affirmation. Nowhere does the Bible assure the person who persists in deliberately sinning that he or she is acceptable to God. The Bible tells such a person, rather: Repent! Quit that sinning!

Though this distinction between two categories of sin is not taught by all advocates of victorious Christian living, it may well help define our hope of victory. Do we speak of sin as deliberately choosing to violate the known will of God? Then the Bible promises full deliverance, consistent victory. No need to ever fail. Do we speak of involuntary failure to measure up to God's likeness? Then the Bible promises us steady growth toward that goal, though we will not be fully delivered from sinful attitudes and behavior until we "become like Him" when we "see Him as He is" at the end of our earthly pilgrimage.

I call this the mediating view of sanctification because it stands midway between those who hold out hope for absolute perfection on one hand and those who hold out no hope for a victorious life on the other. It is much easier to go to a consistent extreme than to stay at the center of biblical tension. In reaction to perfectionist teaching, some have concluded that there is no hope beyond the common Christian experience of struggle and defeat.[15] Their preaching and writing about the inevitability of living in constant, deliberate sin do not sound exactly like Paul's great proclamation of emancipation: sin shall not have dominion over you! (Rom. 6:14). He gives thanks to God who always causes us to triumph (2 Cor. 2:14) and exults in the assurance that we are more than conquerors (Rom. 8:37). These are not isolated proof texts but rather reflect the mood of the entire New Testament from the promise of abundant life (John 10:10) and a bumper crop of Christlike characteristics (John 15) by Jesus Himself to the promises of Peter that we can escape from the world's corruption and experience abounding godliness (2 Peter 1) and on to John's assurance that we must (and can) live out life in the moral light (1 John 1) and if we don't we should question whether we even belong to God at all (1 John 3). The gospel is good news not merely for life beyond the grave, but good news for victory in daily life today.

This does not mean, however, that the victory is easy. Ours is no spectator religion in which we relax and let Christ live out His life in our bodies. Some teachers, like the early message of the Victorious Life Testimony, do hold out such a hope. But such a hope is not biblical, for it ignores the biblical stress on warfare, on the battle with temptation. There is indeed the rest of faith, but there is also the wrestle. Nevertheless, it is warfare with victory assured, not defeat. And those who settle for a life of defeat are "shortsighted, even to blindness, and [have] forgotten that [they were] cleansed from [their] old sins" (2 Peter 1:9). In fact, Paul calls such people "carnal" because they behave like the unconverted (1 Cor. 3:3).

Not all Christians, then, experience a life of victory. The difference among Christians is not merely one of degree, all on a growth track with some growing more rapidly than others. Who are the defeated, the "carnal," the "shortsighted"? Three varieties. Some are ignorant of God's plan for victorious living or the way to experience it; some may know basic principles but have drifted out of a tight relationship with God, perhaps through neglecting the means of grace; and some are in flat-out rebellion, deliberately saying "no" to God in some matter.

What do such people need? They need a fresh encounter with God, a return to the original contract of faith they signed when they received salvation. They need to yield and trust. No person is more than two steps away from a life of victory in Christ: surrender and faith, consciously yielding to God unconditionally and trusting Him to keep His word. Such is the relationship that releases Holy Spirit power for victorious living. It does not provide instantaneous perfection, but it does start the process of transformation from one degree of His glorious character to another until we are finally made complete in Christ when we see Him as He is. That is our glorious hope!

Notes

1. See J. Robertson McQuilkin, "The Keswick Perspective," in *Five Views of Sanctification* (Grand Rapids: Zondervan, 1987), 149–96. Still the most definitive statement of "Keswick," Steven Barabas's *So Great Salvation* (Grand Rapids: Eerdmans, 1952) makes the case for Keswick being a methodology rather than a doctrinal system. His treatment gives a doctrinal definition to the teaching as much as has been done and probably as much as could be done. For a concise example of the Keswick approach see Stephen Olford's essay in this volume (chapter 2).

2. Harold John Ockenga is considered by many to have been the father of resurgent evangelicalism, having coined the term *New Evangelical*, and having himself "fathered" the National Association of Evangelicals, Fuller Theological Seminary, and *Christianity Today*. Though none of these institutions would be noted for "Victorious Life teaching," that teaching was a major driving force for Ockenga himself and he was a leading advocate of it.

3. Charles Gallaudet Trumbull, *Perils of the Victorious Life* (Philadelphia: The Sunday School Times Co., 1919), 6.

4. Charles Gallaudet Trumbull, *The Life That Wins* (Philadelphia: The Sunday School Times Co.), 16. This tract, a message first delivered in 1911, is the most widely read publication of the Victorious Life Testimony, reaching almost one and one-half million copies by 1965.

5. Robert C. McQuilkin, *Victorious Life Studies* (Philadelphia: Christian Life Literature Fund, 1918), 2.

6. Robert C. McQuilkin, *God's Way of Victory Over Sin or If It Isn't Easy It Isn't Good* (Philadelphia: Christian Life Literature Fund, 1920 rev.), 7.

7. Note that this variety of perfectionist teaching is typically Armenian, so that while a person may have had the sin nature eradicated he can lose his salvation altogether. This introduces another dilemma beyond the scope of this essay to examine.

8. An article on "The Victorious Life" by Princeton Seminary professor Benjamin Breckinridge Warfield was published in the *Princeton Theological Review*, 1918, 321–73 and republished posthumously as the final chapter in a massive collection of articles on *Studies in Perfectionism* vol. 2, (New York: Oxford, 1931), 561–611. The annual conference of the Victorious Life Testimony had been held on the Princeton campus for five years until then, so Warfield's caustic attack hit like a bombshell in the fledgling movement. Warfield's stature and superb logic so defined the doctrine of the movement for those outside that Clarence Melvin Loucks in his definitive doctoral dissertation ("The Theological Foundations for the Victorious Life") says that all subsequent attacks on the movement are rooted in Warfield's critique and add little of substantive significance.

9. "Nearly three years after Warfield published his article, [McQuilkin] told the members of the Victorious Life Council that Warfield exposed 'the untenability . . . and utter lack of support of either Scripture, experience or psychology,' for his views on the two natures of the believer" (Loucks, 57).

10. Loucks, "Theological Foundations," 77.

11. *The Evangel*, 3, no. 6 (February 1938).

12. Robert C. McQuilkin, *The Message on Romans: An Exposition* (Grand Rapids: Zondervan, 1947).

13. McQuilkin et al., *Five Views of Sanctification*, chapter 4.

14. The founder of the movement, Charles Trumbull, lived till 1941, well after the mainstream of the movement left its perfectionist heritage. I am not aware that he changed from his original position.

15. Typical of this increasingly prevalent mood among Evangelicals is the volume *Less Than Conquerors: How Evangelicals Entered the 20th Century* by Douglas

Frank (Grand Rapids: Eerdmans, 1986). The volume is no less caustic than Warfield's original attack, but considerably less scholarly and convincing. It does, however, highlight the impatience many younger Evangelicals have with anyone who holds out hope of becoming "more than conquerors."

4

About the Author

Bradford Mullen teaches theology, apologetics, and ethics at Columbia Biblical Seminary and Graduate School of Missions, a division of Columbia International University. His course "The Principles of the Christian Life" introduces entering seminary students to the Victorious Life heritage of the school.

As a young man, Mullen came to Christ after listening to several Billy Graham "Hour of Decision" broadcasts and watching a Billy Graham Crusade on television. Later he made a total commitment of life to Christ under the ministry of Stephen Olford. He served on the pastoral staff of Grace Church, Ridgewood, New Jersey (1975–81), joining the faculty of Columbia Biblical Seminary in 1986. He earned a B.S. from Trinity College (Florida), an M.Div. from Columbia Biblical Seminary, a ThM from Trinity Evangelical Divinity School, and a Ph.D. from Boston University. He and his wife, Noel, have two children, Ian and Amy.

About This Chapter

Get ready for some concentrated theology! Here is a masterful analysis of what the Bible says about legalism. Once we think through the issues surrounding that most deadly of gospel perversions, legalism, we can avoid the trap. Unfortunately, many who are most concerned about personal godliness tend to fall into the legalism trap, and that includes those who advocate a victorious Christian life. So how do we avoid the trap? And are the critics of the Victorious Life Testimony correct in accusing the movement of promoting legalism? Brad Mullen may provide some surprising answers as he lays a solid biblical foundation for defining legalism biblically and avoiding it practically.

The Legalistic Trap: How to Avoid It

by Bradford Mullen

N othing is more deadly, spiritually speaking, than legalism. It lures its adherents into a life of ever-entangling bondage. It lulls its devotees into a false sense of future security. It leads all who follow its siren song away from the grace of God that is in Jesus Christ alone. The end of legalism is death because, "by the deeds of the law no flesh will be justified in His sight" (Rom. 3:20).

A Definition of Legalism

Legalism is a theological, not a biblical, term. Although the word does not appear in the Bible, the concept of living by law as a means of divine approval certainly does. In common parlance, "legalism" refers to any religious system by which a person consciously strives to satisfy the law[1] of a holy God (or gods) by means of personal performance. We generally think of legalists as religious workaholics. This description, however, can be misleading. Paul worked hard. In Colossians 1:29 he characterized his entire ministry as "labor" by "striving." What distinguished Paul from legalists was that Paul testified and believed his intense labor was "according to His [Christ's] working which works in me mightily." Legalism is never identified by the amount or intensity of activity expended. It is measured, rather, according to the mind-set and motive of the one active. Legalists work *in order that* God would grace them. Biblical Christians work *because* God through Christ has graced them.

Legalism Among Unbelievers

When the Bible addresses the subject of the abuse of the law of God, however, it also has a larger constituency in mind than conspicuous recompense-seeking religionists. Paul's words cited above (i.e., Rom. 3:20) end the first section of his explication of the gospel in which he declares that *all* humanity—pagan, cultured, and religious—falls short of God's glorious standard (i.e., God's law). We fall short, but not for lack of trying to hit the mark. Our effort, however, amounts to a ceaseless campaign of coping with the consequences of our failure to satisfy the law of God we know, in whatever form we know it. At a basic level, fallen human beings are engaged in an enterprise of suppressing the truth and exchanging it for a lie (Rom. 1:18–27) and of accusing and excusing themselves vis-à-vis God's law (Rom. 2:14–15).

On first hearing, it might seem odd to suggest that *all* unbelievers are legalists. Does not lawlessness characterize many unbelievers? Do not many rail against or reject the jurisdiction of any law? Certainly! Unbelievers are "lawless," however, not because they do not recognize the existence of law, but because they break the law they instinctively recognize. Ironically, unbelievers are no more able to abide by the laws they set for themselves and for their society than they are to live according to the explicitly stated laws of God. Other lawlessness is founded upon a denial of not only the jurisdiction of, but also the very existence of law. Trying to live consistently with that denial is another matter entirely. An unbeliever who professes not to live by some law is either self-deceived or disingenuous.

Paul reasons in Romans 2:14–15: "For when Gentiles who do not have the Law do instinctively the things of the

Law, these, not having the Law, are a law to themselves, in that they show the work of the Law written in their hearts, their conscience bearing witness, and their thoughts alternately accusing or else defending them" (NASB).

"Lawless" people who reject the concept of law, so-called antinomians, do so as a coping device calculated to silence a guilty conscience provoked by the law. Unbelieving "antinomianism" (literally, a worldview "against law") is, strictly speaking, a misnomer. Antinomians are only formally against law. Psychologically and spiritually their consciences prevent them from adhering consistently to their theory.[2]

In the broadest biblical sense, therefore, anyone who is not a Christian is a legalist. Legalism is the antithesis of Christianity. The essence of Christianity is that a person is made righteous in Christ by grace alone through faith alone. The fundamental premise of legalism is that a person is made righteous by deeds that he or she performs. Since these are the only two possible approaches to God and are mutually exclusive, all persons who are not Christians may be said to be legalists.

Legalism Among Professing Christians

We most commonly use the term *legalism* with reference to overtly religious persons and, for the purposes of this essay, particularly of professing Christians. It is important to establish that legalism denotes the orientation of all that is not Christian in order to appreciate the seriousness of its presence among those who profess to be Christian. It delights to masquerade as a higher stage of Christian growth. But legalism is no less among professing Christians a diabolically inspired deception whose end is death. It is toward an understanding of this kind of legalism that the balance of this essay is devoted.

God hates legalism, especially among those who name Him. God disdained Israel's meticulous adherence even to His prescribed rituals when outward conformity was unaccompanied by a deeper commitment to the God who ordained them (1 Sam. 15:22–23; cf. Mark 12:33–34). The most celebrated legalists of all time, the publicly pious Pharisees, did not worship the wrong God, nor lack rigor in life. The Pharisees erred by resting on their privileged pedigree and ostentatious observance of self-prescribed practices (Matt. 23:13f.). Consequently, the word *pharisee* has become synonymous for legalist. The apostle Paul leveled his most stinging attacks on Jewish legalists, the so-called "judaizers," whose "gospel" was fatally flawed because it demanded a prerequisite—obedience to the Law of Moses (Gal. 1:6–10).

Legalistic Christianity

"Legal*ism*" is a system of thinking, a religion, anti-Christian by definition. The adjective, "legal*istic*," however, can describe acts or attitudes of people who claim to believe the Bible, some genuinely converted and some not. Here is the rub. Strictly speaking, a "Christian legalist" is an oxymoron. The Bible, however, describes some who presumably are Christians, but who behave incongruously to their profession by adopting the premise of legalism. Though formally inconceivable, Paul's admonition to the Galatians indicates the practical possibility exists: "Are you so foolish? Having begun by the Spirit, are you now being perfected by the flesh? . . . Does He then, who provides you with the Spirit and works miracles among you, do it by the works of the Law, or by hearing with faith?" (Gal. 3:3, 5 NASB).

A "legalistic" Christian is in a perilous spiritual no-man's-land—having little or no joy or victory over sin and no biblical grounds for assurance.[3] Legalism sets a trap to ensnare every rebellious, drifting, or ignorant professing Christian. The trap is sprung when the professing Christian moves from a "grace-by-faith" to an "earning-by-works" approach to God.

The Agents of "Legalistic Christianity"

Christian legalism poses an ever-present threat because the agents of legalism exert their influence after conversion as before, and even more virulently, inciting a conceptual conflict concerning the true identity of the professing believer. The world, the flesh, and the devil relentlessly tempt the professing Christian to adopt attitudes and a lifestyle consistent with the preconversion identity.

The *world* is the settled strategy of any culture or aggregate of cultures constituted to assuage guilt and to prescribe a works-righteousness means of salvation. The world constantly floats some regimen, some scheme, some idea—even if it is an antiregimen, antischeme, or anti-idea—in order to hold out hope to sinners groping for personal meaning, fulfillment, and acceptance. Options span the behavioristic spectrum from asceticism to libertinism, or the philosophical spectrum from theistic formalism to nihilism. The worldly trap is often undetected because it is so popular, so expedient. "Group think"—everybody's doing it (Rom. 1:32)—provides a false sense of security. Worldly legalists may just as readily be up-and-coming socialites as down-and-out boozers. The point is that for them the canons of culture confer meaning and guide the "groupie" toward wholeness.

The *flesh,* that voracious appetite for self-aggrandizement and sensual satisfaction, a consequence of the Fall, conspires with the world. Lurking in us all is the attitude, "I am not so bad." When the world entices us to do something to merit God's continued blessing, the flesh says, "I can do it!" "Fleshliness," or as we more commonly say, "carnality," is a legalist trap. A carnally minded person follows the duty-to-self ethic assiduously and passionately, whether in dissipation (unrestrained sensual excess) or in discipline (self-imposed sensual restraint). He remains in bondage because the flesh is insatiable.

The *devil* is the high priest of legalism. Jesus attributed the Pharisees' legalism to their father, the devil (John 8:44). The devil has "doctrines," catechizing his followers to the ways of the world and the flesh (cf. 1 Tim. 4:1–5). He continues to mediate "the big lie," as when he tempted Adam and Eve to seek greater self-fulfillment in accordance with his scheme while ostensibly still serving God's ends. Legalism is the devil's ploy to usurp God's authority. Of course he rarely appeals to professing Christians by directly assaulting God's revelation. Rather, the devil plants the idea that I need spiritual truth beyond, or in addition to, God's revelation in the Bible. If this canard persists, I functionally shift allegiances from God to the devil, though I might publicly still claim allegiance to God's Word alone. Once duped at this point, the evil one can lead me by the nose anywhere he wants.

The Strategies of "Legalistic Christianity"

There are three tried and untrue methods to counteract the agents of legalism. These methods are often hawked as higher stages of Christian maturity. For this reason they are particularly dangerous. They are nothing more, however, than religiously camouflaged legalism.

Some retreat into *monasticism* in hopes of avoiding the world's allurements. "The world cannot influence me if I remove myself from it," the argument goes. However, Jesus said we are in the world, but are not to be of it (John 17:16–18). Since He has overcome the world, I must too (John 16:33; 1 John 5:4–5). Therefore, "victory over," not "retreat from," is the Christian stance toward the world. The world does not contaminate by contact. The world's mind-set corrupts. Monastic withdrawal is legalistic because by it I abdicate my biblically mandated responsibility in favor of the strictures of a mystical spirituality. A spirituality so "heavenly minded" that it forsakes the world generally flows from or leads to legalism.

Many advocate either asceticism or libertinism as response to the temptation of the flesh. *Asceticism* teaches the denial of bodily pleasure in order to enhance spiritual insight. Do not confuse asceticism, as is often done, with self-sacrificial discipleship. The goal of biblical discipleship is to bring bodily appetites under the authority of God so that they can be denied, or enjoyed, for His glory. Asceticism does not distinguish between "the flesh" and "the body," regarding all matter, the body included, as inherently evil. God's creation is good, though fallen. God-given bodily desires need to be ordered and directed, not eradicated.

Another approach to the flesh is *libertinism*. Some gnostics reasoned that since matter "does not matter," and the body is matter, why not let the body "do its thing." The real enduring person, they believed, is pure spirit. But God created us spirit *and* body (Gen. 2:7). The apostle Paul commanded, "Do not let sin reign in your mortal body" (Rom. 6:12 NASB). I am party to this gross distortion whenever I respond to sin by saying something like, "So, I sinned. But, after all, God knows my heart." Christian freedom is not license. Both asceticism and libertinism are legalistic approaches because their adherents calculate success in terms of their own insight and efforts.

Ethical Christianity

God acted lawfully in redemption. He satisfied His own righteousness when He graced me in Jesus Christ (Rom. 3:24–26). Having broken God's law, I stood condemned by it, unable to satisfy its demands. God "legally" removed my condemnation, pronounced by the law, so that I could be free to follow the law. God's goal is that in Christ I will not merely "be" righteous, but also I will "behave" righteously (Rom. 8:3–4). The opposite of "legalistic Christianity," therefore, is not "lawless Christianity," but "legal Christianity" or "ethical Christianity."[4]

I choose the description "ethical Christianity" because many who faithfully advocate living in the power of the Spirit (i.e., the Victorious Christian Life) often do not concern themselves enough with ethics. Perhaps in reaction to classic liberalism, which regards ethics as a means, not an outgrowth, of redemption, evangelicals too often have stressed God's provision to be godly without specifying the ethical norms that characterize a godly life. Furthermore, today the trendy fashionableness of relativism provides a cultural inducement to continue to downplay, or even to deny, that God has a standard.[5]

The Center of Biblical Tension

I am indebted to Robertson McQuilkin for, among other things, the wisdom distilled in his oft-repeated aphorism, "It is easier to go to a consistent extreme than to stay at the center of biblical tension." This aphorism is particularly apt when assessing what the Bible says about the function of law in the Christian life. Certainly we are "not under law, but under grace" (Rom. 6:14 NASB). But, it mangles Paul's argument to claim that he contends that the law no longer exists, or the law has no practical value for the Christian. Ethical Christianity, not unethical license, lies at the center of this biblical tension.

Paul took great pains in the epistle to the Romans to remind his readers that the law's demands are not negated by the gospel. The law is written upon human conscience (Rom. 2:14–15), a faculty Christians employ in order to live godly lives (Rom. 13:5). Faith in the gospel, Paul says, actually "establishes" the law (Rom. 3:31). Also, since Adam's sin was against God's law, even the prefallen, "perfect" man was subject to law as a standard (Rom. 5:12–14). The law, Paul affirms, is "holy and righteous and good" (Rom. 7:12 NASB). The Spirit's presence is the difference between failing to observe the law in the flesh and fulfilling it (Rom. 7:25–8:4). Paul said, "Christ is the end of the law for righteousness" (Rom. 10:4 NASB), not because the law ended, but because now in Christ the righteousness to which the law conforms can be a reality in life by a means other than keeping the law single-handedly. Paul defines love, which fulfills the law (Rom. 13:8f.), according to specific imperatives (i.e., "laws"). The structure of Romans follows Paul's custom, namely, the presentation of "theological" truth followed by detailed "ethical" imperatives derived from that theology.

The Biblical Paradigm of God's Salvation

Christians are "united to Christ." Salvation's blessings come to the believer because the believer is "in Christ." Owing to the merits of Christ, therefore, I can claim *"every spiritual blessing"* (Eph. 1:3, italics mine). If, however, I view justification (God's declaration that I am righteous in Christ) as a formal blessing appropriated at conversion, but sanctification (God setting me apart to live righteously in Christ) as a practical blessing distributed as I grow, then on what basis might I attempt to be sanctified? Too often professing believers strive to be sanctified by conforming to the law. But this approach flies in the face of the Bible's basic premise of salvation—"But the righteous man shall *live* by faith" (Rom. 1:17 NASB, italics mine).

Sanctification is best viewed not simply as a stage that follows justification. Sanctification is living according to the implications of justification.[6] Yes, it involves obedience. But, so does justification. When I was converted, I obeyed the gospel (Rom. 15:18; 2 Thess. 1:8). Obedience, however, is not the means of justification nor of sanctification. Faith is. Because I believe, I obey. Christian obedience is an aspect and outgrowth of faith. There is no sanctification apart from faith-sanctification. Likewise, I am glorified by grace through faith as I live in the light of my certain destiny. By faith I now "sit . . . in the heavenly places in Christ Jesus" (Eph. 2:6).

Grace sanctifies. What is God's grace? Grace is not "what," but "who"—the Lord Jesus Christ. Legalism has me within its clutches the moment I regard grace as a thing to be gained, not a person to be believed. Unless I keep this firmly at the forefront of my mind, I am easy prey for legalism. Christ does not dispense grace as if it were some spiritual substance. Christ *is* grace. I am "graced" by being found by faith "in Christ," otherwise I might wrongly conclude that I need to *do* something to extract sanctifying grace from God. Any time I say something like, "He will grace me if I . . . ," I affirm my belief in a quid pro quo arrangement with God that eviscerates grace. I might not be so crass as to negotiate blessings from God for my cash contributions to Christian causes. I am more likely to ante up something like praying fervently or evangelizing frequently as spiritually appropriate bargaining chips. But, whenever I offer something to God in exchange for grace I expose myself for the legalist I am.

The Effects of Sin

Until I recognize the true nature of my sin, I will swap God's gracious blessing for some legalistic sop. I need grace, nothing more. Sinners—dead and malfunctioning because of sin—need the grace of God's forgiveness and regenerating presence. Jesus can be for sinners what they need—righteousness—only when they recognize that they have none of their own.

Jesus' dinner date with Simon, the Pharisee, perfectly illustrates the biblical perspective on sin and Christian freedom (Luke 7:36–50). Jesus' response to the believing woman who washed Jesus' feet with her tears disturbed Simon. "If this man were a prophet He would know who and what sort of person this woman is who is touching Him, that she is a sinner," Simon said to himself (v. 39 NASB). Jesus *was* a prophet. He did know. Simon was right. She was a sinner. But Jesus said, "Her sins, which are many, have been forgiven, for she loved much; but he who is forgiven little, loves little" (v. 47 NASB). Simon was wrong in his failure to recognize that he was just as great a sinner as the woman. Simon should have loved much, but *he* did not because he was blind to his sin. Each one of us should love much, but . . .

Jesus Our Example

Jesus is the object of my faith. He is more than my sinless substitute. Jesus is also my example. In His dependence on the Father He modeled the same servant disposition that I should adopt (Phil. 2:5–8). Incredibly, God calls me to be as perfect as Jesus, as perfect as our heavenly Father Himself (Matt. 5:48; 1 Peter 1:14–16). Christ perfectly followed and fulfilled the law (Matt. 5:16–20). He actually heightened the law's implications, indicating that the standard of compliance extends beyond the act to the intent (e.g., Matt. 5:21).

The gospel would not be good news if it announced my release from the law's penalty by Christ, but now obliged me to be Christlike (which is equivalent to fulfilling the law) by dint of my ability to live as He did. No amount of gratitude for sins forgiven and no presentation of perfect modeling alone can effect righteous living. How did Christ satisfy the law's demands? It was by grace through faith in the power of the Spirit. And, as the Father sent Him, so He sends us (John 20:21). Everything the Father through the Spirit was to Him to fulfill His humanity and purpose (John 3:34 NIV), He through the Spirit promises to be to us (John 14:16–20).

The Holy Spirit and the Law

God's one provision for us to live lawfully, ethically, is Himself. That is why God commands me to walk "according to the Spirit."

> For what the Law could not do, weak as it was through the flesh, God did: sending His own Son in the likeness of sinful flesh and as an offering for sin, He condemned sin in the flesh, in order that the requirement of the Law might be fulfilled in us, who do not walk according to the flesh, but according to the Spirit. (Rom. 8:3–4 NASB)

Why did Jesus take the curse that the law justly pronounced? *"In order that* the requirement of the Law might be fulfilled in us." The presence of the Holy Spirit ensures that every blessing of Christ is applied to me. The Spirit's name advertises His purpose. He is the *Holy* Spirit, not because He is intrinsically more holy than the Father or the Son. He is named the Holy Spirit because He comes to make me holy (i.e., sanctified), or Christlike. No law speaks against or extends beyond the scope of the fruit of the Spirit (Gal. 5:22–23), because *the fruit the Spirit produces and the standard the law envisions are identical.*

The Word of God

I cannot know the direction in which the Spirit is moving me, and for which I am assured His enablement, apart from the Bible. The Bible tells me with propositional precision what the Spirit in me wants to do. The Spirit inspired the Word and now illumines the Word, directing me to interpret it the way that God gave it (i.e., faithful hermeneutics). The Spirit speaks today in His Word, not in extrabiblical "words" or ephemeral "senses." "Sensing," ironically, is the modus operandi of the world, the flesh, and the devil. Is true loving what I "sense" to be loving, or what God defines in His Word to be loving? Discipline, self-sacrifice, and confrontation, for example, are not bad things when they are performed biblically, yet they may offend a certain sentimental, this-worldly definition of love.

Christian ethics is the discipline of applying the truth of the Bible to life, to the level of detail revealed in the Bible, in order to demonstrate God's functional authority in life. For those life issues not directly addressed in Scripture, or for those life situations where multiple issues collide, the Word provides priorities and principles that engage every Christian in the task of "pressing on" in faith.[7] Prayer, the church, and providence—commonly called "means of grace"—are God-ordained ways the Spirit applies God's Word to life.

It is the task of sound hermeneutics both to understand the meaning of the text and to apply the truth of the text to life, whether I begin with the authoritative text or move from

life to the text.[8] Every Christian is responsible to be in fellowship with the church to identify the specific issues in the contemporary situation that need addressing, to analyze cultural
lenses that may distort perception of the biblical perspective,
and to strategize concerning the best approaches to live God's
will ethically.

Biblical authority ceases to function when I either ignore
the standard of God's righteousness found in it, or when I add
to those standards. Usually the latter is regarded as legalism.
Yet, insisting on going no farther than articulating in vague,
undefined generalities the standards of a godly life only leaves
me with standards derived from the world, the flesh, and the
devil. That is also legalism, as we have seen, in its most decep-
tive form.

Legalism and the Victorious Christian Life

Victorious Life teaching has been criticized as promoting legalism. Is that criticism justified? I've outlined in this
essay how authentic Christian living is the opposite of legalism
and "the victorious life" is another way of saying "authentic
Christian living." How, then, do some critics accuse the teaching of being legalistic? For one thing, some advocates of the
Victorious Life do tend toward legalism. Not the spokesper-
sons so much, but those who seek to apply what they have
heard may stumble into the legalism trap. In fact, any
Christian who is serious about holiness may pursue it with
self-effort, a form of legalism. On the other hand, any Christian
who is successful in areas where he or she formerly experienced defeat may be tempted to take credit for the achievement, and that is a form of legalism. Again, people may not
actually take credit for themselves, but in testifying of God's
enabling grace may appear to some to be spiritually proud,
which would be a sure sign of legalism. So the charge of legalism may have merit or may seem to have merit because of the
speech or behavior of some advocates.

But there is a more common reason for the criticism. Many people misunderstand the term *legalism* and assign it to anyone who is serious about keeping the law of God, who is aggressive in the pursuit of holiness. In such cases the fault lies more with the critic than with those criticized. Many critics hold that the law has no place in the life of a Christian, and for them the person advocating a life of victory over temptation and sin, naming those sins in biblical detail, is misnamed "legalistic." But the teaching of victory in Christ is grace from beginning to end, the antithesis of legalism. Nevertheless, the temptation is there for every Christian, no matter what his or her view of sanctification, to slide back into the legalism trap; so how do we avoid it?

Avoiding Legalism

I can hear someone saying, "Wait a minute. The title for your chapter indicates that you will discuss how to avoid legalism. You have discussed a lot of theology. But, what should I do?" Ah! Do you see the problem? If your first impulse in cultivating your Christian life is to *do* something, you might be illustrating the pervasive and subversive nature of the trap of legalism.

The way to avoid legalism—at least in the first instance—is not to do, but to *think*. Paul says, "Be transformed by the renewing of your *mind*" (Rom. 12:2 NASB, italics mine). Jesus taught that legalists "*suppose* [wrongly] that they will be heard for their many words" (Matt. 6:7 NASB, italics mine), and "think [wrongly] that in them [the Scriptures as interpreted by them]" they had eternal life (John 5:39 NASB). The author of Hebrews declares Abraham to be faithful because, "He *considered* that God is able to raise men even from the dead" (Heb. 11:19 NASB, italics mine). Notice how Peter gives us the proper order—think, then behave—when he writes about Christian living in 1 Peter 1:13–15:

Therefore, gird your minds for action, keep sober in spirit, fix your hope completely on the grace to be brought to you at the revelation of Jesus Christ. As obedient children, do not be conformed to the former lusts which were yours in your ignorance, but like the Holy One who called you, be holy yourselves also in your behavior. (NASB)

So, train yourself to *think biblically*. When you do, you increasingly *will think* thankfully. Legalists think tit for tat. They also "look gift horses in the mouth," deciding whether they want to pay tit for tat. But one who knows grace is overwhelmingly grateful for Christ, knowing that giving thanks in everything is "the will of God" (1 Thess. 5:18).

To think biblically means to *think prayerfully*. A legalist prays to impress God and others. A Christian prays focusedly and continually so God may impress His Word upon every situation and relationship of life. A person who thinks biblically will *think lovingly*. A legalist competes with others to amass more and greater blessings from God. A Christian seeks to be the channel of more and greater blessing to others from God. This is why a Christian will *think evangelistically*. What greater blessing can we give another than the gospel of Christ? Telltale evidence of a legalistic orientation is inordinate occupation with the depth and richness of one's own spirituality in the absence of planting and nurturing the life of Christ in others. And when Christians think biblically they should *think ethically*. God's standards have not changed, because God has not changed. Our sentiments should resonate with the psalmist's, "Oh how I love Thy law!" (Ps. 119:97 NASB). Christ has set us free to identify, detail, and press for full conformity to the law's demands. Biblical freedom is not the right to do what we want to do, but the power to do what we ought to do. Any gospel short of accomplishing this is no gospel at all.

Notes

1. Unless otherwise indicated, I will use the term *law* in this essay to refer to what most call God's "moral law." I define "moral law" as God's righteous standard, the righteousness of God Himself, which He designed human beings to image (Eph. 4:24; Col. 3:10) and to which the biblical imperatives for all human beings conform. The Law of Moses is not coextensive with the "moral law," yet includes the basic outline of it. For more discussion on the way the Bible uses the word *law* see Robertson McQuilkin's chapter, "Law," in his *An Introduction to Biblical Ethics*, 2nd ed. (Wheaton: Tyndale, 1989, 1995), 31–72.

2. Evangelistic strategies, to be biblical, must take into account the presence of the work of the law in the conscience of the unbeliever. The first witness anyone receives is the Holy Spirit who convicts of sin (John 16:7–11; Rom. 1:18f.). Also, biblical counseling must be grounded in the standard of God's law. The reality of humanity's just guilt for breaking God's law and the goal of fulfilling the law in Christ are the necessary foundational pillars of any viable counseling theory. Any model of ministry is inadequate that does not account for humanity's rebellion against God's law (guilt) and humanity's inability to reflect God's image defined by the law (dysfunctionality).

3. The perennial question of "assurance of salvation" interfaces with the biblical definition of legalism and the biblical assumption of the growing, victorious life of the "normal" Christian. The Bible extends the promise of assurance to those who "trust and obey" (cf. 1 John 5:1–5). The Bible is moot and so should we be on whether habitually untrusting and disobedient professing Christians are Christians at all. God does not bargain with me over how untrusting or disobedient I can remain and still enjoy assurance. The aphorism, "If He is not Lord of all, He is not Lord at all," is apropos. The legalistic professing Christian, therefore, rightly worries continually, "Have I done enough?" According to Romans 4:16, however, "it is by *faith*, that it might be in accordance with *grace*, in order that the promise may be *certain*" [(NASB), italics mine].

4. The word *ethical* comes from the Greek *ethos*, meaning "custom" or "law." It is, therefore, appropriate to use when considering the abiding standard to which God calls all Christians.

5. I assisted Robertson McQuilkin with "The Impact of Postmodern Thinking on Evangelical Hermeneutics," a paper read at the annual meeting of the Evangelical Theological Society, Naperville, Ill., in November 1994, and soon to be published in *The Journal of the Evangelical Theological Society*. In it we call for a reaffirmation of biblical authority in the face of an erosion of confidence among evangelicals that the Bible can speak authoritatively today.

6. For a lengthier exposition on the biblical doctrine of sanctification see my article "Sanctification" in Walter Elwell, ed., *The Dictionary of Biblical Theology* (Grand Rapids: Baker, 1994).

7. Robertson McQuilkin's *An Introduction to Biblical Ethics* is an excellent model of this approach to Christian ethics. He tackles the "hard" issues without resorting to platitudes, offering nuanced or open conclusions in instances where an application of the biblical principles is ambiguous, yet direct and uncompromising conclusions where the Bible is unambiguous.

8. The hermeneutics text Columbia International University uses in both the college and seminary is Robertson McQuilkin's *Understanding and Applying the Bible*, 2nd ed. (Chicago: Moody, 1983, 1992). As the title indicates, good hermeneutics must move from the biblical horizon (What does the inspired text mean?) to the present horizon (How do I apply it to life?).

5

About the Author

Stuart Briscoe is one of America's best-known pulpiteers, power-fully proclaiming the message of authentic Christian living from major pulpits and through radio, TV, video- and audiotape. A best-selling author, Briscoe has published more than twenty-five books. His identity with Victorious Life teaching goes back to his youth when he traveled the world as a spokesman for that message under the auspices of Torchbearers, a British movement that emphasizes discipleship in its worldwide network of Bible schools as well as on conference platforms.

A Britisher by birth and a former banker, Briscoe eventually moved to America in 1970 at the invitation of a fledgling new church in Brookfield, Wisconsin—Elmbrook Church, where attendance now tops six thousand. His wife, Jill, also is a best-selling author and conference speaker. They have three adult children.

About This Chapter

In this last chapter on the foundations of Victorious Life teaching, we move beyond the historical review of a movement and theological analyses to what Stuart Briscoe is famous for: clear, exciting exposition of biblical truth from Bible texts. Here the path to freedom from bondage to sin is clearly charted. Those who choose to join Stuart Briscoe in following that path will experience a whole new quality of life, free and fulfilled.

Making It Work: Free At Last!

by Stuart Briscoe

W e are Abraham's descendants and have never been slaves to anyone," the Jews expostulated angrily. "How can you say that we shall be set free?"

Jesus appeared quite unfazed by their reaction. He had just told them, "If you hold to my teaching, you are really my disciples. Then you will know the truth, and the truth will set you free" (John 8:31–32 NIV). While they were angrily insisting that they had no experience of subjugation He could, with some justification, have pointed out to them the Roman soldiers standing guard at that moment outside the Temple gates, and if He had so wished, He could have mentioned Egypt and Babylon and a number of other major powers who had subjugated—or tried to subjugate—the Jews. But He held His peace. The self-evident reality would catch up to them sooner or later.

Were they in total denial, or were Jesus and the Jews at that moment not even on the same page? Jesus knew they did not accept His words; they, on the other hand, were convinced He did not understand their position or He would not have had the temerity to make such an outrageous suggestion. They were Abraham's descendants! That set them apart. They were, in their own estimation, rich in resources and privilege and didn't need a thing from Jesus or anyone else. They most certainly were not in need of freedom! The undeniable fact of their privileged position as the covenant people was undoubtedly blinding their minds to other realities, which Jesus was intent on bringing into the light.

"Everyone who sins is a slave to sin. . . . I know you are Abraham's descendants," He responded (John 8:35–37 NIV). In other words, they had to realize that it was possible to be a descendant of Abraham, a member of the covenant people, spiritually privileged to the nth degree, and still be a slave to sin! And His offer as Messiah was not political liberation from the powers they were reluctant to recognize but emancipation from the slavery of sin, which they were even less prepared to acknowledge.

Self-assured in their status as sons of Abraham, they were shocked to hear Him add, "Now a slave has no permanent place in the family, but a son belongs to it forever" (John 8:35 NIV). The inference was inescapable. He was implying that they were not only slaves to sin but accordingly they were in a precarious spiritual position despite their privileged status. And in case there was any confusion, He then pointed unerringly to Himself—the Son who belonged in the family, adding, "So if the Son sets you free, you will be free indeed"(John 8:36 NIV). These proud men understood neither the tyranny of their enslavement nor the possibility of the emancipation or the availability of Christ's empowerment.

This would lead one to assume that they were "dyed in the wool" opponents of Jesus who were out for His blood, when in actuality, the text tells us, they were new believers in Him! But His pointed and personal teaching, which challenged their presuppositions and required a radical change of mind on their part, so infuriated them that their rage did in fact border on the murderous.

How could believers in Him react like that? Maybe they were only believers in the sense that they believed about Him but not in Him. Or maybe there were two different groups to whom Jesus was talking at the same time. These and other suggestions have been made by scholars. Perhaps these "believers" were examples of the kind of seed that falls on the hard ground and initially springs into life only to wither when the heat is on. As Jesus explained it, "They believe for a while, but in the time of testing they fall away" (Luke 8:13 NIV). Jesus was no stranger to this kind of shallow response to His Word, having been told by some of His followers that His teaching on eating His flesh and drinking His blood was a hard saying and they wanted nothing more to do with Him or His teaching. Whatever their specific spiritual status, there can be no doubt that Jesus was offering to lead them into an experience of emancipation from sin's domination—an experience they were not open to accepting. Their failure to accept was not caused by inadequate teaching but by unwillingness to respond. The teaching was clear:

- They were sinning—this was evident in their refusal to believe, their resistance to His Word, their anger, and their ill-disciplined reaction, which incredibly showed violent potential.
- The fact that they were sinning showed conclusively that they were enslaved by sin, in the sense that sin is a dominating power in the human experience, and the more one sins the more one becomes a slave to that sin.
- There is the possibility of freedom from this enslavement, and there is a connection between knowing the truth and experiencing the freedom.
- This truth and the Son are inextricably linked to each other in that Jesus said He was "the way, the truth, and the life." So the mix of experiencing His person

and following His teaching constitutes knowing the truth.

- This knowledge of the truth is the essence of true discipleship, which is necessary to release Christ's emancipating power in the life of the believer.

The question now to be addressed is, "What is the relevance of this exchange between Jesus and a group of first-century Jews to twenty-first-century people?"

The obvious starting point in answering this question is the fact that we, like they, are prone to sinning, which according to the Lord Jesus, means each of us could legitimately be called "a slave of sin." Granted some of us, like the first-century Jews, might be into denial, albeit with twenty-first-century perspectives. Rather than seeing themselves as slaves of sin, many prefer to regard themselves as pitiful victims of other people's transgressions—which they may well be—or unfortunate inheritors of rogue genes—which they probably are.

There are two possible extremes of which we must be aware. The first "psychologizes" the faith to such a degree that there is no place in the bewildering mix of psychological insights for such old-fashioned realities as "the flesh," "fallenness," and "sin." The second extreme refuses to learn from honest psychological insights the things that help to explain human behavior without in any way contradicting what Scripture reveals concerning human deficiencies. Whatever the circumstances of our lives—the accumulation of trauma, the ramifications of nurture and nature—Christians in this psychologically oriented culture must accept the fact that sin is a dominating factor in human experience. Moreover, whatever propensities to certain behavioral patterns flowing from past experiences may be evident, they are all part of human fallenness and contribute to the mass of sin that enslaves. Accordingly, whatever psychological help may be received in modifying unacceptable behavior, nothing should be regarded as an acceptable substitute for dealing with sin.

I have not the slightest hesitation in applauding therapy that so modifies a man's behavior that he stops beating his wife. By helping him see why he does it and by giving him some ideas how to stop it, valuable help has been given. If there's any doubt, a quick phone call to the wife will put the doubts to rest! But I worry about therapy that refuses to call his behavior sin and thus fails to recognize the spiritual dimension of the problem and administer appropriate spiritual antidotes. Modern-day equivalents to first-century Jews might say, "We were never slaves to anything; we were victims. We resent being told we are the slaves of sin; we are Freud's children." Jesus' words echo down the centuries to us in the twenty-first century as surely as they reverberated in the ears of the first-century Jews: "Everyone who sins is a slave to sin."

"But so what?" says a modern believer. "I'm saved, my sins are forgiven, God loves me unconditionally, He understands my weakness, and nobody's perfect. And by the way, don't forget Jesus said, 'Judge not that you be not judged.' So lay off will you?" However true some of these sentiments might be, the fact remains that Jesus *did* address the subject of setting people free from sin's enslavement! So the "so what?" is not hard to answer! Those whose sins have been forgiven and who bask in God's understanding love for them are to be encouraged to look at their potential for ongoing sinning, and then to ask whether continuing in those sins is normative. Jesus' words clearly point in another direction. He was talking about them enjoying some kind of freedom. But what kind?

Does God in some way offer an experience subsequent to regeneration where He takes away my ability to sin? Or does He in some way impart to me as part of the salvation package the ability not to sin?

Paul, writing to the Romans, dealt further with the theme of slavery to sin that the Lord had introduced. "We know," he said, "that our old self was crucified with him so that the body of sin might be done away with, *that we should no longer be slaves to sin*" (Rom. 6:6 NIV, italics mine). So being freed from sin in Paul's words has to do with being "crucified with Christ." This, he insisted, took place in our baptism, which in his way of looking at things coincided with coming to faith. Remember that in the church's early days those who trusted Christ were promptly baptized, therefore faith and baptism were seen as a complete package. So occasionally the word *baptism* would be used as shorthand for "faith / baptism" in much the same way as "getting a diamond" signifies getting engaged or "putting out a shingle" points to starting up a law practice.

But in what way does Paul mean that we were crucified with Christ and as a result died to sin? Surely he is not suggesting that we are, through faith in Christ, introduced to a spiritual realm in which we are as dead as the proverbial dodo and like that mysterious beast are incapable of doing anything—including sinning? All the evidence points away from our being incapable of sinning. We should be excruciatingly aware that we can continue to sin. But it is clear he does not mean that those baptized into Christ's death have lost all capacity to sin because he tells us "not to let sin reign in your mortal body." If we can't sin, why say don't sin? Conversely, if he says don't, it must be because we could!

No, let's give Paul credit for being consistent about identification with Christ and realistic about our present experience. He means something else by his insistence that we have been "baptized into his death." But what does He mean?

The clue to understanding *our* death must be an understanding of *His* death. Paul explains that when Christ died, He "died to sin once for all." This cannot mean that He stopped sinning, for He had never started sinning. Nor does it mean that He suddenly became immune to sin's seduction. He had never been susceptible to seduction. His death to sin was a collecting of the wages of sin, which is "death." In His dying He assumed sin's consequences, which as we know is death. This is the death into which we have been baptized—or in which we share. Being baptized into Christ's death does not mean that we are no longer capable of sinning. Neither does it imply that sin will no longer be attractive to us. Rather our union with Him in death means that God looks on us as having been at the Cross when the divine act of justification took place. So as Paul said, "Anyone who has died has been justified [literally] from sin." Accordingly, no longer being slaves to sin means we are no longer being held accountable for our sin the same way a dead man can no longer be held accountable for his deeds. In this sense our relationship to sin has been terminated, through baptism into Christ's death, and in the same way that Christ was raised again, so "we too may live a new life."

Take the case of a beautiful, young, single woman. She is surrounded by admirers who constantly ask her for dates. Some of the men she finds attractive but suspects they may be dangerous; others she knows are safe but unattractive. She is unsure how to respond to the former because of her own ambivalence and is fearful of offending the latter. She doesn't know what to do and lives in constant bondage to her indecision, fear, and other assorted emotions. Instead of enjoying her singleness, it is a burden, a bondage. Subsequently she marries. The young men come around not knowing her new status. Now she is no longer unsure how to respond. She smiles sweetly, holds out her hand, shows her ring, and says, "No thanks, I'm married." She has been "freed up"; the ring is the sign and the seal of her new standing. She no longer needs to worry about whether she is doing the right thing; she knows the right thing is to live in the good of having "died" to singleness and she is now free to enjoy being married. This does not mean, of course, that she is incapable of recognizing that other men are attractive, and of course she is capable of being unfaithful. She is not dead to other attractions or deviant possibilities, but in her positional dying she has become free to live in a new realm.

Let's remind ourselves of Jesus' words: "If you hold to my teaching, you are really my disciples. Then you will know the truth, and the truth will set you free" (John 8:31–32 NIV). We have seen that knowing the truth involves responding to His teaching, but also because He personally is the Truth, it includes being in union with His person. This brings us back to Paul. Knowing the Truth, being in union with Christ, is the same as being baptized into His death and resurrection. Holding to Christ's teaching, in Paul's language, means "Count yourselves dead to sin but alive to God." And being a disciple means, "Do not let sin reign in your mortal body. . . . Do not offer the parts of your body to sin . . . offer yourselves to God . . . and offer the parts of your body to him" (Rom. 6:12–13 NIV).

So let's see if we can put it all together. We have come to the point of accepting that in our union with Christ through being regenerated and sealed in baptism we have been transported into a realm of experience where we are no longer held accountable for sin. We have been justified from the consequences of our sin. In fact we have entered into a relationship to sin that is not at all dissimilar to that of a dead criminal's relationship to his crimes. He is no longer in a position to be held accountable—neither are we. But unlike the dead criminal we have been raised into a new life that now offers us the possibility of being dominated by grace rather than subjugated to sin.

The significance of being "under grace" is that grace provides the empowerment to live in the good of the new status. Jesus called it being united to His life in the same way that a branch is united to the vine. Whether we think like Paul of grace as divine enabling, or with Jesus see ourselves as the conduits through which His life flows, the result is the same. We are now enabled through grace / life to live in newness of life.

One of the characteristics of this new life is the ability to say no to the old life to which we have died anyway. This is not the same as Nancy Reagan's "Just Say No" campaign for teenagers; her campaign suffered from being inspiring but not empowering. God doesn't say, "Now don't yield the parts of your body to sin. Go on—do your best." His message is more like, "Don't yield the parts of your body to sinful practices because doing that is not consistent with your new relationship to Me as My disciple. I know how difficult this will be for you but don't worry because I make grace—or the life of Christ—available to you. So in that empowering go ahead, be strong, and stop doing the wrong thing."

There's more. When the opportunity to go wrong comes our way—which it will regularly—we not only count on our new status and in His grace decline to do the wrong thing; additionally, we take the opportunity to do the *right* thing. Being free from sin not only means I can be strong in Him to stop doing wrong, it also means in Him I have the ability to do what's right. So, for example, if I have a problem with my tongue being an instrument of torture, I not only have strength but I am also given ability to use my tongue as an instrument of blessing. If my mind drifts off into unwholesome thought, I can not only corral it, I can channel it into productive thought patterns.

It will be seen from what we have discussed that there are a faith component and an obedience dimension to being made free. This should not surprise us because the whole of spiritual experience runs on the parallel tracks of obedience and dependence—or, as the old hymn insists, "trust and obey." We know this, but it should be noted, nevertheless, simply because there is a tendency in discussions of the life of spiritual maturity or victory to concentrate on one at the expense of the other. I well remember as a young person being mildly confused when asked to sing:

> Buried with Christ and raised with Him too,
> What is there left for me to do?
> Simply to cease from struggle and strife,
> Simply to walk in newness of life.
> Glory be to God.

Simply ceasing to struggle didn't do it for me! I found when I gave up the struggle of obedience and discipline I slipped farther away from my desired objective of maturity and victory. But by the same token I had become greatly discouraged by the struggle, so the thought of giving up on it was most appealing. But that didn't seem to work either! Those advocating only dependence—or ceasing—were right and wrong, while those promoting obedience alone were wrong and right. It is not a matter of either/or but a case of both/and. It is dependence on His grace flowing like the sap of the vine through my branchlike life, which is the result of "being united with Him in His resurrection," which makes obedience possible. And that obedience is clearly demanded by the imperatives that discipleship enjoins and that Paul spelled out. So, as always, it's a matter of dependence and obedience.

To the extent we choose to put these principles into practice we open ourselves up to the possibility of increasing maturity as one by one we chip away at the sinful practices that are so deeply rooted in our fallenness. The bad news is that as we begin to see progress in one area we will be surprised to discover other undreamed of areas waiting for our attention.

The good news is, as Jesus said, "If the Son sets you free, you will be free indeed" (John 8:36 NIV), while Paul's version of the same truth is, "Sin shall not be your master, because you are not under law, but under grace" (Rom. 6:14 NIV). Glory be to God!

PART TWO

Implications

The foundation has been well laid, and that is just as well since the fundamental biblical teaching of a victorious life in Christ has been neglected by much of the church, especially in late twentieth-century America. But in focusing on the foundation we could easily neglect the superstructure—the implications of the teaching for life beyond the individual who experiences "victory in Christ." In this section we will look carefully at how a personal life in the Spirit will impact the church and the world. If my personal experience does not lead to change in my church and community, can it lay claim to being an authentic Christian life?

First, the church. John Oliver gives a wonderful case study of the transforming power of Victorious Life teaching in a local congregation. Next, the world. The primary responsibility of the church toward the world is to win it to faith, so Sanna Barlow Rossi outlines the implications of victorious living for evangelism at home and abroad. The ministry of the church for its own and for the world calls for leadership that experiences life in the Spirit, so Johnny Miller describes, again through a case study, how this kind of leadership can be developed in theological education. Lest, in concentrating on discipling Christians and winning the lost, we neglect the social implications of living free and fulfilled, John Perkins and Crawford

Loritts provide moving testimonials of God's abundant grace in the life of an individual and of a people. These testimonies could prove too personal and specific to move the rest of us to action, so Robert Priest provides a most intriguing analysis of the cultural factors in victorious living—factors we must all live by if we are to be truly free and fulfilled.

6

About the Author

Since the arrival of John W. P. Oliver as pastor of the First Presbyterian Church of Augusta, Georgia, in 1969, the historic downtown church has been transformed. For the twenty-fifth anniversary celebration of his ministry there, I wrote the congregation:

> Twenty-five years ago, the total budget was $68,000, with little or none for missions. This year the missions budget alone is well over a million dollars. Twenty-five years ago, one person was listed as a missionary but no one knew her. Today First Church supports more than 150, many of those sons and daughters of this Church. Twenty-five years ago there was little corporate prayer and none for the missionary cause; today many gather weekly to pray for the world and prayer is pervasive throughout the life of the church.
>
> Some churches are strong on reaching people in distant places, but weak in evangelism at home. Not First Presbyterian Church of Augusta. God has been pleased to bring many to birth in this family. One indication is that twenty-five years ago, about 16 people gathered for the Sunday evening service. . . . Today the sanctuary is full, many of those present won to Christ by members of this body of believers.

Although many factors have contributed to this remarkable story, Pastor Oliver himself believes the transformation is based on regular, clear proclamation of the message of victory in Christ.
Oliver came to Christ as an undergraduate at Denison University, transferred to Wheaton College, and graduated also from Fuller Theological Seminary and Southern Baptist Theological Seminary. He served two churches as assistant pastor before his call to Augusta. John and his wife, Cris, have two grown sons.

About This Chapter

We begin a section on implications of Victorious Life teaching for evangelism and missions, Christian education, and society at large. But we begin with the foundation: the local congregation. In most of these chapters we've asked people who have personally experienced these implications to tell their story.

In this chapter on church we turned to the pastor of a truly remarkable church. It is remarkable because it is strong, not in one or two areas, but in all areas: solid Bible teaching from pulpit and classroom podium, corporate prayer on an astounding scale, strong, steady growth through evangelism, nationwide impact through social activism, huge investment in world missions, a musical program second to none, and on the story goes. It will soon be apparent that Pastor Oliver attributes these developments in large part to the undergirding teaching of victorious Christian living. He only gives a few snapshots, and that rather reservedly, as you will see, but there is enough of the exciting story here to inspire the leadership of any church with the possibilities.

Victorious Living in the Local Church

by John W. P. Oliver

P reaching the Victorious Christian Life provided by the risen Christ is one of three critical elements that will produce a vital and deeply committed congregation of believers. When interwoven with historic Christian orthodoxy and an evangelical standard for cooperation in matters related to God's kingdom on earth, regular proclamation of a life of victory by the power of the Spirit will transform lives and, indeed, the entire congregation.

Our church is Presbyterian and we have found, contrary to the opinion of some, that classical Reformed theology provides room for focus on the life of victory in our risen Head. The Westminster Shorter Catechism asks, "What is sanctification?" and answers, "Sanctification is the work of God's free grace, whereby we are renewed in the whole man after the image of God, and are enabled more and more to die unto sin, and live unto righteousness." The preaching of the provisions of the victorious Lord Jesus Christ through the person and work of the Holy Spirit for the renewal of the whole man and the enabling of the renewed man for righteous living is clearly Reformed truth as well as evangelical biblical truth. No wonder it can produce a company of believers in a local church that is dynamic in life and service.

I'm seriously concerned about spiritual depth in a day of widespread focus on church growth, which, all too often, is spiritually superficial. Preaching the resources the believer has in our victorious Lord is a significant part of the way a congregation can be propelled toward maturity in the Christian faith, leaving behind the elemental things (Heb. 6:1).

Such an emphasis from the pulpit and in the church's Bible classes not only leads to a maturing Christian faith, it directs the mind and heart to the indwelling power available for implementation of the message. And that is always a part of truly preaching the whole counsel of God. It is insufficient to stress what ought to be done. The hearers of the Word of God must know that there is power available, because of our mystical union with Christ, to become doers of that Word. Without the provisions of the Lord Jesus for the right application of the Word received, preaching can degenerate into impartation of knowledge alone, or, worse, a harangue about what ought to be. Is it not the case that there are earnest believers in churches that preach the Scriptures who grow weary in trying to do what they ought because they know little about the victory of Christ that renews and enables them to accomplish the "ought"? Sometimes the frustration is a struggle for personal holiness, sometimes for enduring service for Christ, but there must be a better way.

We have seen at First Church, Augusta, that what Christ has accomplished on the Cross and in the Resurrection, and now ministers to the church through the Holy Spirit, does produce knowledgeable disciples who know both what must be done and wherein lies the strength, beyond their own, to do it. The Victorious Christian Life message reveals the enabling grace of sanctification for the believer who is confronted with the demands and duties of the Word of God and finds himself unable, even after regeneration, to be and to do what the Lord calls him to be and do. The Victorious Life message provides the congregation an ongoing, practical emphasis on the Lord's work of renewing "the whole man after the image of God and enabling him more and more to die unto sin and live unto righteousness."

In the congregation represented by this chapter, after almost thirty years of grounding in this teaching concerning the victorious life, the evidence is clear in every aspect of the ministry. The church cannot be explained in its growth in size, depth, and fruitfulness in any other way. Consider some of the results.

The Victorious Christian Living message has helped to produce numerical growth that has been steady and solid. This has occurred in a location and in facilities that had been deemed unsuitable for rebuilding a vibrant congregation and where only a dwindling, aging congregation existed. Nothing seemed present to attract new and younger people to the downtown location in the congregation's historic and deteriorating buildings. We didn't use popular means of marketing the church nor employ worldly lures to entice the reluctant.

The turning point came when one newly married and newly converted young couple ventured to a morning service in old, dark, poorly maintained facilities. They returned for the evening service. They never left. The two of them, who now comprise part of the church's leadership, were the first of a steady stream of people who have not only been drawn to the church, but who have taken hold of the provisions of our triumphant Lord. The result has been recognizable spiritual depth and productivity for the kingdom of God. Programs and promotions could have provided an initial appeal but could not have created the durability and depth produced by the teaching of the life of victory in Christ. Rather, the programs and promotions become, not appeals to entice the unsuspecting, but avenues for ministry for those already appropriating the church's message.

Repeatedly the question has been posed as to how this congregation has been able to keep leaders and workers in the church for the long haul. The answer has sounded almost pious to some to say that, in large measure, it is the stress on the provisions for victory in our risen Lord. Especially has this been true when the question implied that some secret method has been in operation. While respite and renewal are needed (and provided) for the congregation's leaders and workers so as not to have burnout among the willing servants of Christ, it is arguable nonetheless that it is the provision for victory in the Lord that not only renews the individual believer, but also helps the believer to overcome the inherent tendency to look after the things of self more than the things of others. Durability as well as depth have emerged from the preaching of the message.

Spiritual stability and a serious attention to the Word of God are manifested in large measure because the congregation is receiving more than information in the preaching and teaching week by week. It is not that a "how-to" seminar substitutes for the preaching of the Word. It is that along with biblical content and the call for a verdict, a connection is made with the riches in Christ Jesus so the hearers can understand that the verdict reached in the mind is possible to be lived out through Christ, who strengthens them (Phil. 4:13).

Grasping the means by which the Word may be implemented carries its own benefits. More of the Word is sought. Attendance upon the Word becomes a desired thing. Attendance increasingly is less dependent on convenience, competing interests, or the likes of "who is preaching tonight?" A deep hunger and thirst for the Word of God draw irresistibly. Large numbers return on Sunday evenings, in part, because of the additional and practical benefit of putting the mind and heart under the authority of the Word, knowing that its benefits enable the hearer to do what is expected.

The phenomenon of a crowded sanctuary on Sunday evenings has piqued interest and raised questions not easily answered by sharing methods or ideas. People ask, "How do you get them to attend on Sunday night?" Of course we emphasize commitment to the principle of the Lord's Day as the Christian's Sabbath. And there are additional appealing ingredients in the vibrant Sunday evening service. Principally, however, it is the stable, serious attention to the Word that the Victorious Life message has helped to produce.

Private, daily dependence on the Word apparently has developed as more and more believers claim the guides and schedules made available for regular, personal reading and reflection on God's Word.

This same spirit is seen in an annual Bible and Missionary Conference when it is not uncommon to have Sunday morning size, even overflowing, congregations at successive nightly services. The principal speaker for such meetings is annually given the assignment to preach not just "missions," but also the Lord's abundant and victorious provisions. Thus God's people obediently follow through on the challenge for world evangelization. Compelling illustrations and missionary reports about world evangelization make the challenge to the congregation clear. The source of victory in Christ through grace makes it possible to respond obediently and confidently to the challenge. The riches that empower must accompany challenge in true proclamation.

Were space unlimited, it could be demonstrated that the message of victory has grown a Sunday school in a downtown setting with inadequate facilities for more than two decades. The depth of lay teachers and serious attention to the Word of God have steadily advanced the Sunday school from just over one hundred to an average of eleven hundred in attendance. The Victorious Life message has played its part.

The glad embrace of Christian living standards in marked contrast to their rapid disappearance in many evangelical circles is a direct result of understanding that the sanctifying grace of God includes victory through Christ. In a Protestant tradition no longer noted for separation from questionable practices formerly avoided in evangelical congregations, the congregation has gradually but perceptibly allowed a deep commitment to the Lord to eliminate questionable practices that fall in "the gray area" and on which earnest believers are not always agreed. The general movement in the congregation toward a deep piety is in direct ratio to the move away from things lawful but not expedient. The victory of Christ is at the heart of this steady movement toward separation unto the Lord (1 Thess. 1:9).

The separation unto the Lord because of the life of victory has not in general produced a believer-centered life of piety or an isolation from the opportunities to address the needs and hurts all around the church of Jesus Christ. The more there has been an understanding of victory, the more fervent and innovative the ministries have been beyond the borders of the local church. Compassion and service in the broader community have emerged.

In addition to the general, standard supply of assistance for the hurting through cooperative efforts with other congregations, the people have pioneered in the local community and more widely in the country at large in addressing the welfare and distress of people. Interestingly, it is the congregation with a strong stress on the life of victory in Christ that has established a broad-based and multifaceted work in the economically depressed areas of the city. Without the publicity that surrounds the much-appreciated efforts of Habitat for Humanity, for example, believers have lived out their deep commitment to Christ as triumphant Lord in a program to rehabilitate housing for the poor. Regular tutoring of children in inner-city schools is the outworking of the overcoming life for some. Professionals in the health-care field provide clinics in depressed areas and programs to ensure that needier cases are provided transportation to available medical facilities and services. Often supplementing where tax-supported efforts end, medical professionals provide in their services a Christian presence and ensure adequate care and compassion. The message of victory in Christ has not stopped with personal piety.

Perhaps the clearest example of the blending of true piety resulting from a life of victory through Christ with practical, selfless service among the poor and disenfranchised is the congregation's medical campus ministries and its summer mercy projects manned by medical students and professionals. The church's staff for medical campus ministries and Christian student leadership from the medical campuses, characterized by a strong response to the victorious life through Christ, developed as its main ministry of mercy a summer-long medical institute in the slums of inner-city Philadelphia. Spartan living conditions and long, tiring days on the streets are the fare for all participants, medical students there for the summer and physicians who give a week of their time to provide oversight and expertise. Combing the tenements to find children needing vaccinations and specific childhood medical tests, administering such without charge in mobile facilities, and relating to the children and adults in kindness and compassion have earned the opportunity to tell of the saving grace and dying love of the Lord Jesus Christ. Such a ministry summer after summer, without remuneration or acclaim, has accomplished far more than expensive tax-funded medical programs reaching far fewer children. It has been the overcoming of Christ's victory in the believer's life that has originated and sustained such compassionate service. The Victorious Christian Life rightly implemented brings about selfless, compassionate service in Christ's name.

Knowing that victory for the believer is only in the death, resurrection, and ascension of the Lord Christ, the congregation has not forsaken soul winning and world evangelization in its ministry to hurting humanity. Personal and corporate evangelism have gone beyond seeking an initial decision to leading the penitent to the riches purchased at Calvary for sanctification as well as for justification. Regularly, through the years of preaching and teaching the Victorious Christian Life, people have come to saving faith in Christ alone and moved ahead toward spiritual maturity. While there are ongoing programs for evangelism, the evidence says that evangelism is inevitably a part of the warp and woof of any ministry that includes the message of victory.

Numbers of individuals, predominantly younger adults and young people, have been drawn to the Savior apart from specific, individual evangelistic encounters from the church. From time to time, these conversions have been unexpected if not seemingly impossible. The newer converts seem to sense early on that there is more to be known and appropriated for the believer than the initial work of justification. Evangelism has not only been stimulated by the message of victory, but the fruit has more often than not been conserved by being in the midst of a people serious about living and serving in the strength of the victorious Christ.

The commitment to world evangelization, both in giving and in the sending of families and individuals from the congregation, has inarguably been the fruit, in large measure, of the message of this book. For years the congregation has given 50 percent, and occasionally more than 50 percent, of its regular, annual contributions to benevolences, largely for personnel and agencies involved in world evangelization. This pattern has prevailed even in light of insufficient buildings to accommodate the growing Sunday school, a large part of which has been housed in leased facilities for two decades. Victory is evident in cheerful acceptance of less-than-ideal and crowded classrooms and victory is seen in refusing to reduce benevolences to obtain added space.

While such a "fifty-fifty" ratio has been the goal of the church's leadership, it was not attained through the use of programs or campaigns. The work of victorious grace has quietly moved in the hearts of the people through the years until this goal was achieved and maintained. Matters on the heart of the Lord of the harvest have become the matters on the hearts of His people in the local church.

The departure of business and professional men from their stateside endeavors, in many cases uprooting families in the midst of career development and children's educations, to go to other lands in missionary service has become usual and regular fare after the message of triumph in Christ attained its cumulative effect. The surrender of a promising future in the States by young, career singles is no longer a rarity. Again, the message of victory, along with other biblical emphases, has done its work.

Upon reflection, it is apparent that the progress in every area of the local ministry could not have been realized apart from the truth of the Victorious Christian Life. It can be taught and experienced. Indeed, it must be.

7

About the Author

Sanna Barlow Rossi is best known for her books of mission biography, four for Gospel Recordings and one for Wycliffe Translators. Her most recent volume, *Anthony T. Rossi, Christian Entrepreneur*, chronicles the amazing story of her late husband, the creative genius behind Tropicana.

Following graduation from Columbia Bible College, Rossi taught Bible in the public schools for ten years, then traveled with Joy Ridderhof, founder of Gospel Recordings, for ten years. It was in those pioneer ventures into unreached areas of the world that many of the incredible stories she chronicles took place. When "experts" said there were a couple of thousand languages in the world, Ridderhof and her colleagues had already recorded the gospel message in more than four thousand! The power of the indwelling Christ is the only possible explanation for two young women who penetrated the last frontiers, often where men had feared to go. Ridderhof, also a graduate of Columbia, and Rossi were strongly committed to the Victorious Life message and practiced it with dramatic impact around the world.

About This Chapter

Though Sanna Rossi's experience focused for ten years on pioneer missionary work, in this chapter she demonstrates how the life of victory in Christ incorporates evangelism both at home and abroad. This has been the message of the movement from its beginning. She also demonstrates how essential it is for the messenger to embody the message. The witnessing Christian at home and the pioneering evangelist abroad must live a godly life if that evangelism is to be effective. In this chapter the link between victory in Christ, witness for Christ, and world missions comes into clear focus.

Living in
nd Missions

low Rossi

It is no accident that young Bob McQuilkin came into his initial experience of "victory in Christ" at a missions conference. Victorious living, witness, and missions are inextricably intertwined. One might say that victorious living was linked with evangelism from the outset: "Go therefore and make disciples of all the nations." But how can we do this seemingly impossible task? Adequacy for this work is stated along with the command: "Lo, I am with you always" (Matt. 28:19–20).

Origins of a Movement

Present-day Victorious Life teaching, like Jesus' Great Commission, links Spirit-filled living with world evangelism. In 1910, Charles Trumbull, editor of the *Sunday School Times,* realized in his own life that the secret of victory over sin and defeat is found in the indwelling presence of Christ, and a movement was born. A year later he spoke at a missions conference in New Wilmington, Delaware, where young Robert McQuilkin, eager to know a Christian life more like that of Paul, gave him rapt attention. Following Trumbull's testimony McQuilkin went aside to pray and with almost dramatic suddenness experienced that same surrender and trust in Christ to which Trumbull testified, and it transformed forever his

Christian life. From the start, the teaching on the Spirit-filled life included the call to be witnesses to the uttermost part of the earth.

Victorious Living Includes a Heart for the Lost

In 1912 Trumbull and his associates launched the Victorious Life Testimony and the two secretaries of the organization were Robert McQuilkin and Howard Dinwiddie, both of whom were engaged in a nationwide conference ministry on the Victorious Christian Life.

In 1920 Howard Dinwiddie was sent by the Victorious Life Testimony to hold conferences in Guatemala. There he met Cameron Townsend, who immediately began to share with Dinwiddie his deep burden for the Indians.

As the vision captivated Dinwiddie, he immediately thought of his friend L. L. Legters who was then teaching in Victorious Life Conferences in the States. Dinwiddie knew that Legters had a heart for the Indians and he urged his friend to join the group of men who banded together to reach the Indian tribes. Twelve men gathered for what was to be a historic conference in the highlands of Guatemala. From that meeting came two movements, the Pioneer Mission Agency, associated with America's Keswick, and Wycliffe Bible Translators.[1]

It is not too much to say that Spirit-filled living makes a person a witnessing Christian. Sharing one's faith is an integral part of victorious Christian living. More than that, it makes the Spirit-filled believer a world Christian, and the Victorious Life Testimony proved it from the beginning. To be like Christ is to love the whole world. The Christian's life in Christ and the Christian's mission to the world are inseparable—the cause and effect, life and service, witness and work. "If a person is truly like Christ," states Robertson McQuilkin, "he will be a world Christian, will he not? In other words, witness to one's near neighbors and far neighbors, to the ends of the earth, is part of living victoriously."[2] And that is not just for the full-time missionary.

In London, I talked with a young woman on her way to the Philippines as a missionary. She told me about a friend who was a business entrepreneur. "His whole life is missions," she said. This statement arrested me because she spoke of a man celebrated in Florida, not for his worldwide missionary interests, but as Mr. Tropicana. "He truly loves the Lord," Marianne Seidel affirmed. And as God in His mysterious way eventually led me to leave missionary pioneering and marry that very man, I witnessed firsthand for many years that Anthony Rossi's remarkable success in business was channeled into one purpose: world evangelization. Every Christian who walks in the Spirit and understands the Word of God will be a world Christian. But some are called to direct missionary service.

The Missionary Call Is Heard Best by the Spirit-Filled Heart

Hundreds of people, inspired by the lectures of Dinwiddie and Legters, committed themselves to help meet the challenge of unevangelized Indian peoples. In the early days many of those missionary recruits were channeled into the two mission organizations they were involved in starting, Pioneer Missionary Agency and Wycliffe Bible Translators. That missionary emphasis characterized the Victorious Life Conferences down through the years. For example, Columbia Bible College held Victorious Life Conferences from its beginning and eventually established Ben Lippen Conference Center near Asheville, North Carolina, for that purpose. How well I remember, as a teenager in the 1930s, those Friday evening missionary meetings. At the close, everyone stood in a great circle in Huston Hall. Its open walls were the mountain forest with its orchestration of cicadas and katydids. The song we sang at that time was, "Where He Leads Me, I Will

Follow." We were profoundly committed to the urgent directive—global missions.

Before the Victorious Life Movement was born, Robert McQuilkin was actively involved in leading missionary prayer groups and missionary conferences, but not long after his experience of a new dimension of life in Christ he and his bride felt the tug of the missionary call themselves. Before long they prepared for missionary service in Kenya. But it was not to be. The ship on which they were to sail sank in New York Harbor. That didn't end the missionary vision, however. Soon after, in 1923, when the "praying women" of Columbia, South Carolina, called him to lead their fledgling Southern Bible Institute, McQuilkin joined them to build a school that would proclaim the victorious Christian life and send out thousands of missionaries. It is not by accident that the motto of Columbia International University from the outset was "To Know Him and To Make Him Known." To know Him is the essence of victory, and to make Him known is the force of missions. God's call to vocational missionary service is heard by the person who is in tune with the Spirit.

Victorious Living Is Essential to Effective Witness

Since global missions is intense warfare with forces of spiritual darkness and the adversaries of truth, global missions demands that missionaries be equipped for victory, that they use the "whole armor of God." Otherwise, missionaries can go down in defeat even though they seek to proclaim the message. The experience of victory in the power of a living Christ is essential to the ambassador of the kingdom of light. Thus, victory in Christ and witness for Christ march indivisibly together.

Joy Ridderhof, the first graduate of Columbia International University, became the founder of Gospel Recordings, which has recorded the gospel in almost five thousand languages of the world. When she began her ministry the experts didn't even know there were half that number in existence! She understood victorious living, the energy of her unprecedented missionary enterprise, as simply singing faith. This she learned directly from Robert McQuilkin, in whose home she had lived her first year at Columbia.

McQuilkin said, "The Lord is not saying to us, 'Cheer up, there's nothing to worry about.' On the contrary, He says, 'In the world, ye shall have tribulation, but be of good cheer, I have overcome the world.'"[3] So Joy's special verse was, "With a voice of singing declare ye, tell this, utter it even to the end of the earth; say ye, The LORD hath redeemed his servant Jacob" (Isa. 48:20 KJV). On this she commented, "Keep rejoicing in your spirit throughout your daily tasks. Put cheer into your everyday voice when you answer the phone, in the office—speak with the song of hope and faith. Tell it with the voice of singing—to your family, your neighbors—and to the ends of the earth. It's a wonderful story to tell. It's a wonderful song to sing."[4]

Vigorous faith and effective ministry are intertwined. Ridderhof in her remarkable career, experienced it.

> En route to the Philippines, the devil fought us. He put many suggestions in our minds, such as, "You don't have enough money. They are having guerrilla warfare in Luzon, and you won't be able to travel. You will have no car, and how are you going to cart this heavy equipment from place to place? No one has written inviting you to come and record. You won't be able to get the languages."[5]

Then Joy goes on to state that, in reading encouraging promises from the Word of God, faith overcame the negative thoughts. "Happy art thou, O Israel . . . who is like unto thee, O people saved by the Lord!"

"And what happened?" Joy writes. "Bob Bowman of FEBIAS met us at the boat. We had no duty to pay, and enough money for all our needs. A car was loaned to us for travel. Missionaries cooperated with us most graciously, and we got the languages—our 'quiver full' in one year."

Henry Drummond, in his famous essay on 1 Corinthians 13, "Love Never Faileth," advised missionaries, "You can take nothing greater to the heathen world than the . . . reflection of the love of God upon your own character." Again he writes, "[Love] is the universal language. It will take you years to speak the Chinese or the dialects of India. . . . [but] from the day you land, that language of love, understood by all, will be pouring forth its unconscious eloquence."[6]

A missionary stayed awhile in a bush village in Africa, but never succeeded in grasping the language of the people before he had to leave. Another missionary came later to that same place. After some time, he learned bits of the language and began to tell the people about Jesus. They said to him, "Oh, we've met Him already—He was in our village." As George Hodges wrote a century ago, "The best Christian is he who most reminds the people with whom he lives of the Lord Jesus Christ."

"Thanks be to God who always leads us in triumph in Christ, and through us diffuses the fragrance of His knowledge in every place" (2 Cor. 2:14). These words link triumph with evangelism—making Him known in every place. The witness must walk in the Spirit or the battle is lost before it ever begins.

The Message of Victory Passed on to the Emerging Church

I remember our encounter with Kikuyu Christians in Kenya during the days of the Mau Mau uprising in 1954. Many Christians died for refusing to sign the evil oath that bound them to kill. One after another declared, "I will not take the oath to save myself." This is how the Kikuyu lived out the victorious Christian life in the midst of incredible circumstances:

Cannon Elijah was a rural Dean in one of the strongholds of the Kenya terror. We first met him in December 1954 at the Church Missionary Society station near Embu . . .

Bwana Elijah, in his white toupee, black suit and clerical collar, always smiled as he talked, and often laughed outright, to spill over his heart full of sheer gladness. Why was he happy? Many of his friends had wondered, too, because Elijah was no exception to the Kikuyu Christian and his sufferings . . .

"How is it," they had asked, "that you can always be so happy? We would like to know this, too."

For them, Elijah had one answer, "The Happy is waiting for you to take it! It is at the Cross. You must go there and receive it. But if you go there, you will be broken and empty. And you will see the Lord Jesus—He is everything. In Him is the Happy you are looking for."

It was at this time that Elijah first told us of the martyrdom of his young sister who had been brought up in his own home until the day of her wedding. Then for two brief years she and her husband had lived in their homestead several miles away. The Mau Mau oathing had swept through that place, and she and her husband resisted it, along with others, all of whom were hanged. Elijah told us of the testimony at that funeral when the Christians marched in triumph to the burial of those young people; and the whole crowd of them, their faces reflecting the reality of Heaven, were singing, "Onward, Christian Soldiers," as they marched to those graves.

"God's power is great," Elijah told us. "Hard core Mau Mau are becoming so transformed that now they shine more brightly than we do."[7]

On another occasion I was present with a group of Kikuyu Christians when Elijah testified,

Praise to our Lord Jesus Christ! Just yesterday, I received word that all my coffee trees have been destroyed by Mau Mau. When I heard this, I wondered at the joy and song in my heart. Why can I be so happy? Then I began to realize in a new way what a treasure I have in Jesus. . . . He is with me always in my heart. I can rejoice that my coffee trees are destroyed. This loss makes me see His glory more clearly.[8]

Recently I talked on the phone with Betty Cridland who, along with Mary Beam, was named Distinguished Alumnae by her alma mater, Columbia Bible College. She told me of a visit that she and Mary had made in November 1993 to their Uduk people of the Sudan. They attended a Spiritual Life Conference in Ethiopia held in a Uduk refugee camp in Khor, Bonga. There they found that the thousands of refugees, driven out of their homes in the Sudan by civil unrest in 1985, were the same stalwart Christians Cridland and Beam had been forced to leave behind decades before.

These people had survived years of deprivation, wandering, and hardship. Many had died as martyrs. Yet this remnant of fourteen thousand witnessed, in their wholehearted, triumphant hymn singing, an enduring faith. The message the Uduks had learned by the lives and teaching of their "mothers," as they called Betty and Mary, was the truth that sustained them in crises, and that keeps them yet today. They have so embraced this life of victory in Christ that their enemies comment, "The message the Uduks know is that which sustains them."[9]

With awe, Betty Cridland and Mary Beam realized that these Uduk Christians had been loyal to their Lord and Savior at any cost. For years, the "mothers" had sought to help the Uduks prepare for leadership in their churches. And, indeed, they had succeeded. Now, today, elder leaders pray that the younger generation will continue in the truths they themselves earlier discovered. This prayer is being answered before their eyes. United Nations officials say of the Uduks, "They're different from other people. They share their food and ask only for Bibles." Muslims say, "We don't understand why they have such love for people."

Victorious living, that is, knowing Christ, not only empowers the believer to make Him known but is, in itself, the very means of introducing Him to others.

In its conviction that victorious living, witness, and missions are inextricably intertwined, Columbia International University has been dedicated from the outset to train global Christians to serve God with excellence. Of the graduates over these seventy-five years, about 75 percent have entered Christian vocations, and at least 25 percent serve overseas. Third president Robertson McQuilkin, said, "Part of being like Christ is to love the whole world."[10]

And the victorious Christian, whoever he is, and whatever his vocation may be, can demonstrate today that indeed, "to know Him" *is* "to make Him known."

Notes

1. For a detailed record of the connection between the Victorious Life Testimony and Wycliffe origins, see Annamarie Dahlquist, *Trailblazers for Translation* (Pasadena: William Carey, 1995).
2. Personal letter, 1995.
3. Marguerite McQuilkin, *Always in Triumph* (Old Tappan, N.J.: Revell, 1956), 229.
4. Joy Ridderhof, *Count It All Joy* (Glendale, Calif.: Geddes Press, 1978), day 13.
5. Ibid., day 18.
6. Henry Drummond, *The Greatest Thing in the World* (London and Glasgow: Collins), 24.
7. Sanna Morrison Barlow, *Light Is Sown* (Chicago: Moody Press, 1956), 29–31.
8. Ibid., 46.
9. "Was It Worth It?" *SIMNow* (Fall 1994), 14–15.
10. Personal letter to author.

About the Author

Johnny Miller was well prepared to accept the presidency of Columbia International University in 1990. His background was diverse: newspaper reporter, public school English teacher, missionary, founder and pastor of Cypress Bible Church in a Houston suburb, and professor of New Testament at Columbia for five years. Cypress provided thirteen years of experience in pastoring a small church at the beginning, then a medium-sized church, and finally a large church. So he has a deep understanding and love for churches of all varieties. He graduated from a secular institution with honors (Arizona State) and earned both master's (High Honors) and doctorate degrees from Dallas Theological Seminary.

Miller married his high-school sweetheart, Jeanne, and they have two married children, both headed for missionary service. He serves as president of the American Association of Bible Colleges and on the board of administration of the National Association of Evangelicals.

About This Chapter

This is a case study, and an exciting one. We have seen how the normal Christian life of being filled with the Spirit impacts the local congregation and the congregation's central function: witness and evangelism. Now we look at the implications of that teaching for preparing those who minister. Johnny Miller describes his philosophy of education for Christian ministry and illustrates that philosophy from Columbia International University. As you read, it will soon become apparent that he views teaching and discipling in victorious Christian living as the cornerstone of any valid theological education.

Victorious Living in Theological Education

by Johnny V. Miller

Columbia Bible College was founded for the purpose of proclaiming the Victorious Life message and molding lives according to the likeness of Jesus Christ. That is still the goal of Columbia International University. We call it "Total Life Training," preparing a whole person for God for an entire life. We want to produce graduates who live the victorious Christian life. This is what makes Columbia unique; no other Bible college was founded specifically to inculcate this message and life.

Wherever I go I hear that Columbia graduates are different—intent on a daily walk with God, and practical in orientation toward ministry. I take no credit for the fruit of seventy-five years of labor. My association with Columbia has shaped me more than I have shaped it. Furthermore, most students who come to Columbia already have at least a fledgling desire (often a mature, passionate longing) to know Christ and to make Him known. Our stewardship is to help develop the spiritual life, to nurture that passion toward maturity, and to equip that person to be an agent of the same kind of change in others.

The simplest definition of the Victorious Life is a daily walk of faith and obedience in conscious dependence on the indwelling Spirit of God. Such a life must be one of the primary fruits of a theological education that is pleasing to God. Theological education that does not produce godliness is worse than a waste; it flaunts the purposes of God. What is essential in developing victorious Christian living within a program of theological training? How does such change take place? And what does the product look like? That is the subject of this chapter.

The Power to Change

The Power of Godly Relationships

Whenever I ask graduates what influenced them most at Columbia, they usually tell me a *who,* not a *what.* People change people. God uses relationships to do His work of priming, preparing, and polishing for ministry.

This is evident in those who studied under the first president, Robert C. McQuilkin. He had boundless energy, brilliant intellect, and a remarkably consistent and joyous walk with God. In the school's early days he was practically the only instructor, and therefore his life was the curriculum. That life was fruitful in producing his passion for Christ, for the Word, and for world evangelism, which are still the heartbeat of CIU. Those whom I have met who studied under him strike me as being "different," reflecting the qualities of the first president.

My point is that victorious Christian living must be caught as well as taught. The faculty is always the primary curriculum of Columbia Bible College and Columbia Biblical Seminary (even though other relationships are a crucial element of one's education). Our faculty handbook states: "Teaching, then, is the very complex process of causing the behavior of another to be changed into the image which the teacher personally reflects." Not every called and gifted teacher is equally winsome. Some are energized by being alone, some by being with people. Some bend toward writing, others toward debating. But each one must care for people, especially their students, and be open to share their lives with learners, to mentor in one form or another.

This is what Scripture teaches, both by precept and example: Godliness is taught and caught through caring relationships that are centered on Scripture.

The Lord Jesus taught that the purpose and product of a teaching relationship is a changed student: "A disciple is not above his teacher, but everyone who is perfectly trained will be like his teacher" (Luke 6:40). That can be a wonderful promise or a dire threat. But the point is plain—we reflect our teacher(s).

Our Lord Jesus exemplified that philosophy in training His disciples (Mark 3:14), devoting the majority of His short sojourn to preparing them for life and ministry after the Ascension. He set limits and high standards for them (Matt. 10), admonished and corrected them (Matt. 16), and held to His message and purpose even when many found the demands too stringent (John 6:66; Luke 9:57–62). There is no discipleship without discipline.

Ultimately the disciples were transformed into "Christians," Christlike individuals (Acts 4:13). Through their Spirit-filled lives the gospel would change others. The Great Commission assumes ministry through relationships. Jesus could have commanded us merely to duplicate the scrolls or distribute the Scriptures, but He commanded us to go personally and make disciples.

Paul mirrored Christ's philosophy. He gathered individuals and small groups whom he trained, and he wrote to the churches to "imitate me, just as I also imitate Christ" (1 Cor. 11:1; Phil. 3:17). He encouraged Timothy to suffer for the Lord, based on their mutual relationship in the Word (2 Tim. 3:14). And he told Timothy to pass on what he had learned through Paul (2 Tim. 2:2).

The second president of Columbia Bible College, G. Allen Fleece, captured this truth in an unpublished paper, "The Culture of the Spiritual Life." "It is not enough that the message be true, it is also necessary that the messenger be true" (p. 5). He continues,

> God's Word is light, but a blind man needs more than light, he also needs sight. Only the Holy Spirit can give sight. Only when the light of God's truth is given through a channel filled with the Holy Spirit is there the possibility of imparting sight to blind hearts. (p. 7)

The point doesn't need belaboring: Education is relational. It can reproduce hypocrisy, formalism (truth without piety), imbalance. Or it can produce godliness of heart and life. Students, as well as children, "learn what they live." Therefore, teachers who would reproduce victorious Christian living must first experience it themselves.

The Power of the Word of God

Relationships are always instructive, but relationships alone do not produce godly living. To do that they must be mutually centered upon and submissive to the Word of God.

It should be the delight of every Christian to meditate daily on Scripture (Josh. 1:8; Ps. 119:9–11; Col. 3:2) and to make a lifelong pursuit of knowing God's written revelation. Since the source of all truth is God, no valid education can leave God out. There is no other path to victorious Christian living.

Obviously, then, theological education for victorious Christian living must major on Scripture. The goal is not to reproduce the life of the teacher, but the life of Christ through the teacher. One of our principles of operation states:

> CIU accepts the Bible alone, and in its totality, as the absolute authority in faith and life. Since the objective of this training is to make servants who know God, the Bible is to be

the heart of the curriculum. In all of its academic program CIU must guard against adding to or subtracting from this authority in any way. On the positive side, we must be sure that every regularly enrolled student is dedicated to pursuing direct study of the Bible to gain a general knowledge of its content, and a growing discipline in its mastery.

When the Bible speaks, God speaks. The only proper response is to love, worship, and obey Him. We are under the authority of His inerrant revelation. The minister of God must master the interpretation and application of Scripture (hermeneutics), and be able to instruct others (exposition). But that instruction must come through a life that has been nurtured and changed by it before passing it on (1 Tim. 4:6). We should be like trees that are nurtured by water instead of like pipelines that merely pass it along.

The Scriptures are not exhaustive, telling us everything there is to know. But they are complete and sufficient, telling us everything we need to know for life and godliness. While "all truth is God's truth," only the Scriptures are absolute, or "true truth." Not everything that appears true to the student of natural revelation is actually "God's truth." All must be tested by the Scriptures.

Scripture testifies to its own effectiveness and sufficiency in equipping for ministry and godly living: "All Scripture is given by inspiration of God, and is profitable for doctrine, for reproof, for correction, for instruction in righteousness, that the man of God may be complete, thoroughly equipped for every good work" (2 Tim. 3:16–17).

Scripture also testifies to its own primacy in instructing and shaping the believer as the Holy Spirit wields it in an individual's life: "But you have an anointing from the Holy One, and you know all things. I have not written to you because you do not know the truth, but because you know it, and that no lie is of the truth" (1 John 2:20–21; cf. also John 16:13; Acts 10:38). The Holy Spirit uses the Word of God to do the work of God. The inculcation of Scripture effectively changes and equips us for ministry through the power of the Holy Spirit.

This is not to say that the Spirit directly teaches us everything we need to know apart from human teachers. The Bible says that the Holy Spirit gives the gift of teaching to individuals for instructing the body of Christ (Rom. 12:7). That brings us back to the subject of relationships focused on the Word of God. As Paul told Timothy, "And the things that you have heard from me among many witnesses, commit these to faithful men who will be able to teach others also" (2 Tim. 2:2). As student and teacher gather around the Word of God in classroom, chapel, office, small group, and home, it is essential that Scripture be handled with the awe and reverence that a love letter from God deserves.

The Power of Ministry Experience

Godly relationships and the study of Scripture are two key elements in theological training for victorious Christian living. But these are not enough. One of the banes of formal biblical education is that many students *lose* passion for Scripture, for ministry, and even for God during their training. The stress of studies can turn the Bible from a love letter into a dry textbook, especially if one studies for grades instead of for Spirit-mediated truth.

As a result, dynamic Christianity may evaporate, leaving a residue of formal Christianity. A student can learn more *about* Christ while knowing less of Christ. A faculty member removed from frontline ministry may substitute faith in his knowledge or principles for faith in God Himself. We may know much truth, but be helpless in the face of demonic oppression, or enslaved to addictions, ungodly attitudes, or worldly values. We may be prayerless and powerless.

The best antidote is to be involved in situations that force us to live by prayer and faith, that challenge us to walk in dependence on God's Spirit and to apply our understanding of Scripture to ourselves and to others. Since we learn by doing, we learn victorious Christian living by having to live victoriously.

Therefore, theological education must let students test their faith and understanding in the battlefield of real-life ministry. Ministry experience must be integrated throughout the curriculum to keep a student from becoming a Dead Sea or a clogged spring. When we hoard truth we become spiritually unfit, overloading the mind and fattening the spirit. We become arrogant (because we "know," 1 Cor. 8:1), or else timid because we fear we don't know enough, and we are trusting in what we know instead of in the Lord to do His work through us (2 Tim. 1:6–8). Ministry experience helps make us conscious of our absolute dependence on Christ for adequacy, and of the Lord's provision of His adequacy through prayer and faith.

This is how the Lord Jesus taught, involving His disciples in ministry from the beginning. In the early stages of their training they watched Him and discussed what they saw. Then He sent out the Twelve (Luke 9:1–6, 10), and later the seventy (Luke 10:1–20), on their own. They reported their experiences, and spent another season with Him. Finally they were ready to fly solo.

Perhaps the major missing element in theological education today is this ministry *alongside* the faculty. We tend to be specialized and professionalized. There are theological scholars gifted for research and writing who make a valuable contribution to the cause of Christ. But since teachers reproduce themselves, faculty who are uninvolved with students and with a wider world of ministry through the church will produce stagnation in their students.

Columbia has several responses to this challenge. First, we search for faculty with successful ministry experience before entering education. I even prefer faculty who are mildly frustrated at being faculty, because they would rather be doing frontline ministry instead of (or as well as) training others for such ministry. But having concluded that God has called them to a training ministry, they tolerate their frustration. This kind of teacher will be able to integrate every course with the practice of ministry, both by illustrations (positive and negative) from experience and by carefully crafted assignments that require practical application during the course.

Second, we encourage and foster continual growth and renewal among the faculty through cross-cultural exposure and ministry-on-study leave and term breaks.

Third, we have ministry practitioners involved with students as trainers and evaluators in field education and internships, where the rubber meets the road. These are not merely laboratory experiments, but real-life opportunities to trust God to work through a prayerfully dependent servant.

Fourth, our financial support system requires us to look to God in prayer and faith to provide through gift income a portion of each employee's monthly salary. This both fosters prayerful dependence among the faculty and staff, and models it to students. Since the Lord Jesus instructed us to pray for our daily bread, it is a privilege to look to Him corporately to provide our needs. God has honored that faith. No salary has gone permanently unpaid, a testimony of God's faithfulness to each student generation for seventy-five years. We take a day each month for extended times of corporate prayer for our needs, and also those of the world.

There is more to knowing Him than just getting our food. There is the power of the Resurrection in our daily lives (Phil. 3:10). Confidence in Him. Obedience to Him. Suffering for Him. Victorious Christian living is the trusting submission of our wills to God and obedience to the truth of Scripture in the face of spiritual warfare, elements learned only in ministry's front lines.

The Product of Change

Personal Piety—To Know Him

The outcome of this combination of godly instructors, the centrality of Scripture, and well-coached ministry experience should be maturing a twofold longing on the part of the student—a longing to know Christ ever more intimately, and a desire to make Christ known ever more broadly. That has been the motto of Columbia from the beginning: "To Know Him and To Make Him Known."

Columbia International University tries to integrate victorious Christian living into every aspect of the program. We study it specifically, include it in every course, and try to live it out. What element(s) of the training process yield "victory"? They all contribute. But, while such growth can be fostered (or frustrated), it cannot be forced.

There is only one way ultimately to account for a passion to know the Lord Jesus—the fruit of the Holy Spirit's life within us. When we apply biblical truth by the power of the Holy Spirit, there is victory. We live in conscious awareness of the immediacy of the presence of God.

How does this life manifest itself in the life of a graduate? Along with growth in the knowledge of the Word and increased skill in ministry, there will be developed character qualities that evidence the life of the Spirit. Some are especially relevant to our era:

Love. The greatest biblical value is love, first for God and then for others. That has been transformed in our age into self-love. The victorious Christian must understand what the Scripture teaches about love, and then choose to lay aside sinful self-interest for godly self-sacrifice. This is a vital foundation for enduring service to God.

Integrity/Accountability. We must inculcate integrity; what we are in the private corners of our lives is what we really are. And we must hold ourselves accountable to others for the expression of that integrity. God means for believers to live in community (church), and in accountability to that community. We can foster such accountability in the educational setting through small-group relationships that provide encouragement, consolation, and admonishment as necessary, and which also help develop relational skills. But then it must be followed through for life.

Holiness. Because of Satan's invasion of our homes and minds through public media, most of us are deeply influenced by ungodly philosophy and values. It is increasingly difficult even to recognize evil, much less hate it. A period of separation (even isolation) can clarify our thinking and sharpen our senses. Holiness, however, is a life of intimacy with God, not simply separation from external worldliness. That which devastates believers is more often a worldliness of attitude, thought, or values than of contact with ungodly things or people. Biblical holiness searches out the inner recesses of our lives and roots out our pride, arrogance, bitterness, selfishness, willfulness, and divisiveness, and lays these repeatedly at the foot of the cross.

Discipline. The development of holiness is paralleled by the development of a disciplined daily spiritual life and the ability to endure hardship in order to be faithful. A Bible college or a seminary may be a boot camp where new disciplines are learned. Or it may be a "health club" or even a "rehabilitation center." Whatever the image, it must be a place where students learn both the internal and external spiritual disciplines necessary for victory in spiritual warfare.

Prayer and Faith. The power for victory over sin and for fruitfulness in ministry is not our power but His. The one channel of that power is dependent prayer as a way of life.

Concern for Ministry—To Make Him Known

If we know Him, then we will be concerned about the things that concern Him. Victorious Christian living is not simply about *my* relationship with God, but also about God's love for the world. To love Him is to obey Him.

What is God doing in the world today? He is "bringing many sons to glory" (Heb. 2:10). He is reaching into the unreached pockets of humanity in order to add to His family many other sons and daughters to be conformed to the image of His beloved Son, the Lord Jesus (Rom. 8:29). That should be our preoccupation also.

The Great Commission was our Lord's simple mission statement entrusted to the church two thousand years ago. The church has never forsaken all other pursuits to give itself to this mandate for even one year. According to Matthew 24:14, the Lord's plan for the world will not be accomplished until the Commission is fulfilled. Some debate whether this will take place before or after the rapture of the church. That is irrelevant—it is the heart of God to see the job done! It is our opportunity to hasten that day (2 Peter 3:12).

The victorious Christian life is consumed with the immediate presence and power and promises of God. These are granted to enable us to walk with Him and to serve Him. Theological education that fosters victorious Christian living must focus on the preparation of world Christians who will seek to reproduce that victorious life among those yet unreached. This is the unsheathing of the sword of the Spirit—the Word of God—and this is the focus of Columbia International University. We prepare world Christians to know Him and to make Him known.

9

About the Author

Born dirt poor into a Mississippi bootlegger clan and having dropped out of school after three years, John Perkins met Christ in California at the age of twenty-seven and has become an international symbol of reconciliation. Perkins founded Mendenhall Ministries in Mississippi, Voice of Life Ministries in Jackson, and Harambee Christian Family Center in Pasadena, California—ministries devoted to evangelism, church, day care, adult education, tutoring, health care, thrift stores, vocational training, low-cost housing, summer camp—the list goes on. Publisher of *Urban Family* magazine, Perkins has authored nine books, including the best-selling *Let Justice Roll Down*. He has preached in major conventions and conferences around the world and lectured at more than two hundred colleges and universities.

About This Chapter

Victorious Life teaching often concentrates on the personal, internal life of the Christian and his or her responsibility to witness to those outside the community of faith—evangelism and missions. Little is said of the implications of Spirit-filled living for the external needs of hurting people, of one's responsibility for redeeming the community at large, for seeking reconciliation. This powerful story of one who embodies the whole gospel should change that forever. If this chapter doesn't change us into people who demonstrate the love of Christ by reaching out in reconciliation and healing the hurts of our communities, I'm not sure what would. Victorious living must have a social dimension to be truly godly.

Social Dimensions of Victorious Living

by John M. Perkins

He has showed you, O man, what is good.
And what does the LORD require of you?
To act justly and to love mercy
  and to walk humbly with your God. (Mic. 6:8 NIV)

For me, the gospel has always been social. Had it not been, I would have eventually rejected it.

I did reject it for the first twenty-seven years of my life. You see, I grew up in Mississippi in the thirties and forties. And as a young black man, I could not, for the life of me, see how Christianity was relevant to anything important in my life.

Almost all the black religious folks in those days seemed weak and cowardly to me. Their religion may have enabled them to handle their oppression without going crazy. But meanwhile, it seemed to make them easy for the white folks to control.

And the white folks who called themselves Christians (most of them did) appeared no different from the non-Christians, especially when it came to how they treated the "colored folks." Their brand of Christianity did not have the power to make them see that we were all children of God and were brothers and sisters in His sight.

I felt that if these people, both black and white, were the ones who had the answers, then we were all in big trouble. Besides, if the only thing that Christianity did was to give you a ticket to heaven, as a young man, I was not sure that I wanted to suffer through being a Christian my whole life just for that. I figured I might as well wait until I was on my dying bed to confess my sins, or maybe I would ask Jesus into my life when I was an old man, by which time it wouldn't matter very much one way or the other.

I believe that there are many people who are just like I was—who want and need to see a Jesus of courage—a Jesus who is relevant to their everyday lives—a Jesus who would be good news to the poor, not just someone to help them tolerate their situation.

God Uses Who We Are

As I look back on my life, I have come to believe that God uses our life experiences to prepare us for whatever He has planned for our life and mission.

I did not grow up in a Christian home. My mother died when I was seven months old, and my father gave the five of us children to his mother, Grandma Babe, to raise. Grandma Babe had mothered nineteen children of her own. My family were gamblers and bootleggers. We were looked down on by the black religious folks for our lifestyle.

But we were proud of what we did. We did not bow down to the system and take the crumbs from the white oppressive system. We knew we were outlaws and, in a sense, thought we were smarter than those religious folks who humbly accepted their oppression.

My older brother, Clyde, and I were very close. Clyde had gone away to fight in World War II and was wounded. He received a Purple Heart. To us, he was a war hero. But to most of the white townspeople, he was still just a nigger.

Not more than six months after surviving a war and returning home, Clyde was shot down and killed by a policeman for making too much noise while standing in line for a movie. He died in my arms on the way to the hospital.

It was this kind of incident that shaped my young life. Finally, when I was nineteen years old, I left Mississippi for California. I had no intentions of ever returning to live in the South.

On one of my short visits back to Mississippi I met the woman who would become my wife. We were married shortly after that, moved out west, and began to raise a family in California. We were on the fast track, had left the poverty and violence of our youth, and had finally got our piece of the pie. Single-minded and focused, I fully intended to be rich one day. And I would have realized my ambition, if God had not made other plans for me.

It was through my four-year-old son, Spencer, that God finally got through to me. Spencer had been attending a little church Sunday school down the street from our home. He talked me into going to church with him. On one of those Sundays, the pastor preached from Romans 6:23: "For the wages of sin is death, but the gift of God is eternal life."

I understood wages. Since leaving Mississippi, my whole life was about earning wages. I had left Mississippi because the system was too oppressive for a black man. Here in California, I could earn a fair wage. But was the sinful lifestyle that I was living earning me death? Although I was doing pretty good for a poor bootlegger's son from Mississippi, I was not content. I knew deep down that something was not right.

God used wages, something that was important to me, to get my attention. I gave my life to Jesus that day. Ever since that day, I have been attempting to introduce this Jesus to others and, at the same time, reconcile the contradictions of the Christian faith—the inconsistencies that keep us from demonstrating our love for each other. This love is so central, so important, that Jesus said it would be our mark of recognition, the way the world could identify us as Christians. In short, I believe God has given me a clear mission: reconcile the two great commandments. To love God and to love our neighborhood mean reconciling evangelism and social action, reconciling people to God and to each other.

As a young man, I couldn't see that loving God meant that you loved your neighbor, so Christianity held no credibility for me. Now, because this Christianity had turned my life around, I wanted it to have meaning. I wanted others to see Christianity—its nature and potential—not what others had self-servingly made of it.

I began to be discipled and to study the Scriptures on my own. Because of my background and upbringing, some Scriptures began to jump out at me, passages that had the potential to make a difference in my life and in the lives of my family and my home state of Mississippi. Finally I was beginning to see and hear the relevance of the gospel:

> The Spirit of the Lord is on me,
> because he has anointed me
> to preach good news to the poor.
> He has sent me to proclaim freedom for the prisoners
> and recovery of sight for the blind,
> to release the oppressed,
> to proclaim the year of the Lord's favor. (Luke 4:18–19
>   NIV)

Why hadn't I heard passages like this before? Yes, this Jesus did come for everyone, but especially for people like me. And there were more Scriptures that didn't seem to fit into the Christianity that I had witnessed all my life.

> Then the King will say to those on his right, "Come, you who are blessed by my Father; take your inheritance, the kingdom prepared for you since the creation of the world. For I was hungry and you gave me something to

eat, I was thirsty and you gave me something to drink, I
was a stranger and you invited me in, I needed clothes
and you clothed me, I was sick and you looked after me,
I was in prison and you came to visit me."
Then the righteous will answer him, "Lord, when did we
see you hungry and feed you, or thirsty and give you
something to drink? When did we see you a stranger and
invite you in, or needing clothes and clothe you? When
did we see you sick or in prison and go to visit you?"
The King will reply, "I tell you the truth, whatever you
did for one of the least of these brothers of mine, you did
for me."
Then he will say to those on his left, "Depart from me,
you who are cursed, into the eternal fire prepared for the
devil and his angels." (Matt. 25:34–41 NIV)

I was struck with wonder. Did this Word mean to say that
feeding the hungry, clothing the naked, visiting the prisoner,
and inviting in the stranger are all signs of whether or not you
are a Christian? What was going on here? It looked as though
someone had been misrepresenting Jesus and Christianity.

Can This New Christianity Make a Difference at Home?

It was as clear to me as if He had said it out loud. God
was calling me to return to Mississippi, to my own people, to
share with them what He had done for me. But since I had
very little respect for the Christianity that I had seen when I
was there, how would this more "holistic" Christianity play
itself out? Would it be dangerous? Would my own black people listen to me? What would the white folks think?

The answers were very quick in coming. When we moved
into the little town of Mendenhall, Mississippi, we moved into
the "colored quarters" on the other side of the tracks, right
into the same oppression and poverty that we had left behind
thirteen years earlier. But this time, my wife, Vera Mae, and I
were armed with a gospel that we believed could not only save

people from their sins, but if lived out fully, could also improve their quality of life.

Naturally, the first place that I tried to share this gospel was in the church. The typical black church at that time, at least in the rural areas, was served by a pastor who did not live in the community or even in the town. He was the pastor of three or four other churches. He would visit a different one each Sunday of the month, so that each church had a preacher only one Sunday a month.

In Mendenhall, usually the pastor drove in from Jackson in his big new car, preached, collected an offering, and drove out. He had no part in the day-to-day lives of the people. When I began teaching Sunday school in one of the local churches—showing how the gospel should have an effect on our day-to-day lives—I became a threat to the pastor and was kindly kicked out of the church.

Although I wouldn't dare think of comparing myself to Jesus, it was comforting to know that the same thing happened to Him when he tried to influence the religious establishment of His day.

It was as though God was reminding us that you can't put new wine in old wineskins. Our rejection was the motivation that we needed to organize our own church and begin our youth ministry in earnest.

This was around the violent time when Medgar Evers and three civil rights workers were murdered. Churches were being bombed and burned. There were hostility and conflict all around us. I saw Mendenhall as a microcosm of the larger society. Most blacks who were getting a formal education were leaving the town and moving north. The neighborhood was left with the very old and the young. Success meant escape, leaving Mendenhall and never coming back.

Young people were not being educated to improve the conditions around them. God gives us a vision of what true education is in Genesis 1:27–28, when He tells Adam to subdue the earth—to bring the earth under control so that it could be used for the good of humanity. Learning how to use the earth's resources for your own good and the good of your neighbor is the whole purpose of education. But for many young blacks, education instead became the way to buy things, and to get out of Mississippi. I could see that our little town would never get any better with this mentality.

I saw that if we were going to change our environment, then we would have to change the mind-set of our most valuable resources, our young people. First we had to win some of the kids to Christ and help them stay in school. Then we could encourage them to go to college, where they could acquire some skills and return to the community and use their education to make life better for their neighbors.

Some of the young people started going to college. Dolphus Weary and I began summer tutoring programs through the churches, helping kids academically and encouraging them to stay in school.

We learned that the deep socioeconomic needs of a neighborhood could be met by organizing the people around their own needs as they perceive them. We worked side by side with the neighborhood's people, developing health centers, housing projects, day care centers, and recreation facilities. The community began to change as we discovered that we could not, in good conscience, separate loving God from loving our neighbors. We could not separate our faith from our works.

Let me make this clear. We did not then and do not now believe that our works are what saves us. We only believed that our works are the evidence of the faith within us. Because "faith by itself, if it does not have works, is dead" (James 2:17).

Who Else Is My Neighbor?

There is no way to have grown up black in the South and not have had race play a major role in the way you looked at the world. My whole Christianity was summed up in Jesus' two great commandments: love God and love your neighbor. I understood very clearly that loving my neighbor in the little ghetto of Mendenhall meant helping to improve the quality of life for my hurting brothers and sisters. But how did that apply to white folks?

Well, for the most part, I didn't care how this applied to white folks. I had no more respect for their brand of Christianity than I did for the "religious" black folks. In fact, I was not sure I believed these folks were Christians at all. But I didn't have too much time to think about that, because now, added to everything that we were involved in, the civil rights movement was in full swing in Mississippi. What, we wondered, did this mean for us?

It was not a very big jump for us to get involved with a peaceful, nonviolent movement that only asked that black folks be brought into full citizenship in this country. If our peaceful demonstrations broke unjust laws, then, like the apostle Paul, we would go to jail.

Well, go to jail is exactly what we did. Our peaceful demonstrations landed us in jail on several occasions. In one of those jailings, five of my children were thrown into jail with me.

But the incident that God used to answer the question of "How do white folks fit into the neighbor equation?" will probably always be the longest night of my life. It was February 7, 1970.

After a peaceful demonstration in Mendenhall, twenty-two of us were arrested and taken to jail. Three of us were nearly beaten to death that night by state troopers and white local police. I have written about this in several places, so I won't take the time and space to write about it in detail here. But I was beaten and tortured to within an inch of my life. I truly thought I was going to die that night.

But this was the first time in my life I considered what racism had done to white folks. Sure, I knew what it had done to me and my people. We were victims of the oppression and the unjust laws designed to keep us as second-class citizens. But that night, I saw and experienced firsthand what these men had to become in order to keep us oppressed.

I tried to bargain with God. I prayed as hard as I could. I remember saying something to this effect: "God, if You let me live to get out of this jail tonight, I will live and preach a gospel not only to free my own people, but a gospel that will cross racial and social barriers." I guess God must have heard me that night.

Although God delivered me from what I thought was my death sentence, I still had trouble keeping that bargain that I made with Him. The abuse that my body took affected my soul. While lying in the hospital waiting for my body to recover, my spirit was wrestling with God. How could a just God allow something like this to happen? Why did white Christians allow this system of oppression to continue?

It was while wrestling with God and struggling with my faith that God began to change my heart. My flesh wanted to hate the people who had done this to me, but God wouldn't allow me to hate. Had I not had the love of Christ in me, I could easily have hated back. And that was the difference— Christ's love inside me.

At first it was a subtle change. But I saw clearly that we were not doing enough. Yes, changing the laws would improve the quality of life for my people, but just changing the laws did not change people's hearts. True change comes through the love of Christ, and this change happened from the inside out.

No longer would I talk about integration. From now on I would preach reconciliation. No longer would I talk about a black church and a white church; I would preach to the whole church. I read the passage in 2 Corinthians 5:17–19 through different lenses. "Therefore, if anyone is in Christ, he is a new creation; the old has gone, the new has come! All this is from God, who reconciled us to himself through Christ and gave us the ministry of reconciliation: that God was reconciling the world to himself in Christ, not counting men's sins against them. And he has committed to us the message of reconciliation" (NIV).

Because we are in Christ, we are new creatures. We are no longer Blacks or Whites. We are Christians. As Peter puts it in 1 Peter 2:9 we are a "new race." And Paul makes it very clear here that God has given us the ministry of reconciliation.

Being reconciled to God and to each other is the gospel in a nutshell. It sums up who we are and what we are to be about. And these two commandments, that we love God with all our heart and soul, with all our strength and mind, and that we love our neighbor as ourselves, are never again to be split apart. They are two sides of the same coin—they reflect each other. The way we demonstrate our love for God is by loving our neighbor.

It is when we can fulfill these two mandates together that we witness to the unbelieving world a gospel with power enough to be relevant even in the most desperate situations. But when we allow them to be sundered—when we allow Christians to claim to love God and not prove that by loving their neighbor—then we don't have much to offer the hurting people of the world. It was Jesus who said that "when they look at you, they will know you are My disciples by the way you love one another." If we are not loving each other across worldly barriers, then we do a disservice to the gospel.

Victorious living is discovered in living out a gospel that does not separate loving God from loving each other. This is a gospel that doesn't allow us to claim we have faith without works, or claim to be righteous without doing justice. Victorious living is keeping the vertical and the horizontal in balance. And for me, it has also meant challenging others to do the same.

10

About the Author

Born in the high Andes and raised in the Amazon River basin of Bolivia by his Wycliffe Bible Translator parents, Robert Priest knew the Siriono culture from the inside. Following his education at Columbia Bible College, Trinity Evangelical Divinity School, and the University of Chicago, he did his doctoral research for the University of California at Berkeley among the Aguaruna of Peru. Recognized during his work at both the University of Chicago and Berkeley for groundbreaking concepts in cultural anthropology, Priest has been published in both religious and secular journals and books. He has taught missions and intercultural studies at Columbia Biblical Seminary since 1990. Priest and his wife, Kersten, have four children.

About This Chapter

Here we have a masterful and fascinating analysis of the interplay of culture and biblical standards. Dull is the reader who will not feel the prick of conscience as we see our own culturally induced spiritual blind spots and our clumsy intrusion into the lives of others who have been formed by a different culture. Victorious Life teaching focuses on three aspects of Christian life: God's standard for Christian living, God's provision for Christian living, and our responsibility for appropriating that provision. This chapter focuses on the first aspect: God's standard. Priest's background and present responsibilities would lead us to anticipate special help for the cross-cultural missionary who seeks to disciple those of another culture. That anticipation will not be disappointed.

Cultural Factors in Victorious Living

by Robert J. Priest

A
s Lin Wuji[1] grew up he was told to remember all that his parents had done for him, that while debts to friends could be numbered, debts to parents are beyond number. He should, therefore, show unswerving respect and veneration for his parents, as they had for theirs. He was told "water flows downwards but not upwards," which meant that love for one's children could be taken for granted, but that love for parents must be taught: that while a natural man loves his children, a moral man loves his parents.

Outwardly Lin Wuji did what was expected, but inwardly he resented parental demands and was more interested in his own future and that of his children. Then he became a Christian. Remorse for his sins focused on the sin of ingratitude and lack of filial love and respect. Others soon began to comment on his changed life—a life of virtue evident in the way he treated his parents. Then Lin Wuji went to seminary. There he studied under Europeans. He surprised his Old Testament professor with his thesis topic: "Filial Piety in the Old Testament." Yet, when his professor read the thesis, he discovered that this theme really was an important one in the

Old Testament. He wondered why no one had written about it before.

Upon graduation Lin Wuji entered the pastorate. One Sunday, Bill, a visiting missionary, heard him preach,

> I exhort you to be filial; it is not easy to repay parents for their kindness. They cleaned your dirty bottom and held you out to urinate. Who knows how often they lay [with you] in your wet bed? When her son was ill, your mother feared for you; she neither slept nor ate, but prayed day and night. Only after she nearly died of worry did her son recover. When he was four or five, she was always watching out for him, afraid he would swim in the river or climb a tree in search of birds' nests. When he reached the age of fifteen or sixteen, he became impolite, neither respecting the elderly nor loving the young, and forgetting his parents' kindness. When her son married and prospered, he indulged himself in eating and drinking. When he had a baby son, he embraced him and provided him with beautiful clothes and hats, calling him pet names while taking walks with him. You love your own children, why do you forget how much your parents loved you? Sweet water cannot be taken from a bitter well; brambles will not grow grapes, nor pumpkin vines grow yellow silk. There is reward for evil and reward for good; the moving cart leaves its tracks, and the unfilial parent will have unfilial progeny.[2]

Bill was startled to hear a sermon so similar to ones preached by Confucianists. Disturbed by what seemed to him like syncretism, he invited Lin Wuji over for a meal, hoping to straighten him out. But when Lin asked him about his parents—whom he had recently placed in a nursing home—he became uncomfortable. Clearly Lin found it hard to understand how a man of God could do such a thing. Somehow Bill lost the desire to correct his brother's preaching. Hoping to lighten the mood, Bill suggested they join his children who were watching the Academy Awards on TV. Silently Lin Wuji watched as each award winner expressed thanks—thanks to their makeup artists, counselors, fellow actors, children, spouses, lovers, the family dog—but never in the hour he watched the show was thanks or gratitude expressed toward the ones above all who should be thanked, one's parents. Lin left Bill's home deeply disturbed by the immorality of a nation that no longer honored its parents, and deeply concerned for the spiritual life of a missionary so obviously corrupted by an immoral culture.

Theologians and preachers who reflect on sanctification and the Christian life have seldom sufficiently understood the human realities that need to be related to the biblical truths they faithfully exposit. One such human reality is culture. One searches works on sanctification in vain if one attempts to find any treatment of culture in relation to sanctification. Yet culture profoundly influences the sanctification process, and basic principles about culture in relation to sanctification need to be explored. It is particularly important that such things be understood, given the fact that tens of thousands of missionaries are involved in cross-cultural ministries intimately concerned with the sanctification process in the lives of others—ministries that include teaching, discipling, counseling, rebuking, correcting, and encouraging. That is, there are profound practical ramifications of our understanding of culture in relation to sanctification for pastoral and missiological practice. This paper will begin by suggesting certain basic principles about culture in relation to sanctification, and will then suggest a number of practical principles that cross-cultural Christian workers need to keep in mind as they work toward the sanctification of others.

Basic Principles About Culture in Relation to Sanctification

Culture as Aid to Sanctification

Missionaries often see things about other cultures that they perceive as antithetical to the Christian life. They must first, however, recognize that culture often serves (at least potentially) as an aid to sanctification—as inculcator of conscience and instiller of moral virtues.

Culture as Inculcator of Conscience. While cultures vary significantly in the moral norms they stress, every society attempts to inculcate moral norms in its members. Many of the most strongly held moral convictions of such cultures are congruent with, and supportive of, biblical values. Thus traditional Chinese culture stresses the importance of honoring and caring for parents, Thai Buddhism stresses the importance of generous hospitality, the Utku stress the moral evils of irritability and anger and the virtue of patience and self-control in the face of adversity, and the Aguaruna[3] of Peru stress the evils of gluttony and of failure to restrain appetite in the presence of needy others. This, of course, does not mean that the members of such societies actually fully live up to the moral values they affirm. As Romans 2:1ff. tells us, all humanity fails to live up to the standards they consciously affirm and judge others by. When members of these societies become Christians, they experience conversion—an "about-face." There is a new center to their lives—God; a new motivation in life—love (and gratitude) for Christ; a new source of power for living—the indwelling Holy Spirit; a new social community—the church; and a new source of authority—the Bible. But they do not instantly thereby have a mind that is fully reprogrammed. Instead, their new love for God will often take the form of a morally changed life in areas where they already know themselves to be deficient because of what their culture has taught them. A rebellious Chinese son is transformed into one who honors his parents; a Thai who practiced grudging hospitality becomes known as one who practices generous hospitality; and an Utku who struggles with temper finds new resources for being patient, loving, and kind. Where culture affirms the same moral values as found in Scripture, Christians of that culture are less likely to miss or ignore those specific pressing moral obligations. But where culture is silent on a matter, or opposes the biblical norms, even more mature Christians may be unwittingly deficient.

And so we have the paradox of mature missionaries from the United States—with a culture that values youth over age and that stresses obligations to children over obligations to parents—being deficient with reference to the fourth commandment to a greater extent than recent Chinese converts with a much more limited knowledge of the Word. Or American missionaries, whose upbringings stress that anger is a natural emotion that ought to be expressed rather than repressed, and whose occasional expressions of irritability, impatience, and anger are not thought of as particularly reprehensible, may go to cultures of New Guinea, Paraguay, or northern Canada, which vigorously stress the evils of irritability and anger. Such missionaries may be completely unaware that people are not nearly as impressed by their fidelity to truth as they are struck by the missionaries' immoral impatience and tendency toward anger, an area where even young converts exemplify much higher character.

Culture as Instiller of Moral Virtues. Culture not only serves to instill ideas of right and wrong that are often congruent with and supportive of biblical teaching, but culture also works to instill virtues—personal habits, dispositions, and moral skills, many of which are similar to the moral character traits the Bible stresses should come to characterize the believer. Thus Utku culture not only teaches cognitive lessons about the immorality of anger, but it produces in its members habits and dispositions with reference to difficult circumstances and personal offense. An Utku child grows up in a harsh physical setting where he or she learns to face suffering and hardship with equanimity and humor. A child accidentally upsets the urine pot onto the igloo floor. With no trace of irritability or anger, only gentle laughter, the mother begins the laborious job of cleaning up the frozen mess. Utku culture teaches habits of response—of responding to unforeseen difficulties with gentle humor, for example, rather than with irritated outbursts or imprecations.

Children in the United States do not face the physical difficulties faced by Utku or Lengua children and are not subjected to the same cultural disciplines intended to harden them against pain, hunger, and frustration. In many ways they grow up soft and pampered. Such children may love the Lord, but nonetheless discover in adulthood, if they become missionaries, that their character traits with reference to endurance of hardship and patience under adversity are vastly underdeveloped in comparison even to Utku or Lengua unbelievers.

Missionaries need to recognize that the cultures to which they go are often highly supportive of moral virtues and character traits that should characterize all believers. Such cultural support actually contributes to the likelihood of believers in that culture exemplifying such biblical virtues.

Culture as Hindrance to Sanctification

But culture not only works in support of the moral life, culture also has the effect of opposing morality as defined by Scripture. Thus South Carolinian white culture of the 1930s, 1940s, and 1950s was supportive of racist talk and humor and of action taken to exclude blacks from white social settings. In such a context, many godly members of this subculture, with clear consciences and without fear of social disapproval, acted to exclude blacks from white social settings and told jokes that today would be recognized by all as racist and sinful. Culture thus frequently blinds us to moral issues. Just because our consciences do not condemn us does not mean that we are truly in the right (1 Cor. 4:4).

Aguaruna culture stresses a morality linked to family. Everyone who is not a relative (*patag*) is an enemy (*shiwag*). Thus it is okay and even admirable to lie to, steal from, commit adultery with the wife of, or kill someone who is not *patag*. The Bible, of course teaches a universal ethic, not just a family ethic. Aguaruna culture stresses that one should carefully note any offense (by nonfamily) and respond with retaliation and revenge, theft for theft, life for life. Honor is directly associated with being quick to take note of any offense and with vigorously avenging any affront. Only men who have killed in revenge reach the highest levels of respect and honor. Do the Aguaruna ever forgive? "Never!" is the response. The message of Jesus directly contradicts this ethic. When a young man in this traditional context becomes a Christian, the culture itself calls him a woman and a coward if he fails to avenge a death. The culture itself refuses to grant him honor until he first kills another. An Aguaruna believer who wishes to forgive others faces a greater moral battle than someone whose culture prescribes nonretaliation.

But culture not only contributes to moral blind spots and affirms values directly contradictory to biblical ones, it also provides ready-made justifications and rationalizations for behavior that violates scriptural norm. Thus certain cultures instruct their members that male sexuality is a "natural" drive not subject to a man's control, that if a man is seductively approached by an attractive woman while alone, it is simply not possible for him to control himself and he is not responsible for availing himself of the opportunity. Certain strands of thinking in Western culture would stress that anger is a "natural" emotion we are not responsible for and that really ought to be expressed, not "repressed" lest it damage the inner psyche. Western Christians with sinful pride may readily invoke cultural justifications excusing their sinful pride in terms of positive self-esteem, something their culture stresses is basic to good mental health. Christians in such cultures may excuse their sexual failures, their pride, or their irritability, quickness to take offense, and occasional explosions of rage in terms of the justifications provided by their cultures—and not be nearly as remorseful as God, or people from other cultures, would deem appropriate.

Culture as Neutrally Different: Complications for Sanctification. But we must not simply categorize each cultural trait as good or bad. Many cultural assumptions and norms involve conventional elements that appropriately vary from one culture to another. American Christians, in a land of abundance, think of gluttony as a sin against the self—against the body, the temple of the Holy Spirit. The worst foods to indulge in are therefore those high in sugar and fat. Aguaruna Christians also condemn gluttony, though not as a sin against the self. Since they face periodic scarcity, they think of gluttony as a sin against others—as a failure to restrain one's own appetite on behalf of those around. The worst food to overindulge in is therefore meat, the principal source of protein, a food seldom available in abundance. And so, the Aguaruna have a special word for the worst kind of glutton—*etsemjau*—a "meat glutton." Which culture is right about gluttony? Both, in their own context, are.

Cultures vary in what is thought of as erotic, and thus in what modesty entails. For many medieval Europeans a woman's bare feet were thought highly erotic, while the bosom was associated primarily with nursing. In such a context, paintings of the Virgin Mary with bosom uncovered were common and deemed appropriate. But Murillo's portrait of Mary with her bare feet showing was thought shockingly immodest, and it merited a rebuke by the inquisition. Similarly, contemporary Fulani men say it is the sight of a woman's thighs that stimulates lustful desires. They find it hilarious that Western women go swimming in suits that carefully cover the bosom, a matter of relative indifference to modesty, while flagrantly uncovering their thighs to the world. For American men, kissing has sexual or romantic overtones. Thus moral men do not kiss other men. What Arab and Russian men are comfortable with, and New Testament Christians routinely practiced—men kissing men—is morally repugnant to most American men. For many Arab men, on the other hand, the mere sight of a woman's hair tends to stimulate lustful thoughts. Modest Arab women cover their hair in public. Behavior and dress that are appropriately modest in one cultural context may be deemed shockingly immodest in another context. Christian modesty in the U.S. will look quite different from Christian modesty in Iran. An Iranian Christian missionary is probably not the best person to legislate standards of modesty for American Christians, nor are American missionaries well-positioned to legislate standards of modesty for Fulani or Iranian believers.

Again, cultures vary enormously in what may be owned and by whom—that is, what counts as property. A Sirionó growing up in a hunter-gatherer society may be astounded initially to realize that fruit trees are objects that certain individuals can lay exclusive claim to. Fruit trees, like the air that we breathe, are simply there for use by those who need them. An Old Testament Israelite, on the other hand, would recognize that fruit trees are privately owned, but would also know that travelers may legitimately pick an occasional fruit for their own consumption (Deut. 23:24). Both the Sirionó and the Israelite would offend if they exercised such prerogatives on the American or German missionary's fruit trees. It is cultural convention and law that determine what may be owned and by whom, as well as what ownership implies, and such conventions vary from one culture to another. Thus what would be theft in one culture would not necessarily be so in another. The problem comes when such cultures come into contact: when a Sirionó man climbs an American missionary's fruit tree, for example. The Sirionó's cheerful friendliness and utter lack of embarrassment when seen by the missionary become doubly disturbing. From the American standpoint, here is someone who not only steals, but who steals without shame. But in fact, this problem is not a moral problem indicative of a failure of sanctification. Rather it is a problem of cultural differences over conventional understandings of property rights.

Culture, then, is an intervening variable that plays a critical role in many of the specifics of the sanctification process. It is particularly important that cross-cultural missionaries, whose ministries concern the sanctification of national believers, understand and take into account such realities. Here are a few of the practical implications that follow from the basic truths just outlined.[4]

Practical Implications for Cross-Cultural Christian Workers

Anyone responsible for the spiritual growth and well-being of others invariably attempts to discern and make judgments about their spiritual condition. And here is where the trouble often begins.

Of Logs and Specks (Matt. 7:2–5)

Jesus warns against the natural tendency to discover even the smallest of faults in others while simultaneously failing to recognize substantive failures in one's own life. This common human failing is exacerbated when one looks at those of other cultures. Since our culture encourages us to be particularly sensitive to certain kinds of faults, we go to people of other cultures that do not sensitize them to the same issues and we are able to detect and criticize even the smallest speck in our brother's eye—when it comes to these issues. At the same time we fail to recognize the great moral vices in our own lives that our culture has blinded us to—vices that people of another culture may rightfully see as logs. The natural tendency, when ministering cross-culturally, is

> (1) to emphasize as sin what one's own culture recognizes to be sin but that the culture one is entering does not recognize as sinful—and for that very reason allows and practices openly, while
> (2) failing to address issues that to the native people are substantive moral failings. Few people enjoy being told they have a speck in their eye by someone who obviously has a log in his.

Heart Vs. Outward Appearance

Sanctification, above all, concerns the heart. Heart-love for "God is the taproot of all true holiness," writes J. I. Packer. When a person's motivating aim is to please God, when one's basis of trust is God and His Word, then we may speak of such a person as holy or sanctified. When one's heart is right with God, it will result in changed outward behavior. But it is not true that observers who look at that behavior, who look on the outward appearance, can accurately infer the state of another's heart. This is true for several reasons. First, many people do the right things for the wrong motives—as did the Pharisees. External conformity to (or emphasis on) a moral code may be associated with evil, and not just with good. Second, behavior that to the observer seems sinful need not imply a rebellious, unsanctified heart. This is because, as we've seen, people from different cultural backgrounds differ in many of their convictions and understandings of right and wrong. Unless one understands his culture, and the meanings things have for him, one cannot reliably infer the "heart" condition of the individual from that culture. Only with a deep understanding of native culture and conscience can one determine with some reliability whether the perceived moral failure is (1) "unwitting," or (2) deliberate and "presumptuous," or (3) perhaps not a moral failure at all.

It has been said that the mark of a truly indigenous church is that the missionaries don't like it. It is an amazing fact, but true, that believers from two different cultures can each love the Lord, keep short accounts with God on all known sin, regularly practice the disciplines of the Christian life, be growing in their walk with God, and yet, when they come in contact with each other, see things about the other that they dislike and even condemn.

Missionaries will probably struggle with such negative feelings throughout their ministry, unless . . . unless they acquire deep cultural understandings of those with whom they work; unless they develop deep understandings of how their own culture has shaped them; unless they deeply appreciate the moral values and disciplines their host culture shares with the Bible; unless they learn to humbly acknowledge their own weakness and sin in some of these areas; and above all, unless they love people they are with to the extent that they are not easily offended (1 Cor. 13:5, 7), do not judge by appearances (Judg. 7:24; Matt. 7:1), and assume the best about others (1 Cor. 13:5, 7). "Love covers over a multitude of sins" (1 Peter 4:8 NIV).

How then should cross-cultural missionaries proceed?

(1) Missionaries need to make it a high priority to gain an understanding of the culture and conscience of the people with whom they are ministering.

(2) The focus when instructing new converts about sin and sanctification should be on the Christian life as a relationship with God. Rather than trying to instantly straighten out every aspect of his conscience that one deems to be faulty, one assumes that the new believer's conscience is operative. As one teaches the basics about the nature of sin, temptation, confession, forgiveness, and the importance of keeping a clear conscience before God, one does so initially with reference to moral understandings with which his or her conscience is already in agreement with Scripture. Even the newest believer should be given the understandings and resources needed for confessing and repenting of known sin, receiving God's forgiveness, and appropriating God's power for resisting temptation in the area of that sin.

(3) The process of discipling and pastoring new believers continues with a search together for ever more biblical understandings of God's standards for life. Scripture itself must be the only absolute standard for the Christian.

(4) Having a conscience and mind fully conformed to God's ideal is not something that instantly happens after

conversion. Indeed, it is something toward which believers grow, but which none will fully experience in this life.

Victory in the Christian life is compatible with growth and diversity. Victory may be experienced by new Christians as well as old, though its actual outworking may differ for each. Victory may be experienced by Aguaruna, Japanese, German, or American Christians. Yet the precise mix of deep moral understandings and blind spots, of moral character strengths and weaknesses, will vary not only from one individual to another, but from one culture to another. Christians of different cultures will follow somewhat different trajectories of sanctifying growth.

In dealing with such a growth process, several things should be stressed. (1) The consciences of believers have been shaped by their culture, by Scripture, and by an interplay of the two. As a result, believers from different cultures will differ in their moral assessments of many things—such as what parts of the body should be covered in order to be modest. This means that missionaries' consciences will speak to moral issues in ways that are informed by their cultures as well as by Scripture. They should be sure that what they teach is not the authority of a moral code they bring with them (a mix of Bible and home culture), but the authority of the Bible—to be read and understood by indigenous believers. The goal then is for believers individually, and the indigenous church corporately, to be studying and submitting themselves and their consciences to the Scriptures.

(2) Change of conscience occurs through gradual transformation of inner understandings and convictions out of a spiritual walk that includes the transforming influence of the Word of God. Outer conformity to an extrabiblical code of behavior imposed by the missionary, on the other hand, fails to adequately and appropriately engage the inner conviction of conscience.

(3) The missionary should not hesitate to teach and preach biblical passages setting forth basic moral and ethical teaching and should provide input and guidance in raising questions and searching the Scriptures, but the missionary should encourage the indigenous church itself to determine the specifics of how the Scriptures apply morally to their situations in life. The goal is a sanctified body of believers acting out of inner convictions of conscience, not out of concerns with conforming pragmatically to a code of behavior that the missionary obviously values but that fails to make moral and biblical sense to the indigenous believers involved.

Sanctification is something that occurs in social communities, not just to isolated individuals. The goal in every culture is a thriving indigenous church—a social community that faithfully communicates the Word, applies it to life, guides its members in the disciplines of the Christian life (prayer, Bible study, confession, etc.), and exercises discipline over its members.[5]

We are shaped by our cultures. God is not. Yet He accommodates Himself to our cultures. Christians have long recognized that God did this in the Scriptures. But it is equally true that He does this in sanctifying each believer. In sanctification, we gradually become, as it were, what Christ would be were He a member of our society. This means that we come to stand in tension with our society and its norms, and that we also remain distinctively incarnate in that culture. On the one hand, Christians of different cultures may be thought of as gradually becoming more alike in certain respects. As Japanese Christians, reared on the proverb "A lie also is a useful thing!" become more Christlike, they will come to share an un-Japanese commitment to truth—which may make them more like American Christians than like Japanese non-Christians. American Christians will come to honor their parents in a way that makes them atypical of their own society—and much more similar to Asian Christians. On the other hand, a sanctified Japanese believer will still be distinctively Japanese. An Aguaruna living a victorious Christian life will do it in a distinctively Aguaruna fashion. Modesty for a Sirionó Christian woman will look quite different from modesty for an Iranian believer. Sanctification is for all believers. But its outworking is culturally variable.

Reference List

Briggs, Jean. 1970. *Never in Anger: Portrait of an Eskimo Family*. Cambridge: Harvard University Press.

Konig, Otto. 1978. *The Pineapple Story*. Oak Brook, Ill.: Institute in Basic Youth Conflicts.

Loewen, Jacob. 1975. *Culture and Human Values: Christian Intervention in Anthropological Perspective*. Pasadena, Calif.: William Carey Library.

Priest, Robert J. 1994. Missionary Elenctics: Conscience and Culture. *Missiology* 22:291–315.

Zheng, Kaitang. 1991. The Rich Soil on Which Christianity Grows in an Anhui County. In *Religion Under Socialism in China* (Ed. by Luo Zhufent. Trans. by Donald E. MacInnis and Zeng Xi'an). New York: M.E. Sharpe, Inc., pp. 232–41.

Notes

1. Lin Wuji is a fictional character—a composite of true-to-life experiences of many Chinese Christians.
2. Although this account is fictional, I wish it to be as culturally true to life as possible, and so I quote a portion of an actual Chinese sermon recorded by Zheng Kaitang. (1991): 235–36.
3. An Amazonian tribal group among whom the author did fieldwork.
4. For a fuller treatment of conscience and culture in relation to the missionary task, see Robert J. Priest, "Missionary Elenctics: Conscience and Culture," *Missiology* 22 (1994): 291–315.
5. Jacob Loewen, *Culture and Human Values: Christian Intervention in Anthropological Perspective* (Pasadena, Calif.: William Carey Library, 1975), 211–84.

11

About the Author

Crawford Loritts is national director of Legacy, an organization he founded in 1982 as Here's Life Black America, a ministry of Campus Crusade. The major focus of Legacy is to act as a catalyst in helping to rebuild and restore strong, godly families in Urban America. A major ministry of Legacy is to hold conferences of national and international scope, such as CHICAGO '81 and DESTINY '87, as well as local Urban Family Conferences across the nation. Loritts has often spoken at other major events such as Promise Keepers. Heard regularly on Moody Broadcast Network, he is also known widely through numerous articles. Though a recognized leader in the African-American evangelical church, Loritts serves just as easily in leadership of predominantly white movements and organizations. He and his wife, Karen, have four children.

About This Chapter

Crawford Loritts, speaking from generations of experience and deep passion, gives us a glimpse of what victorious living means to the African-American. Here is a powerful demonstration of what Robert Priest has pointed out in the preceding chapter, "Cultural Factors in Victorious Living." We can see clearly that the black perspective is very different from the white, yet so biblically authentic. We could wish Loritts had expanded on this unique view of the problems of contemporary African-Americans and the solution, but what he has done is very effective—a brief essay that deliberately leaves out much that might be said to focus clearly on the essentials of what it means to live victoriously in the black community.

This insight is needed as much by the white community as by the black. In surveying generations of graduate students, asking them to identify in order of priority the "big twenty" problems facing America, I made a startling discovery. Black students consistently listed racism as number one; white students rarely included racism at all. Though in this essay he addresses African-Americans, if we are to help one another grow in Christlikeness and not provide further stumbling blocks to those who differ, white *and* black, we need to listen to Crawford Loritts.

Victorious Living from an African-American Perspective

by Crawford Loritts

Not long ago I preached at a large, predominantly Caucasian church in suburban Washington, D.C. Before I stood to preach, the choir sang a very moving song. The congregation listened in rapt attention. Although obviously moved, no one said a word or responded in any way until the worship leader said, "And all God's people said . . ." Then in unison the entire congregation said a hearty "Amen!" This struck me as somewhat humorous because in my mind I contrasted what the response in my home church, or most black churches, would have been. After hearing such a worshipful, deeply moving song no one would have had to give us permission to say "Amen," or to shout for that matter!

Emotions have always played a significant part in our worship and in our Christian experience as African-Americans. By nature we are an expressive people. This dynamic signature is clearly seen in almost every facet of the religious life in our community. And this is particularly true as it relates to the ministry of the Holy Spirit (or the victorious Christian life). Freedom, joy, and personal triumph and victory over sin and weakness are meant, we feel, to be exuberantly shared with fellow believers so that together we can celebrate God's deliverance. In this way we affirm and validate each other.

This perspective is deeply rooted not only in our African heritage but also in our journey and pilgrimage through oppression in this country. Historically the black church was the only institution that was legitimately ours. For many years it was the only place we could go that would provide us with a sense of worth, dignity, and direction. It gave us hope in the midst of our despair and, most significantly, it interpreted and applied God's plan for dealing with the painful daily struggles of our people with the issues facing our personal lives as well as the ever-present injustices of a system that shouted to us every day that we were worthless and less than human.

It is in this context and against this backdrop that most African-Americans view and experience the victorious Christian life. For the black Christian the history of oppression in our experience has made us aware of the need to daily rely upon God for strength to face our struggles. That is why historically the black church did not separate "theology" from everyday life. Their preaching and teaching had to relate to the people. It can be argued that the theme of the black church during slavery and the early days of reconstruction was God's deliverance from our painful predicament. And since at times any hope of deliverance in this life seemed impossible, heaven became our focus and our encouragement to persevere down here. The Negro spirituals attest to this as we looked past our circumstances to a brighter day. In that way we could keep going. Although we were in physical bondage, we could experience freedom and victory in our spirits.

However, between WWI and WWII many African-Americans moved from the rural South to the northern industrial cities looking for work. Historians call this the Great Northern Migration. We went from a rural, agricultural people to urban dwellers faced with the unique challenges that came with city life. With this also came a shift in perspective and in the message that the black church preached. In the words of the black historian E. Franklin Frazier, the church became increasingly secular. There was a gradual shift from the daily reliance on the supernatural with a strong emphasis on heaven to the social and political structures and solutions for our deliverance here and now.

At this point you may be wondering what all of this has to do with the victorious Christian life in the African-American experience. In my view, everything. Although during slavery and the early part of this century there was not a clearly defined theology of the Holy Spirit as related to the Christian's daily walk with God, the black church did preach out of necessity the need for a passionate reliance upon God. We may not have completely understood the theological specifics concerning the ministry of the Holy Spirit but nevertheless we depended on Him. However, the church, in response to the pressures of urbanization and thus the development of other organizations (the NAACP, the Urban League, etc.) as well as political and governmental solutions to the struggles of African-Americans, began to share the responsibility for the direction and "deliverance" of our people with these institutions. But this also produced a shift in reliance from the God of our "weary years" to the promises of programs, politicians, and the judicial system.

Further complicating matters was the horrendous racism practiced by evangelical seminaries and Bible colleges that taught a biblically sound message on the victorious Christian life but would not recruit African-Americans and/or allow us to attend their institutions. This failure to "practice what they preached" not only solidified mistrust for years to come but it also denied many of us of the powerfully liberating truth concerning what the Bible teaches about our position in Christ and how to be overcomers in this life. Many of the theologically liberal institutions went after our brightest, most promising preachers and gave them an education, albeit without biblical substance. I have often wondered what would have happened if evangelicals would have put out the welcome mat and opened their doors?

I don't want to suggest, however, that God's great sanctifying work in the hearts and lives of African-American Christians was thwarted or hindered by the offenses of the dominant culture and the "urbanization" of our people. My understanding of the sovereignty of our great God, His grace and mercy, and thus His ability to cut through the layers of human opposition, indifference, and the schemes of Satan to get truth to all of His people is the source of encouragement and hope. Nothing and no one stops God! Despite other voices that have called for a departure from our reliance on the Spirit of God to overcome our struggles, there have always been faithful men and women of God in the black community who have turned a deaf ear to the noise of the world and the nonsense of carnal Christians. Again, we may not have understood the "theological implications of the victorious Christian life," but many understood it profoundly in their souls and in their experiences. This faith has weathered the storms and tests of time. So when my mother (and thousands of other African-American Christians from her generation) says, "Pray, trust God, and obey Him, and He will make a way," she knows from her understanding of the Scriptures and her walk with the Master exactly what she is talking about!

I am not minimizing the need for biblical accuracy and doctrinal clarity concerning our victory in Christ. Indeed, wrong thinking leads to wrong living. Neither am I suggesting that there has been blatant ignorance in the African-American Christian experience concerning the victorious Christian life. I am declaring that this great truth has been attacked and "muddied" as a result of the historical challenges and battles that the black church and our people have been through. But I believe that God once again is putting this truth on the front burner in our community. There are encouraging signs and a refreshing sense of spiritual momentum developing among our people. Allow me to share a few of them with you.

First, there are the increased awareness and acceptance of the powerlessness of the political process and government programs to provide lasting solutions to the challenges facing the African-American community. A moral vacuum has been created that the body of Christ can step in to fill. Once again the church is stepping up to the plate and solutions based on the Word of God and demonstrated by transformed lives are gaining increased recognition, attention, and acceptance. God is orchestrating the environment for His voice to be heard.

Second, there are stronger, biblically balanced preaching and teaching coming from our pulpits. The increased numbers of blacks attending conservative seminaries and Bible colleges over the past few decades are having a powerful impact in our churches and in the community. In addition, pastor and leadership conferences sponsored by biblically based, successful churches and ministries in our community have multiplied the prominence and popularity of expository preaching. Lives are being changed!

Third, the "discipleship" movement, with its emphasis on the application of truth, personal accountability, and spiritual multiplication, is gaining momentum throughout the African-American Christian community. At this writing some of the fastest growing churches in the black community point to discipleship as a critical component to their success. In addition, biblical, Spirit-filled preaching is driving people toward godly living. Again, I believe that the failure of the government and other institutions to provide meaningful, lasting solutions to the challenges and problems facing our community has caused Christians to realize that we need a Christianity that offers victory and deliverance both individually and throughout our community. However, we cannot go it alone. We need to help each other in experiencing the victory and hope of Christ.

This leads to the fourth observation. There are early, positive signs of revival and spiritual awakening in black America. The disintegration of our families, the proliferation of drugs and crime, the chronic problem of the absentee male, and the seeming avalanche of other assorted challenges and dilemmas have dramatically set the stage for God to get our attention. And it appears He is doing just that. Men and women in our community are turning to Christ in unprecedented numbers. Through my preaching in recent years I have seen a great increase in the number of people committing their lives to Christ. Historically, black church membership rolls have been heavily populated with women. That too is changing. Men are being won to Christ and filtering into the church. Springing up throughout our community are needs-based, relevant ministries offering the hope and help of Christ to broken people. Fresh, young leadership is emerging that is committed to the Word of God and is not afraid to trust God to translate vision to reality. There is a renewed emphasis on and a celebration of the spiritual dynamics (prayer, faith, and the ministry of the Holy Spirit) as the power base for our lives and ministry. God indeed is at work.

In summary, what, then, does all of this mean or imply with regard to the victorious Christian life in the African-American experience? At the expense of stating the obvious, let me clearly say that the biblical requirements for experiencing the ongoing victory in Christ are the same for every person and therefore for every culture. God's truth is unchanging and the objective standard by and through which all of life must be adjusted and measured. However, God has made us (African-Americans) a beautifully free, expressive people. We tend to exuberantly celebrate the joy of the Lord and victory in our pilgrimage. This is our signature! The great moral and spiritual challenges facing our community are driving many of us back to our spiritual heritage for direction and solutions. This renewed hunger and thirst have set the stage for spiritual awakening. This is exciting because, historically, black Christians have not separated our personal walk with the Savior from the issues facing our community. We are positioned to be a powerful vehicle for hope and deliverance.

Please join me in praying that revival will burst forth throughout black America. The psalmist expresses the desire of my heart,

> Wilt Thou not Thyself revive us again,
> That Thy people may rejoice in Thee?
> Show us Thy lovingkindness, O LORD,
> And grant us Thy salvation. (Ps. 85:6–7 NASB)

Oh, God, do it I pray!

PART THREE

Victory for Hurting People

In contemporary society there is one major impediment to living victoriously, getting free, and finding fulfillment: major trauma. It may have happened long ago; it may be present bad circumstances. You may have brought it on yourself by wrong choices, but the chances are you have been victimized—someone else hurt you. Whatever the source, a person is so badly damaged he or she can't get free, can't find fulfillment. This section faces that dilemma squarely.

First Joni Eareckson Tada tells her compelling story of struggling to be free and, step by painful step, how God delivered her from the grip of attitudes that were destroying her. Then, lest we fear we might not have what it takes to follow in her steps, two counselors explain in practical detail, not merely how we can adjust our thinking toward greater wholeness, but how we can find freedom and fulfillment in Christ. First we hear from a world-renowned professor and author of standard textbooks, George Rekers; then we hear from a psychologist who founded the counseling program in one of America's leading churches, Allan McKechnie. In this section we'll explore theory developed in the context of biblical understanding of human nature and how to be free and fulfilled. But we'll also see graphic examples of how it has happened.

In a day when many Christians turn to psychological theory and the professional counselor to straighten out personal problems, the sad fact is that many are given only what humans can produce, unaided by the Spirit or the Book He has given to reveal God's truth about human nature, wholeness, and how to have it. This section is critical to point a different way, bringing psychological theory under the authority of Scripture and thus bringing hope. Here we find the message of victory in the context of psychological theory, guideposts on the path to freedom and fulfillment.

About the Author

Joni Eareckson Tada is the founder and president of JAF Ministries, an organization accelerating Christian ministry in the disability community. A diving accident in 1967 left her a quadriplegic in a wheelchair, unable to use her hands. During two years of rehabilitation, she spent long months learning how to paint, holding a brush between her teeth. Today, she is an internationally known mouth artist. Her first name is recognized in many countries due to her many best-selling books, including her autobiography, *Joni*. World Wide Picture's full-length feature film *Joni*, in which Tada re-created her own life, has been translated into numerous languages and shown in scores of countries around the world. Her daily broadcast is heard on more than eight hundred outlets. She is also an accomplished recording artist, has served on many boards and commissions, and has received many awards for her humanitarian service.

About This Chapter

As we move into a special section of "Victory for Hurting People," Joni Eareckson Tada starts us off with a riveting account of her personal pilgrimage from crushing spiritual defeat to glorious victory in Christ. Through her experience of wrestling with biblical truth, we can see clearly the pathway from despair to hope, from despondency to joy, from the bondage of self-pity to freedom. In the two chapters following there are fine expositions of the theological and psychological dimensions of victory for hurting people, but Joni Eareckson Tada begins with the bright light of personal experience. We focus at this point on "hurting people," because, if God's promises of victory in this world are not for hurting people, who might they be for? All of us qualify! But Joni qualifies in a special way.

Victorious Life and Pain

by Joni Eareckson Tada

I am the victim of a terrible diving accident," I said in a flat and factual way to the lawyer. "It has left me completely paralyzed from the shoulders down."

My dad's lawyer quietly jotted copious notes as I droned on. I was numb and hurting; I didn't flinch at all at the idea of making Maryland Beach, Inc., pay. As far as I was concerned, it was their fault the water was too shallow.

In fact, I thought my diving accident was everybody's fault. I wanted everyone to pay. The Department of Vocational Rehabilitation owed me a good case manager who would plan out my career. My church (which I really wasn't involved much with back then) should take responsibility for doing things for me. After all, that's what churches were supposed to do. I *really* pushed this victimization thing on my parents. They "owed" me; they should somehow pay for the damages I sustained. I fumed at them as they stood at my hospital bedside: "You were the ones who brought me into this world. It's all your fault, Mom and Dad!"

Looking back, I'm certain that most of my anger and depression was rooted in the "victim thing." I was a victim of spinal cord injury much as people are victims of polio, AIDS, or strokes. People, in our culture of comfort, feel swindled by life. And not just as it relates to a disability. People feel victimized in their marriages or by abusive childhoods. Others feel victimized by violent crime or unfair employment practices. Some would swear they are trapped by lack of finances or held back by prejudice and discrimination. Many have convinced themselves that someone else should either pay for the damages owed them or help take responsibility for their lives. People who choose to see themselves as victims are those who choose self-pity, self-centeredness, and plain old selfishness.

I dug in for the long haul. Not only with a court case that seemed to drag on forever, but with a cloud of deep depression from which I would never escape.

The Path Away from Pity

Frankly, after only a year of adjusting to life in a wheelchair, I began to tire of the self-pity. In my innermost being, I realized that the path away from self-destruction was traced somewhere in the pages of the Bible, but I was a novice as to where to look. Thankfully, the Holy Spirit and a neighbor friend named Steve were my guides.[1]

"Look, I'd like to be able to put on a Colgate smile like you," I said to Steve, "but there's no way I can face a life of total paralysis with a happy attitude. It's just too much, too big."

He had a wise and ready reply: "I couldn't agree more. It is too much to ask."

I looked at him askew.

"And God doesn't ask it of you either. He only asks you to take one day at a time."

I realized this wasn't simply a pious platitude plucked off a cross-stitched plaque; this was a powerful and fundamental signpost from Scripture pointing to the path away from pain. I began to "wheel" the path starting with Lamentations 3:22–23, "Because of the LORD's great love we are not consumed, / for his compassions never fail. / They are new every morning; / great is your faithfulness" (NIV). I quickly learned this was the only way to life: one day at a time with God's enabling.

Actually, it's the biblical way to live, Steve reminded me. God promises His mercies are "new every morning." My friend showed how the Bible beautifully pictured this when the manna fell from heaven with the breaking of every dawn—God's people couldn't store up the manna for the next day; no, they had to rely on God's provision for strength one day at a time.

Little wonder the Lord Jesus, the Bread of Heaven, took such pains to remind us not to worry, not to be consumed with the cares of tomorrow. He spent paragraphs repeating Himself in Matthew, chapter 6, saying "Do not worry" five times. He even added why when He reminded us that the troubles we face in a twenty-four-hour slice of time are enough for one day (Matt. 6:25–34).

There is no grace available for next year's worries, next month's anxieties, or tomorrow's problems. Only strength for today. To me, it was a revolutionary idea. It was even echoed in my daily devotional, "God's training is for now, not later. His purpose is for this very minute, not for sometime in the future. If we have a further goal in mind, we are not paying enough attention to the present time."[2]

With this idea firmly imbedded, I could at least face the pain of living with paralysis "today." At Steve's prompting, I purposed to go to God in empty-handed spiritual poverty (that's faith) and ask for strength each morning. Strength to face the, at best, boring routine of someone giving me exercises, bathing and dressing me, lifting me out of my bed and into my wheelchair. Slowly (definitely not overnight), I began to relax into the habit of asking God for help every morning. And for a while, I was satisfied.

But still, questions nagged. I had to resolve this thing about being a victim.

Just Who's in Control?

You can understand. You can identify. We've all—yes, even Christians—felt cheated when hard times have hit. And although we can live on God's grace "one day at a time," sooner or later, those prickly questions begin needling. Questions such as, "Well, if I'm not a victim of unfortunate circumstances out of my control, then just who *is* in control?"

You could be a devoted young mother who must watch her two-year-old die slowly of cancer while you overhear other parents worry about their children's scratched knees and bruised elbows. You could be a thirty-nine-year-old single woman who has served God faithfully for decades and has always longed to be married; you watch your spiritually shallow twenty-five-year-old friend wed a wonderful godly man. You could be a hardworking salesman who holds fast to good ethics, but a conniving coworker cheats his way to the top, receiving praise and promotion.

Life isn't fair. It's full of injustice. Inequities hit us from all sides, prompting those wretched "I'm a victim" feelings. The odd thing is, God has *designed* it this way. Ephesians 1:11 says that "In him [the young mother, the single woman, and the salesman] were also chosen, having been predestined according to the plan of him who works out everything [children with cancer, girls who get all the blessings, and conniving coworkers] in conformity with the purpose of his will" (NIV). Proverbs 16:4 says, "The LORD works out *everything* for his own ends" (NIV, italics mine), and not just the wicked for a day of disaster, but even diving accidents into shallow water.

Exactly why God has designed it this way has been the subject of theological books throughout the ages, and I'm not about to solve it in this short chapter. But a hint as to the "whys and wherefores" behind insults and injuries may be found in the second half of Ephesians 1:12, ". . . in order that we . . . might be for the praise of his glory" (NIV). Cut and dried. Short and simple.

It's all for our good and His glory.

This was one of those truths that was hard for me, at first, to swallow. "It's all for our good and His glory? You've got to be kidding," I said to Steve one night after our Bible study. The very idea seemed to add insult to my diving injury. It was like rubbing salt into the wound on my spinal cord. Even as I flipped through the pages of my Bible with my mouthstick, it was the same. Wherever I looked, Scripture was replete with what sounded like God's bravado—He's in charge for our good and His glory, so snap out of it and learn to "rejoice in suffering"!

Steve helped shed light on this. He explained that Scripture presents us with a view of life from the eternal perspective. This perspective separates what is transitory from what is lasting. What is transitory, such as injustice and injury, will not endure; what is lasting, such as the eternal weight of glory accrued from that pain, will remain forever. Everything else—numbing heartache, deep disappointment, and total paralysis—everything else, no matter how real it seems to us on earth, is treated as inconsequential. Hardships are hardly worth noticing.

With an open Bible, Steve pointed out some amazing Scriptures: "The apostle Paul had this perspective when he said, 'For our light and momentary troubles are achieving for us an eternal glory that far outweighs them all.' And regarding his own experiences with suffering, Paul said, 'I consider them rubbish.' It says this in 2 Corinthians 4:17 and Philippians 3:8 [NIV]."

I protested at first. "Wait a minute," I said. "Did he say, 'Troubles, light? Inequities, rubbish'?"

"Yeah," my friend said, smiling, "and the apostle Peter had this perspective too when he wrote to Christian friends being flogged and beaten. 'In this you greatly rejoice, though now for a little while you may have had to suffer grief in all kinds of trials" (1 Peter 1:6 NIV).

This was a little incredulous. "Rejoice?" I laughed. "When you're cheated out of a fair trial and thrown to lions? The apostle expected believers to view their problems as lasting . . . *a little while?* What sort of wristwatch was he using?"

These verses did not, at first, comfort me when I began to study the Bible. In fact, this kind of biblical nonchalance about gut-wrenching suffering used to drive me crazy. I wondered, *Lord, I will never walk again. I've got a leaky legbag . . . I smell like urine . . . my back aches. Maybe I can get by on Your grace one day at a time, and maybe You see all of this achieving an eternal glory, but all I see is one awful day after the next in this stinking wheelchair. It's not fair!*

Our pain and sense of fairness always scream for our undivided attention, insisting, "Forget the future! What's God going to do to make it right *now*?" Time does that. It rivets our attention on temporal things. And suffering doesn't make it any easier. It tightens the screw on the moment, making us anxious to find quick fix-its or escape hatches. It makes us feel like victims of our circumstances. When I read in Romans 5:3, "rejoice in our sufferings"(NIV), my first thought was, *Sure, God, I'll rejoice the day You make things fair! And if You don't, what's going on? Are You trying to convince me I'm in spiritual denial? That my hurt and pain are imaginary?* When it came to my affliction being light and momentary, God was obviously using a different dictionary.

The Lord, however, does not use a different lexicon when He picks words such as *light* and *momentary* to define earthly inequities. Even if it means being sawn asunder, torn apart by lions, or injured in an accident and plopped in a wheelchair for the rest of one's life. The Spirit-inspired writers of the Bible simply had a different perspective, an end-of-time view. Tim Stafford says, "This is why scripture can seem at times so blithely and irritatingly out of touch with reality, brushing past huge philosophical problems and personal agony. But that is just how life is when you are looking from the end. Perspective changes everything. What seems so important at the time has no significance at all."[3]

It's a matter of perspective. The scales of justice are *meant* to tip off kilter on earth. Our unsatisfied sense of human fairness is not meant to be balanced. But that's good: it is to our benefit that we are not satisfied in a world destined for decay. "Therefore we do not lose heart," 2 Corinthians 4:16–17 says, ". . . For our light and momentary troubles are *achieving for us an eternal glory that far outweighs them all*" (NIV, italics mine). What could possibly outweigh the pain of permanent paralysis? The pain of a life of singleness? The loss of a child from cancer? "We fix our eyes not on what is seen, but on what is unseen. For what is seen is *temporary*, but what is unseen is *eternal*" (2 Cor. 4:18 NIV, italics mine). The greater weight of eternal glory is clear. One day the scales of justice will not only balance, but they will be weighted heavily— almost beyond comprehension—to our good and God's glory. It will mean . . .

Greater glory to God.

A new appreciation for the justice of God—not fairness, but justice.

The final destruction of death, disease, and devilish men. The vindication of God's holy name. The restoration of all things under Christ.

This means an eternal weight of glory for the young mother who holds fast to God's grace as she watches her two-year-old die of cancer. It means a richer reward for the single woman who perseveres patiently. It means a more exalted eternal estate for the salesman who holds fast to good ethics.

And these things outweigh thousands of afternoons of not feeling or moving for me. Mind you, I'm not saying that cancer or singleness or my paralysis is light in and of itself. Paralysis, disappointment in marriage, or cancer only *becomes* light in contrast to the far greater weight on the other side of the scale. And although I wouldn't normally call almost thirty years in a wheelchair "momentary," it *is* when you realize that you and I "are a mist that appears for a little while and then vanishes" (James 4:14 NIV).

Hardships and Heaven

There is a direct relationship between earth's suffering and heaven's glory. I'm not glorifying suffering here. There's no inherent goodness in my spinal cord injury. There's nothing applaudable about the pain. Problems are real and I'm not denying that suffering hurts. I'm just denying that it *matters* in the grander scheme of things. Remember, it is only light and momentary *compared* with what our response is producing for us in heaven—yes, suffering is pivotal to future glory.

For example, the greatest suffering that ever occurred happened on the cross. And the greatest glory ever given in response to suffering was the glory ascribed to Christ when He ascended. He suffered "death on a cross. . . . *Therefore* God exalted Him to the highest place" (Phil. 2:8, 9 NIV, italics mine). There is a direct correspondence between suffering and glory.

When the mother of James and John approached the Lord and asked if her sons could please enjoy a position of prominence in the kingdom of heaven, the Lord replied, "You don't know what you are asking." Then He said to her sons, "Can you drink the cup I am going to drink?"

"We can," they answered.

Jesus said to them, "You will indeed drink from my cup" (Matt. 20:20–23 NIV).

The Lord implied that if His followers were to share in His glory, they would also have to share in His sufferings. And the deeper the suffering, the higher the glory. This is why the apostle could say in 1 Peter 4:13 that to the degree one suffers, keep on rejoicing: "*Rejoice* that you participate in the sufferings of Christ, *so that you may be overjoyed* when his glory is revealed" (NIV, italics mine). We rejoice on earth . . . so that we may be overjoyed in heaven.

Does this mean that those who suffer greatly, yet nobly, will have a bigger halo? A shinier face? No, but it does mean that those who suffer beyond comparison will, if they honor Christ with an uncomplaining spirit, be glorified beyond all comparison.

As Steve and I grew together in our study of God's Word, there were occasional times when, yes, I smirked as I read Romans 8:18: "I consider that our present sufferings are not worth comparing with the glory that will be revealed in us" (NIV). True, every now and then I went through cycles, thinking, *Is the Bible being flippant about my lot in life?* But as long as I kept my nose in God's Word (as well as continuing that habit of leaning on His grace afresh everyday) I remained on the high road home. I became more devoted to the spiritual than the physical. More devoted to eternal realities than temporal ones. I became free from the "victim thing."

Victim or Victor?

Remember my blubbering to my dad's lawyer about my anger against the owners of the beach where I broke my neck? We never won that court case. Looking back, I'm glad and relieved there was only a modest settlement out of court. The truth was, I made a stupid mistake. I took a reckless dive and I'm grateful I finally saw the truth. It was the truth that set me free, along with other truths like leaning daily on God's grace and trusting His sovereignty in every painful circumstance. Most of all, I discovered that playing the victim role is not consistent with living for Jesus Christ. God's children are never victims. Everything that touches the lives of God's children, He permits.

But you know what's odd? The irony is that you can't *imagine* a more victimized person than Jesus. The Scriptures tell us He had no real home. His friends were, for the most part, the fair-weather sort. He was brought like a lamb to the slaughter. He was betrayed and unjustly crucified, suffering a death He did not deserve. Yet when He died, He did not say, "*I* am finished," but "*It* is finished." He did not play the victim and thus He emerged as the victor; and it is *this* example He has set for us.

Forget the self-pity. True, your circumstances might be downright awful. Your supervisor at work may be trying to push you out of your job. Your marriage may, indeed, be a fiery trial. You might be living below the poverty level and life itself is just one big hardship. But victory is ours in Christ. His grace is sufficient; His sovereignty is supreme. Know this truth and it will set you free!

Notes

1. I benefited greatly in the early years of my paralysis from a friendship with a young man who graduated from what was then Columbia Bible College. Steve Estes guided me through most of the biblical insights mentioned in this chapter.
2. Oswald Chambers, *My Utmost for His Highest* (Grand Rapids: Discovery House Publishers, 1992), July 28.
3. Stafford, *Knowing the Face of God* (Grand Rapids: Zondervan, 1986), 221.

13

About the Author

George Rekers is an internationally recognized clinical child psychologist who has held important posts at three major research universities and is currently professor of neuropsychiatry and behavioral science at the University of South Carolina School of Medicine. He has also taught as an adjunct professor at Fuller Theological Seminary School of Psychology, Tyndale Theological Seminary (the Netherlands), and Columbia International University, and served as a visiting scholar at Harvard University. He has been an invited lecturer in many universities and scientific societies around the world. He has authored nine books, some of which have become standard texts. Rekers's education is both secular (UCLA, Ph.D.) and theological (M.Div. from Columbia International University and ThD candidate at the University of South Africa). He and his wife, Sharon, live with their five sons in Columbia, South Carolina.

About This Chapter

Why is this chapter twice the length of other chapters and loaded with documentation? Because the author is staking out new territory for his profession, new territory of profound importance for contemporary Christians. Without realizing it, we tend to absorb the approach of a godless psychology that makes the quest for freedom and fulfillment purely natural. In contrast, George Rekers does three things in this chapter:

1. He documents from research data the reality of the problem. Early environment really can radically handicap a person, mentally, emotionally, and spiritually.

2. He outlines clearly the scriptural basis for the hope we have through God's intervention in broken lives.

3. He demonstrates from empirical data that the biblical approach to finding freedom and fulfillment really does work. Not only the twenty-five years of personal experience of being a distinguished clinical psychologist himself, but the evidence of extensive research assures us that a scriptural approach to therapy not only works, but that it works better than the secular model.

Escaping the Bondage of Early Environment

by George A. Rekers

T he contemporary Western cultural milieu is pervasively influenced by psychological and therapeutic concepts. In this context, it seems quite reasonable (and even compassionate) to many to assume that a person cannot be expected to live a victorious Christian life if one's early childhood environment has been significantly abnormal, dysfunctional, or debilitating. Many individuals feel hopelessly trapped by the tight box of their past.

Perceived hopelessness and helplessness are common indicators of the depressive disorders, but this chapter addresses the question, "Is victorious Christian living actually impossible for some individuals because of their early adverse experiences?"

Handicapping Conditions

Deriving theory from Darwinian biology, D. W. Winnicott attempted to explain how an individual develops a distinctive sense of self through natural processes of development that occur in the context of one's early environment.[1] Thus, Winnicott viewed distractions in one's early development as a cause of psychopathology.[2] In the form of determinism found in the writings of S. Freud, the individual's present is viewed as determined by his or her past.[3] Empirical research has indeed linked adverse childhood experiences with adulthood adjustment difficulties and psychological disorder. Disruptions, deprivation, or deviance in the parent-child relationship interfere with the developing child's ability to adapt to the environment, and thereby have been theoretically considered to be especially potent causes in the formation of subsequent adult psychological orders.

In general, the way a child is treated by parents influences later adulthood occurrence of psychological disorders, including anxiety, depression, and the experience of hopelessness.[4] Loss of a parent in childhood, by death or separation, has been associated with adult mental disorder.[5] Multiple early childhood disadvantages (such as family disruption) have been found to have a cumulative deleterious effect upon children, producing adulthood depression and anxiety.[6] Disruptions in a child's early environment also appear to be linked to the co-occurrence of significant personality disorders with major depression.[7] Perceived lack of family support in the face of a significant loss is associated with perceived hopelessness in depressed adolescents, and greater degrees of helplessness are associated with higher rates of suicide attempt.[8] Children who experience neglect and rejection from their mothers, disrupted personal attachments, multiple mother and father substitutes, grossly inappropriate parenting, physical abuse, and/or sexual abuse are more likely to develop a borderline personality disorder in adulthood; thus, a chaotic, traumatic early environment contributes to serious, chronic personality disorder in adolescents and adults.[9]

Some boys growing up with a hostile, rejecting, or absent father, or some boys who are sexually abused by a male, develop strong homosexual temptations in adolescence or adulthood.[10]

The experience of incest in childhood is an evil that can result in rage,[11] post-traumatic stress disorder,[12] and feelings of helplessness that can disrupt adult adjustment[13] and interfere with the development of a sense of "person-hood." Experiences of "depersonalization" carry over into adulthood and such adults may adopt a "surrender pattern" to cope with subsequent illicit sexual overtures to the degree that they even become vulnerable to sexual abuse by an unethical psychotherapist.[14] Tragically, some child victims of sexual abuse experience that trauma in the context of ritual satanic abuse.[15]

Illustrative Case

On October 25, 1994, Susan Smith caused her automobile to become the underwater death chamber for her two preschool sons. In my book, *Susan Smith: Victim or Murderer,*[16] I describe how mental health experts testified in her trial as to the tragic loss of her father to suicide, her sexual abuse by her stepfather, and her growing up in a dysfunctional family with a family tree replete with multiple cases of depression and alcoholism. Longitudinal psychological studies have found that

> the trauma of losing a parent through death, divorce, or neglect shatters people's feelings of security, adequacy, and worth and leaves psychological scars that never completely heal. When children perceive themselves to be abandoned, feelings of inadequacy and self-devaluation develop. While the effect of abandonment varies . . . many children experiencing loss of a parent show disruption in normal personality development. The extent and impact of early childhood separation of the offender from a loved one may be a causative factor in violent offenses, including murder, rape, and assault.[17]

And psychological research studies have reported an increased risk of suicidal gestures[18] and suicide[19] in people following the death of a parent.

Sexual abuse causes a loss of a sense of security and protection.[20] Such psychological dynamics induce self-defeating behavior patterns in the girl who may be prone to degrade herself with sexual promiscuity while seeking male affection[21]—a pattern observed in Susan Smith's life.

It is no surprise that some think it downright impossible for a person such as Susan Smith to escape the bondage of early environment. Others would contend that only God Himself could cause such a massive transformation. But dramatic personality reorganization with major positive shifts in behavior and mental states has been scientifically documented with Christian conversion.[22] A research psychologist suggested that conversion experiences should be more closely studied by the behavioral sciences because the potency of conversion compared with psychotherapy's potency "looks like atomic power compared with dynamite."[23]

In prison, Susan Smith reportedly prayed to receive full forgiveness by God. If Susan's Christian conversion is genuine, will it affect her criminal nature? Will it affect both her moral guilt and psychological guilt feelings?[24] Is it possible for her to substantially escape the emotional and spiritual bondage of her tragic upbringing and her sins to live a successful Christian life?

Successful Christian Living
for the Environmentally Challenged

Individuals with strong beliefs in psychosocial determinism or religious/philosophical determinism view the control of personal events as being caused by external factors.[25] But those with belief in free will see more possibilities for internal control of one's life, and do not view their lives as determined solely by causes outside themselves, but view causes as "interexisting" with the self.[26] The Bible describes God as the Creator of human beings (Gen. 1:27), who are designed with personalities that reflect His personality—with intellect, emotions, and *will*.

If all cause-and-effect operated in a closed system, all human thought, decisions, emotions, and actions would be determined by an interaction with one's genetics and one's past and present environment. But it is more biblical and accurate to conceptualize cause-and-effect operating in an open system—open to interventions by human choice and by God. Therefore there is hope for freedom from bondage to one's early environment because of the reality of human responsibility to exercise one's will in obedience to God, together with the reality of God's available power exercised through the indwelling Holy Spirit.

Consider, for example, that a variety of forms of substance abuse incurred in childhood or adolescence have been successfully treated in adulthood, by intensive inpatient hospitalization for detoxification and medical therapy, aftercare, vocational/educational counseling and interventions, psychotherapy, cognitive/behavioral, group therapy, and psychopharmacotherapy.[27] If specific humanly devised therapies are scientifically proved to be effective in many cases, how much more should we expect power from God's Spirit to overcome an individual's bondage created by adverse childhood traumas?

All human beings were created for God (Col. 1:16), but spend time living for themselves, as though saying, "God, You run the universe, and I'll run my own life." This sin produces hostility toward God (Rom. 8:7–8). So instead of enjoying the power of God to transform one's life, one possesses only limited human resources to cope with the results of poor early environment and the consequences of one's own sin and the sin of others. This tragic alienation from God and His healing power is not produced by one's early environment, but is a result of one's bondage to sin. In fact, the more a person insists in running one's own life, the more one becomes trapped.

But God wants us to have a full, abundant life both now and for eternity (John 10:10; Rom. 6:23). The first step to freedom from this bondage involves a life-changing decision of repentance and faith. It's like driving south and suddenly realizing that you're headed in the wrong direction. So you've got to make a U-turn.

Scripture uses the word *repent* to refer to a "U-turn" in life: "Repent . . . and turn to God, so that your sins may be wiped out" (Acts 3:19 NIV). "Repent and turn to God and prove . . . repentance by . . . deeds" (Acts 26:20 NIV). Repentance is a U-turn away from our "I'll be God" sinful approach to living, and a radical turn to God through faith in Jesus—something that is proved real by deeds (see Luke 19:8).

With repentance and faith in the finished work of the Lord Jesus Christ, God forgives sin, removes moral guilt, and sets the person free "from the controlling authority of a sinful disposition."[28] First Peter 1:1–2 contains the phrase, "sanctified by the Spirit for obedience to Jesus Christ," where the Greek word translated "sanctified" connotes being "set apart as sacred to God," involving a process of making one holy, purified, or cleansed.

> Though there is continuity with the same human personality, as in the case of birth or death, in regeneration also there is passage into a totally different dimension of human life, with totally different characteristics of personal being. Sin is the prevailing characteristic of persons who live apart from God. They do not have the desire or power to choose consistently the right or to change their condition. Upon union with God the process is reversed, and right begins to prevail. A new life-force has been introduced that has power to prevail against a sinful disposition.[29]

"Experiential sanctification" involves salvation from sinful attitudes and actions (2 Cor. 7:1), and is accomplished by God's grace, involving God's discipline of the believer "that we may share in his holiness" (Heb. 12:10 NIV).

Created in God's image with a will, the spiritual Christian can choose to obey God and do His will (John 7:17), living a life of spiritual success because he or she is willingly dominated by the Spirit of God (1 Cor. 3:1–16; Eph. 5:18–21). God and His resources are available to the person who lives by faith, who chooses to obey the rule of the Lord Jesus.[30] This covenant relationship of faith produces a new self, a new relationship, and a new potential.

A New Self

"You were taught, with regard to your former way of life, to put off your old self, which is being corrupted by its deceitful desires; to be made new in the attitude of your minds; and to put on the new self, created to be like God in true righteousness and holiness" (Eph. 4:21–24 NIV). By the regenerating power of the Holy Spirit, the believer is a new person. "You have taken off your old self with its practices and have put on the new self, which is being renewed in knowledge in the image of its Creator" (Col. 3:9–10 NIV). Thus, the new person is

> . . . no longer subject to the controlling tyranny of the sinful disposition. . . . Thus believers have the ability consistently to choose the right. They still fall short of God's perfect disposition in failing to love as He loves, to be as self-controlled, contented, humble, and selfless as Jesus was. But when the thought or activity rises to the level of the conscious choice, they can choose God's way. Even then, however, they do not do so in their own strength, not even in their own "new person" strength.[31]

A New Relationship

Freedom from the bondage of early environment is only possible because of the indwelling Spirit of God, with all His power and creativity to make things new (Rom. 12:1–2; 2 Cor. 5:17). We are not merely talking of the individual human psychology of a changed person, but the effect in the yielded believer's life of being filled with God's Spirit. It is the grace and power of God and His indwelling that enable such a believer not to sin (Gal. 5:16) and to be a fruitful witness for Christ (Acts 1:8; John 15:1–8).

One's relationship with God can be a special constant companionship between the believer and God's indwelling Spirit (John 14:16–17, 20, 23; Gal. 2:20; Col. 1:26–29). God the Father will "strengthen you with power through his Spirit in your inner being, so that Christ may dwell in your hearts through faith" (Eph. 3:16–17 NIV), and God is "able to do immeasurably more than all we ask or imagine, according to his power that is at work within us" (3:20 NIV). Thus, the apostle Paul can describe a believer as "controlled not by the sinful nature but by the Spirit" (Rom. 8:9 NIV).

Those who live "in accordance with the Spirit have their minds set on what the Spirit desires" (Rom. 8:5 NIV). A victorious Christian life by one who has suffered a tragic early environment does not essentially depend on the person's human psychological dynamics, because the key to victorious living is "Christ in you" (Col. 1:27 NIV); that is, God's personality indwelling the human personality, renewing the new self after God's likeness (Col. 3:10).

When the apostle Paul exhorted believers to be "*filled* with the Spirit" (Eph. 5:18 NIV, italics mine), he used a form of the Greek word *pleroo,* which means to be completed, to be pervasively influenced by, or fully supplied. It implies a relationship of trusting obedience[32] in which one is willingly dominated or controlled by the Holy Spirit (see Rom. 8:9). Paul also used this word, *pleroo,* in Ephesians 3:16–19, pointing to the link between the Holy Spirit and the power of God. McQuilkin observed:

> "Filled with the Spirit" is a figurative, poetic expression that refers primarily to the relationship between two persons in which one is in charge, a relationship that began as a specific event that was intended to initiate a continuing condition.

> The relationship normally results in a glorious sense of the divine presence and certainly results in a transformed life.[33]

Although we receive the Holy Spirit only once at the "new birth" (as we are physically born only once), Paul's use of *pleroo* communicates that we are to be constantly and continually controlled and empowered by the Holy Spirit (just as we are to continually breathe physically).

A New Potential

The normal Christian life involves spiritual growth in which the believer is transformed toward increasingly greater likeness to Jesus Christ (Rom. 12:2; 2 Cor. 3:18; Eph. 4:15–16; Phil. 3:12–14; Col. 3:10; 1 Thess. 4:1–11; 2 Peter 1:3–8) in areas of unconscious sin or sins of omission.

Believers do not "grow" in this way in areas of deliberate sin. For example, if she truly became a believer, Susan Smith would not gradually cut down on lying, murdering, or adultery. Deliberately chosen sin is consistently listed to identify individuals who are unredeemed and still under God's judgment (for example, 1 Cor. 6:9–11, "people of this world who are immoral, or the greedy and swindler, or idolaters" "or a slanderer, a drunkard"; Gal. 5:19–21, "the acts of the sinful nature are obvious: sexual immorality, impurity and debauchery; idolatry and witchcraft; hatred, discord, jealousy, fits of rage, selfish ambition, dissensions, factions and envy; drunkenness, orgies, and the like"[NIV]; and Rev. 21:8, "the cowardly, the unbelieving, the vile, the murderers, the sexually immoral, those who practice magic arts, the idolaters and all liars"[NIV]).

In the area of falling short involuntarily or unconsciously, God brings spiritual growth to the believer's life through the conduits called the "means of grace"—prayer, Scripture, the church, and suffering.[34] Here there is a responsibility of the believer not only to willingly cooperate with God, but also to "continue to work out your salvation with fear and trembling, for it is God who works in you to will and to act according to his good purpose" (Phil. 2:12–13 NIV).

The new person in Christ has the capability to consistently choose to do the right thing. This new person is free to never deliberately violate the known will of God. "Freedom from sin is not freedom from temptation and the fallenness of our humanity but freedom from any necessity to respond willingly to the many temptations to which that fallenness exposes us."[35] This is the victorious Christian life.

Evidence Gives Hope

Numerous studies have demonstrated a positive association between *Christian living* (especially as measured by reliably observed Christian behavior and particularly for those with an "intrinsic" faith as opposed to "extrinsic"/social motivations for religious participation) and *mental health,* as measured in terms of possessing self-control and better personality functioning, and in terms of experiencing freedom from depression, anxiety, alcohol abuse, and dependence.[36] In recent years, hundreds of research studies have demonstrated the positive, healing effects of Christian living. In the limited space of this chapter, only a brief overview can be provided for a representative number of these studies.

Scientific studies have demonstrated that devout Christian living has "a wide range of positive effects on well-being and psychological stability in mature adults."[37] Empirical studies specifically indicate that devout Christian spirituality frees individuals from anxiety and depression, especially in later life.[38] A close relationship with God was found to be positively associated with overcoming hostility.[39] Those with an intrinsic faith have greater spiritual well-being and experience higher levels of hope and lower levels of loneliness, even in difficult situations (such as being diagnosed with cancer or AIDS).[40] Psychological and psychiatric research have also demonstrated the impact that Christian

living has on "buffering against adverse effects of environ-
mental stress."[41]

Empirical research has found that individuals experiencing support from God (called "spiritual support" in the study)
also live free from depression and have high levels of well-
being and self-esteem, even under high levels of stress (for
example when parents are bereaved over the recent loss of a
child); feeling valued, loved, and cared for by God enhances
adjustment and reduces negative emotions for individuals
who are psychologically vulnerable due to high levels of
stress.[42] "Spiritual support" was defined as "support perceived in the context of an individual's relationship with God,
focusing on perceptions and experiences of God's personal
love, presence, constancy, guidance, and available for the
self."[43] A mature faith relationship with God thereby buffers
a person from the otherwise negative effects of highly stress-
ful life events and is a "contributor to effective coping."[44]
Research demonstrated that spiritual maturity does not
directly reduce psychological distress, but it "buffers the deleterious effects of stress on mental health."[45] Spiritual well-
being provides the individual "meaning, memory, systems of
support, mutual aid, a means of coping, and comfort in the
face of difficulty."[46]

Spiritual well-being is positively correlated with marital
adjustment as measured in terms of satisfaction, cohesion,
consensus, and effectual expression; a study supported the
hypothesis that "lived-out spirituality is an important factor in
perception of marital happiness."[47] Other empirical research
clearly indicates that there are far lower prevalences of separation or divorce and greater marital satisfaction among
devout Christians compared to the less religious.[48]
Furthermore, extensive secular research has demonstrated
that one of the characteristics of strong families is living with
a shared strong faith in God.[49] Those who suffer a divorce
need not remain in bondage to the hurt of that tragedy; tap-

ping into spiritual strength has been demonstrated to be a significant factor in healing and postdivorce recovery.[50]

A study of adult Christians investigated *empowerment,* which was defined as interpersonal behavior change in the direction of becoming more like Jesus; the investigators found that those who were seen by themselves and by others as empowered for such life changes were committed to a relationship with God and with others. These individuals had experienced a life crisis in their lives, but they sensed "that God was in control of the events of their life."[51]

In another study, spirituality—involving prayer and meditation—was associated with spiritual healing of Vietnam veterans suffering from post-traumatic stress disorder.[52]

A scientific study demonstrated that spiritual growth through participation in a pentecostal church fellowship resulted in documented changes in sexual orientation from exclusive homosexuality to exclusive heterosexuality; this release from a deviant sexual behavior pattern was achieved without explicit psychotherapy and was found to be durable at the four-year follow-up.[53]

Although a Harvard University researcher classified religiosity under "offbeat and non-traditional treatment methods," she conceded that the research indicates that Christian spirituality has been discovered to be helpful in rehabilitating the alcoholic in terms of preventing alcohol drinking, reducing tension, and improving psychological insight.[54] Decreases in complaints and symptoms for a wide spectrum of personal problems have been reported with church-based lay Christian counseling.[55]

A recent survey of 193 Christian psychiatrists reported that after they became "born again," they "experienced a decrease in emotional distress" in their personal lives. With the biblical teaching and published empirical evidence for the liberating effects of sanctification for psychological problems, it is not surprising that these psychiatrists highly rated the

Bible and prayer as effective treatment for suicidal intent, grief reaction, sociopathy, and alcoholism.[56]

Christian group therapy has helped individuals turn hostility into hospitality and alienation into hope.[57] Research indicates that verbal prayer is an effective intervention for those in some form of bondage[58] and is a constructive coping strategy.[59] It is the active ministry of the Holy Spirit that empowers the spiritual resources of prayer, Scripture, and participation in the life of the church.[60]

Conclusion

God has revealed His caring work of freeing hurting people from the bondage of their early environment so they can live a victorious and successful Christian life through the power of the indwelling Holy Spirit. The primary and highest authority for understanding God's powerfully transforming work of sanctification in the believer's life is *special revelation* from God Himself—i.e., the Bible. But in recent years, scientific research has produced substantial further secondary knowledge regarding how this works out in daily living, based on systematic studies of *natural revelation*—that is, empirical knowledge from human observations through behavioral science research and the newer field of empirical theology.[61] As a result, the professional counselor, using the tools of empirical psychology, can be of significant assistance to many, including Christians. But the goal of the Christian psychotherapist and pastoral counselor, using the resources God provides together with empirical knowledge, should ever be to help people experience the fullness of life in Christ.

In my twenty-five years of ministry and practice as a Christian in clinical psychology, I have repeatedly observed the transforming power of God to substantially heal and provide freedom from the constricting limitations and traps imposed by tragic conditions suffered in my counselees' early environments. But now, just in recent years, numerous scientific studies have accumulated that provide increasingly detailed and convincing empirical evidence that individuals with an intimate relationship with God have greater spiritual well-being and better personal life adjustment, with the power to live free from the bondage of imposed psychological handicaps.[62] Now, any suffering individual can receive great hope and comfort not only from the teachings of the inerrant Scriptures on sanctification but also from recent scientific studies that have provided extensive detail on the confirmed beneficial effects that victorious Christian living has upon personal adjustment, mental health, family relationships, and even some aspects of physical health.[63] Although we still live in a fallen world marred by sin and suffering, God has demonstrated His power to provide substantial psychological and spiritual healing to empower believers to live the abundant, victorious Christian life in the present age as His fruitful witnesses.

Notes

1. A. Phillips, "Winnicott: An Introduction," *British Journal of Psychiatry* 155 (1989): 612–18.
2. Ibid.
3. J. Laplanche, "Interpretation Between Determinism and Hermeneutics: A Restatement of the Problem," *International Journal of Psycho-Analysis* 73(3) (1992): 429–45.
4. D. T. Shek, "Perceptions of Parental Treatment Styles and Psychological Well-being of Chinese College Students," *Psychologia: An International Journal of Psychology in the Orient* 36(3) (1993): 159–66.
5. T. Harris, G. W. Brown, and A. T. Bilfulco, "Loss of Parent in Childhood and Adult Psychiatric Disorder," *Development and Psychopathology* 2(3) (1990): 311–28.
6. B. Rogers, "Adult Affective Disorder and Early Environment," *British Journal of Psychiatry* 157 (1990): 539–50.
7. R. T. Mulder, P. R. Joyce, and C. R. Cloninger, "Temperament and Early Environment Influence Comorbidity and Personality Disorders in Major Depression," *Comprehensive Psychiatry* 35(3) (1994): 225–33.
8. C. D. Morano, R. A. Cisler, and J. Lemerond, "Risk Factors for Adolescent Suicidal Behavior," *Adolescence* 28(112) (1993): 851–65.
9. P. S. Ludolph et al., "The Borderline Diagnosis in Adolescents: Symptoms and Development History," *American Journal of Psychiatry* 147(4) (1990): 470–76.
10. G. A. Rekers, "The Formation of a Homosexual Orientation," in *Hope for Homosexuality*, ed. P. F. Fagan (Washington, D.C.: Center for Child and Family Policy of the Free Congress Research and Education Foundation, 1988); M. S. Lundy and G. A. Rekers, "Homosexuality: Development, Risks, Parental Views,

and Controversies," in *Handbook of Child and Adolescent Sexual Problems* (New York: Lexington Books/Macmillan of Jossey-Bass/Simon and Schuster, 1995) ed. G. A. Rekers. This handbook can be ordered from publisher at 1-800-956-7739.

11. R. T. Frazier, "Space and Holding: Beginning Pastoral Counseling with Incest Victims," *Pastoral Psychology* 42(2) (1993): 81–94.

12. J. A. McNew and N. Abell, "Posttraumatic Stress Symptomatology: Similarities and Differences Between Vietnam Veterans and Adult Survivors of Childhood Sexual Abuse," *Social Work* 40 (1995): 115–26.

13. Rekers, *Handbook of Child and Adolescent Sexual Problems*, 135–251; S. A. Jumper, "A Meta-Analysis of the Relationship of Child Sexual Abuse to Adult Psychological Adjustment," *Child Abuse and Neglect* 19 (1995): 715–28.

14. M. W. Armsworth, "A Qualitative Analysis of Adult Incest Survivors' Responses to Sexual Involvement with Therapists," *Child Abuse and Neglect* 14(4) (1990): 451–554.

15. J. Ladd, "Logotherapy's Place for the Ritually Abused," *International Forum for Logotherapy* 14(2) (1991): 82–86.

16. G. A. Rekers, *Susan Smith: Victim or Murderer* (Lakewood, Colo.: Glenbridge Publishing Ltd., 1996). Chapter 10 provides details of Susan Smith's prison conversion to Christianity. This book can be ordered directly from the publisher at 1-800-986-4135.

17. These are the conclusions of a study (see page 57) by Faith H. Leibman, "Childhood Abandonment/Adult Rage: The Root of Violent Criminal Acts," *American Journal of Forensic Psychology* 10(4) (1992): 57–64.

18. J. Birtchnell, "The Relationship Between Attempted Suicide, Depression, and Parent Death," *British Journal of Psychiatry* 116 (1970): 307–13.

19. G. E. Murphy, "Suicide and Alcoholism," *Archives of General Psychiatry* 36 (1979): 65–69.

20. C. Bagley, "Early Sexual Experience and Sexual Victimization of Children and Adolescents," in Rekers's *Handbook of Child and Adolescent Sexual Problems*, 135–63.

21. Ibid.

22. L. R. Rambo, *Understanding Religious Conversion* (New Haven, Conn.: Yale University, 1993).

23. As Allen Bergin quoted in I. M. Marks, "Behavioral Psychotherapy of Adult Neurosis," in *Handbook of Psychotherapy and Behavior Change* ed. S. L. Garfield and A. E. Bergin (New York: Wiley, 1978); quote from Allen E. Bergin, "Religiosity and Mental Health: A Critical Reevaluation and Meta-Analysis," *Professional Psychology: Research and Practice* 14(2) (1983): 170–84.

24. Guilt has been described as a place where religious faith and psychology meet. See, for example, David Belgum, *Guilt: Where Religion and Psychology Meet* (Minneapolis: Augsburg Publishing House, 1963); Peter Homans, ed., *The Dialogue Between Theology and Psychology* (Chicago: The Univ. of Chicago Press, 1968).

25. S. J. Stroessner and C. W. Green, "Effects of Belief in Free Will or Determinism on Attitudes Toward Punishment and Locus of Control," *Journal of Social Psychology* 130(6) (1990): 789–99.

26. P. Sauvayre and C. Auerback, "Free Will, Identity, and Primary Creativity," *New Ideas in Psychology* 8(2) (1990): 221–30.

27. See, for example, V. A. Kelly, F. B. Kropp, and M. Manhal-Baugus, "The Association of Program-Related Variables to Length of Sobriety," *Journal of Addictions and Offender Counseling* 15(2) (1995): 42–50; B. T. Jones and J. McMahon, "Negative Alcohol Expectancy Predicts Post-Treatment Abstinence Survivorship," *Addiction* 89(12) (1994): 1653–65; J. E. Zweben, "Recovery Oriented Psychotherapy: A Model for Addiction Treatment," *Psychotherapy*

30(2) (1993): 259–68; W. W. Weddington, "Cocaine: Diagnosis and Treatment," *Psychiatric Clinics of North America* 16(1) (1993): 87–95.

28. J. R. McQuilkin, "The Keswick Perspective," in M. E. Dieter et al., *Five Views on Sanctification* (Grand Rapids: Zondervan, 1987), 158–59.
29. Ibid.
30. Ibid., 171.
31. Ibid., 174.
32. Ibid., 177.
33. Ibid., 177.
34. Ibid., 180–81.
35. M. E. Dieter, "Response to McQuilkin," in M. E. Dieter et al., *Five Views on Sanctification*, 186.
36. Ibid.; see also J. Gartner, D. B. Larson, and G. D. Allen, "Religious Commitment and Mental Health: A Review of the Empirical Literature," *Journal of Psychology and Theology* 19(1) (1991): 6–25; A. E. Bergin, K. S. Master, and P. S. Richards, "Religiousness and Mental Health Considered: A Study of an Intrinsically Religious Sample," *Journal of Counseling Psychology* 34(2) (1987): 197–204; and H. G. Koenig, "Religion and Prevention of Illness in Later Life," *Prevention in Human Services* 10(1) (1991): 69–89; Stayhorn, Wiedman, and Larson, 1990; D. B. Larson, et al., "Associations Between Dimensions of Religious Commitment and Mental Health Reported in the American Journal of Psychiatry and Archives of General Psychiatry," *American Journal of Psychiatry* 149(4) (1992): 557–59; E. L. Idler and S. V. Kasi, "Religion, Disability, Depression and the Timing of Death," *American Journal of Sociology* 97(4) (1992): 1052–79.
37. H. G. Koenig, "The Relationship Between Judeo-Christian Religion and Mental Health Among Middle-Aged and Older Adults," *Advances* 9(4) (1993): 33.
38. H. G. Koenig, "Religion and Aging," *Reviews in Clinical Gerontology* 3(2) (1993): 195–203; P. Pressman et al., "Religious Belief, Depression, and Ambulation Status in Elderly Women with Broken Hips," *American Journal of Psychiatry* 147(6) (1990): 758–60.
39. J. M. Strayhorn, C. S. Weidman, and D. Larson, "A Measure of Religiousness, and Its Relations to Parent and Child Mental Health Variables," *Journal of Community Psychology* 18 (1990): 34–43.
40. J. R. Mickley, K. Soeken, and A. Belcher, "Spiritual Well-being, Religiousness and Hope Among Women with Breast Cancer," *IMAGE: Journal of Nursing Scholarship* 24(4) (1992): 267–72; V. Carson, K. O. L. Soeken, and P. M. Grimm, "Hope and Its Relationship with Spiritual Well-being," *Journal of Psychology and Theology* 16(2) (1988): 159–67; V. B. Carson et al., "Hope and Spiritual Well-being: Essentials for Living with AIDS," *Perspectives in Psychiatric Care* 26(2) (1990): 28–34; C. G. Walton et al., "Psychological Correlates of Loneliness with the Older Adult," *Archives of Psychiatric Nursing* 5(3) (1991): 165–70.
41. Koenig, "Judeo-Christian Religion and Mental Health," 33–39.
42. K. I. Maton, "The Stress-Buffering Role of Spiritual Support: Cross-sectional and Prospective Investigations," *Journal for the Scientific Study of Religion* 28(3) (1989): 310–23; C. M. Rutledge et al., "The Importance of Religion for Parents Coping with a Chronically Ill Child," *Journal of Psychology and Christianity* 14(1) (1995): 50–57.
43. Ibid., 319.
44. Ibid., 311, 320; see also C. M. Rutledge et al., "The Importance of Religion for Parents Coping with a Chronically Ill Child," *Journal of Psychology and Christianity* 14(1) (1995): 50–57.
45. D. R. Williams, D. B. Larson, and R. E. Buckler, "Religion and Psychological Distress in a Community Sample," *Social Science and Medicine* 9(2) (1991): 41–64.

46. J. S. Levin and H. Y. Vanderpool, "Religious Factors in Physical Health and the Prevention of Illness," *Prevention in Human Services* 9(2) (1991): 41–64.
47. P. D. Roth, "Spiritual Well-being and Marital Adjustment," *Journal of Psychology and Theology* 16(2) (1988): 153–58.
48. D. B. Larson, "Religious Improvement," in *Family Building: Six Qualities of a Strong Family*, ed. G. A. Rekers (Ventura, Calif.: Regal Books, 1985), 121–47.
49. G. A. Rekers, ed., *Family Building: Six Qualities of a Strong Family* (Ventura, Calif.: Regal Books, 1985); N. Stinnett, "In Search of Strong Families," in N. Stinnett et al., *Building Family Strengths* (Lincoln, Nebr.: University of Nebraska Press, 1971); N. Stinnett and J. DeFrain, *Secrets of Strong Families* (Boston: Little, Brown & Company, 1985).
50. I. G. Nathanson, "Divorce and Women's Spirituality," *Journal of Divorce and Remarriage* 22(3–4) (1995): 179–88.
51. K. I. Maton and J. Rappaport, "Empowerment in a Religious Setting: A Multivariate Investigation," *Prevention in Human Services* 3(2–3) (1984): 37–72.
52. M. J. Jimenez, "The Spiritual Healing of Post-traumatic Stress Disorder at the Menlo Park Veteran's Hospital," *Studies in Formative Spirituality* 14(2) (1993): 175–87.
53. E. M. Pattison and M. L. Pattison, "Ex-gays: Religiously Mediated Change in Homosexuals," *American Journal of Psychiatry* 137(12) (1980): 1553–62.
54. M. Bean, "Offbeat and Non-traditional Treatment Methods in Alcoholism," *Journal of Psychiatric Treatment and Evaluation* 5(6) (1983): 496–503; see also W. R. Miller and E. Kurtz, "Models of Alcoholism Used in Treatment," 55(2) (1994): 159–66.
55. Y. M. Toh et al., "The Evaluation of a Church-Based Lay Counseling Program: Some Preliminary Data," *Journal of Psychology and Christianity* 13(3) (1994): 270–75.
56. M. Galanter, D. Larson, and E. Rubenstone, "Christian Psychiatry: The Impact of Evangelical Belief on Clinical Practice," *American Journal of Psychiatry* 148(1) (1991): 90–95.
57. J. M. Siwy and C. E. Smith, "Christian Group Therapy: Sitting with Job," *Journal of Psychology and Theology* 16(4) (1988): 318–23.
58. J. R. Finney and H. N. Malony, "Empirical Studies of Christian Prayer: A Review of the Literature," *Journal of Psychology and Theology* 13(2) (1985): 104–15.
59. J. Janssen, J. DeHart, and C. Den Draak, "Praying Practices," *Journal of Empirical Theology* 2(2) (1989): 28–39.
60. S. Y. Tan, "Lay Counseling: A Christian Approach," *Journal of Psychology and Christianity* 13(3) (1994): 264–69; K. Daiber, I. Lukatis, and W. Lukatis, "The Bible in Protestant Religious Life in Germany," *Journal of Empirical Theology* 6(2) (1993): 32–59.
61. J. A. van der Ven, "Practical Theology: From Applied to Empirical Theology," *Journal of Empirical Theology* 1(2) (1988): 7–27; K. E. Nipkow, "Empirical Research Within Practical Theology," *Journal of Empirical Theology* 6(1) (1993): 50–63; J. A. van der Ven, *Practical Theology: An Empirical Approach* (Kampen, The Netherlands: Kok Pharos Publishing House, 1993); J. A. van der Ven, "Empirical Methodology in Practical Theology: Why and How," *Practical Theology in South Africa* 9(2) (1994): 29–44.
62. See, for example, C. W. Ellison, "Spiritual Well-being: Conceptualization and Measurement," *Journal of Psychology and Theology* 11(4) (1983): 330–40.
63. D. B. Larson, G. G. Wood, and S. S. Larson, "A Paradigm Shift in Medicine Toward Spirituality?" *Advances* 9(4) (1993): 39–49; see also review by A. D. Bergin, "Religiosity and Mental Health: A Critical Reevaluation and Meta-Analysis," *Professional Psychology: Research and Practice* 14(2) (1983): 170–84; I. G. Nathanson, "Divorce and Women's Spirituality," *Journal of Divorce and*

Remarriage 22(3–4): 179–88; J. S. Levin and P. L. Schiller, "Is There a Religious Factor in Health?" *Journal of Religion and Health* 26(1) (1987): 9–36; J. S. Levin, "Religion and Health," *Social Science and Medicine* 38(11) (1994): 1475–82.

14

About the Author

Allan McKechnie was for six years a counselor at Willow Creek Community Church, South Barrington, Illinois, first as staff therapist, then as director of the church's in-house counseling center with a staff of thirteen. Since then he has directed the counseling program at Columbia International University, first in the undergraduate and then in the graduate program. He has pastoral and extensive counseling experience and has taught numerous seminars, retreats, and workshops. McKechnie is committed to two strategic models of counseling that set him apart from some therapists: (1) he is convinced that the best counseling is integrated into the life of the local congregation, and (2) he believes that all counseling must be integrated with spiritual truth and practiced under the functional authority of Scripture. Allan and Peggy McKechnie have three children, two teens and one preteen.

About This Chapter

In an objective and irenic spirit the author introduces the various arguments swirling around the question of whether psychological counseling is legitimate for the Christian and is part of the ministry of the church. He charts a mediating course in the controversy, pointing out both the benefits and the dangers of using secular psychological theory, while insisting on making scriptural truth about human nature the ultimate guide for the Christian counselor. The counselor needs to define the client's goal by Scripture—Christlikeness—and the means for reaching that goal as well—the power of the indwelling Spirit. We have here the outline of a biblical integration of psychological insights and divinely produced sanctification.

14

Therapy and the Victorious Christian Life

by Allan McKechnie

Victorious Christian living is the goal and opportunity for every believer. Within the realm of the Victorious Christian Life is the freedom from the control of the flesh and the sinful world around us. "The change is so radical as to be comparable to the change that a person experiences at birth or death. . . . Sin is the prevailing characteristic of persons who live apart from God. They do not have the desire or power to choose consistently the right or to change their condition. Upon union with God the process is reversed, and right begins to prevail. A new life-force has been introduced that has power to prevail against sinful disposition."[1] This power that changes the sinful disposition enables the believer to leave the control of sin behind. The believer not only avoids sin but eventually finds sin, in all of its variations, repugnant. In place of sin the believer chooses righteousness and holy living, and in this way becomes more and more like Christ (1 Peter 1:13–16).

The Victorious Christian Life is the work of the Holy Spirit, a gift from God, given to those who have chosen to commit themselves to God.[2] Scriptures such as 2 Timothy 3:16–17 state that in Scripture we have what we need to do to be equipped for every good work. Second Corinthians 12:9

and 1 Corinthians 10:13 promise that God and His power will be enough to enable us to choose righteousness and avoid temptation. With these great promises of victory that free us from being prisoners to the flesh and the snares and temptations of the evil one, Christians have the resources for true victory.

Why Are Christians Pursuing Counseling and Therapy?

If Christians can enter into the joy of the Victorious Christian Life through their commitment to God and His scriptural truths, then why are Christians seeking out counseling and therapy in increasing numbers? Why are churches incorporating counselors and therapists onto their church staffs and counseling principles into their sermons? For what purpose would a Christian even go for counseling? It is understandable that those who do not know or who are not actively practicing the truths of Scripture would struggle with depression, anxiety, or a host of other painful emotions, addictions, and sinful lifestyles. But why would the Christian, who has the power of God and the teaching of the Scriptures, need additional help? It is important to take a close look at why therapy and the church have been embracing one another in the past one hundred years.

There have been several negative trends that have set the stage for counseling and psychology being so much a part of the American church culture. First, counseling, therapy, and psychology made their biggest gains into the church during the end of the nineteenth century when science and industry were on the increase and religion was on the decline.[3] As the faith of Americans shifted to the comforts and solutions that industry and the sciences could offer and religious preaching did not seem to address, Christians rushed headlong into counseling and psychological theories. This was further compounded by the message communicated by many churches that if you have emotional problems or doubts, then you are probably living in sin and are a second-class Christian. Many people decided that it was much easier to go outside the church for their answers than to be branded as a sinner or weak Christian within their local church. At the same time some churches that wanted to continue to attract large crowds became particularly adept at reframing their scriptural understanding of humankind into psychological articulations. This has continued throughout the twentieth century as well.

Second, as liberalism set in, psychology seemed to offer new solutions to old problems without the outdated trappings of religion.[4] In other words, religion was no longer in vogue, and what was needed was a new approach that was different and contemporary.

Third, with the increased reliance upon sciences, sin issues and emotional problems now became the realm of the physician or psychologist rather than of the clergy. As Szasa put it, "The cure of sinful souls was recast as the cure of sick minds."[5]

Fourth, religion also set the stage for the influx of psychology through Pietism. "Historically, Pietism and Puritan variations of it have involved a subjective psychological focus on interior experiences." This spiritual introspection, what Holifield calls a preoccupation with inwardness, rebirth, conversion, and revival, was basic to American consciousness. It was therefore only a small step to translate introspective spiritual piety into secular psychological piety.[6] Christianity in itself had begun to focus on the self, shifting the focus away from God.

Fifth, in many ways psychology seemed to be proving the validity of religion. People who are weak in their faith often cling tenaciously to anything that seems to vindicate what they struggle to believe.[7] Even today, when a university study suggests that faith is a tonic for physical health,[8] many Christians rush to use the research as a means to bolster their sagging faith, placing emphasis on sources outside of Scripture for

their faith. The critics of counseling therapy are partly right—
this movement was to a large extent an attempt to get from
therapy what people did not think they could get from their
church or perhaps even from God.

Christianity Is at Its Heart Psychological

The first positive reason why counseling and psychology
have entered the church is that they have so much in common.
Both ask: Who are we, what is our worth, how do we relate to
others, where do we get our security, what are our needs and
how do we get them met, who controls our lives, and what do
we do with guilt and suffering? Robert Roberts has suggested
that Christianity is a psychology in that it is a view of human
beings and what makes them tick and what they are like when
they are maladjusted or adjusted. The local church is in the
business of "transforming persons from being damaged,
poorly functioning, unfulfilled, hostile, and anxious, to being
whole, well functioning, fulfilled, loving, and at peace. From
the earliest days a central task of the church has been to form
and restore persons. In other words, the church has always
dealt in practical psychology."[9]

History of Spiritual Guidance

The second positive reason for the attraction of counseling and therapy into the church is that the church has had a
history of counseling, which it has called spiritual guidance
and soul care. Benner, in his book *Psychotherapy and the
Spiritual Quest,*[10] has done a fine job of synthesizing the history of spiritual care and counseling in the church and the
recent attempt by psychology to distance itself from religion.
He states that psychology is really about soul care. Soul care
was well established with the wise men of ancient Israel who
"were practical counselors of souls, proclaiming reverence for
God and justice to men, making plain the path of right conduct."[11] He traces soul care through Christ, through the
church fathers, to Luther, who called sin the "curvature of the

self in upon the self," which led to an inability to trust God.[12] He tracks the early Puritans, such as William Perkins, who established stages of spiritual growth. Benner suggests that after the Council of Trent, soul care greatly changed with the Catholics moving toward defending orthodoxy and the Protestants moving toward a gentle shepherding that focused upon pulling a brother back from sin gently. Later the Protestants moved toward righteousness being accomplished more by the intervention of God than by the activities of man and soul care. Soul care, now relabeled *pastoral counseling,* reemerged in 1905 in the Emanuel Movement in Boston. This movement attempted to combine biblical and scientific principles in caring for Christians, eventually moving from the salvation of souls to self-realization.[13] The key elements in most of soul care were the issues of sin and spiritual growth. Benner suggests that Freud, Jung, and other contemporary psychology theorists were well aware of the Christian history of soul care.[14]

Why Do We Need the Teachings of Secular Psychology?

While it is true that the church has had a long history of soul care and that many of the issues that psychology attempts to address are similar to the vital issues of the church, there is much concern voiced about the secular psychology that has been eagerly embraced by many Christians. Writers such as John McArthur, Charles Solomon, and Jay Adams vehemently fight the inclusion of secular psychology into the Christian church. These authors have several key disagreements with secular psychology. The first is that secular psychology teaches a different religion. Solomon and the Bobgans state that secular psychology makes a god of the "self." The old nature is strengthened rather than being crucified.[15]

Secular therapists such as Rogers teach a phenomenology in which reality is subjective to the individual. How you view your world is the correct way for you. His humanistic approach teaches that the client is basically good, and if allowed, will find the good within himself or herself. Therefore, if you have a problem it is probably what another did to you that hurt you or inhibited your natural goodness, thereby freeing you from responsibility. Again the focus is on oneself rather than others or God. If the Victorious Christian Life comes by faith and obedience, then these secular therapies err by redirecting that faith toward himself or herself. This according to Scripture is blasphemy (Ex. 20:3). Scripture teaches us to "love your neighbor as yourself," and "to seek ye first the kingdom of God." We are commanded to be other-focused not self-focused.

The second objection to the use of secular psychology is that most counseling and psychological theories are anti-Christian. It is true that many counselors and therapists view religion as an attempt of the client to avoid dealing with truth and responsibility. And sometimes that is a valid assessment. It could also be true that many therapists may have a neurotic avoidance of religion and issues of faith and God.[16] Avoidance and fear of religion and Christianity are less and less an issue for most therapists as they are learning that humans are essentially religious and religious issues must be addressed. An example is psychiatrist M. Scott Peck, who wrote the best-seller *The Road Less Traveled,* which addressed some of his spiritual journey. In his more recent book, *Further Along the Road Less Traveled,* he details his acceptance of Christ as the cure for his sin problem. Religious experience is becoming more a viable aspect of one's personality and growth.

A third concern for some authors is that secular therapy focuses on evil, or at least nonbiblical techniques and philosophies. Techniques are questioned that allow the client to feel good but do not make a real spiritual or mental difference. Techniques that violate or disregard God and His Word should be suspect. Some secular techniques do violate God's standards, and many aspects of secular treatment pull a person away from the health that can only come through a relationship with God. However, just because a technique is not addressed directly in Scripture does not make it inherently wrong.

What We Can Learn from Secular Psychology

We have established that true joy and peace come from the freedom that God gives us as we respond to Him in faith and obedience. Any teaching or technique that contradicts that basic truth is to be shunned. There is, however, much in the secular field of psychology that can teach us about how to help people understand their true needs in their search for God. As Roberts puts it, "entering into a dialogue with the secular psychologist opens our eyes to see things about Christian psychology that we would have missed. Also we learn about the possible pitfalls that we would have otherwise missed."[17] Benner states that "Christian psychology is Augustinian in affirming that our hearts are 'restless' until they 'rest' in God. We were made to 'praise' God, to honor and trust Him, to find our joy in Him, to admire His beauty and holiness and power, and to serve Him. Unless we live in His presence, we will not function as we were designed to do; we will be subject to anxiety, depression, a sense of emptiness, and poor relationships with our fellow human beings. We are all children, then, children who tolerate poorly being outside of the presence of our heavenly Father."[18]

Secular psychology has done extensive study and research into human behavior and emotions. The results of this research can be used by Christian therapists to help bring people into an intimate relationship with God. For example, the Object Relations school of psychology has researched the thinking and relationships of young children. This school of psychological thought teaches that the young child attempts to idealize the mother and then internalize the good in her. The child expects in the mother attributes that are similar to God's. If those attributes are not found in the mother (are there any perfect mothers?), then the child will either go through life longing for those attributes or give up looking and lower the expectations.[19] Contrary to their conclusions that one must give up the hope for a loving, kind, just, generous, and protective perfect being, Christianity has an answer to that longing. That answer is God. We have much to learn from the school of Object Relations about how to nurture that longing for God in a child and how to diagnose and treat barriers that have been built through poor parenting. There are many other secular research conclusions that are beneficial to believers in ministry.

God's Counselors and Therapy

God's counselors and therapists can best create long-term change by introducing their clients to the power of Christ that can bring about growth, healing, and change. The book of Colossians addresses five means by which God causes spiritual growth in the life of the believer. The work of Christ (1:18–23), the Word of Christ (3:16), the indwelling of Christ (1:27–29), the Body of Christ (2:19; 3:12–15), and creation in general (1:16–17).[20] These five avenues through which the power and teaching of Christ flow are vital for each believer. Most Christians acknowledge the importance of the first four means. Every believer has been impacted by the intervention of Christ. Every believer must take advantage of the teaching of Scriptures and the Spirit that lives within us to make us more like Christ. The believer needs to submit himself to the body life, confrontation, discipline, fellowship, and authority of the local church.

The fifth avenue of spiritual growth, knowledge from creation, is often neglected. The earth still declares the glory of God, and study of God's handiwork and creation will benefit the believer as it did the sages and writers in the Old Testament. Granted, creation and our accurate understanding of it have been marred by the Fall, but Christ still shows His wisdom and work through it. As John White suggests, the study of humankind is similar to a broken mirror: it reflects, but not perfectly. It does give us some accuracy and some distortion about who we are.[21]

God's counselors and therapists must be students of all five of the means of Christ's work. Students will occasionally tell me that they do not need to study psychology, counseling, and sociology since they have all they need in Scripture, but then they sign up for additional hours of training in homiletics, hermeneutics, and evangelism skills classes. All of these courses, studies, and disciplines are merely vehicles for the truth, which once embraced, can aid in the understanding of and presentation of God's truths. If counseling and therapy studies have any validity, they will also open the Word of God to the student in a new and refreshing way, forcing that student to evaluate himself or herself in the light of these new truths, while at the same time learning how to teach others these same insights.

Issues in Therapy

Christian therapists can serve people by helping them discover and deal with the following therapeutic/spiritual issues.

Ignorance

People have never been told. They honestly do not know how to communicate, how to pray, how to problem solve, how to treat a spouse. As we move into this postmodern and post-Christian era, less and less of what is right and good is an inherent part of what is taught in families, schools, churches, and society. Therapists are required more and more to teach people how to live and get along. When the local church, family, and culture have not done their respective jobs teaching people how to live successfully, there is a vacuum of information that can be filled with all sorts of nontruths in their desperate search for understanding. Ignorance is not only an issue when one does not know what good to do, but it is also an issue when one does not know when one is doing wrong. Therapists can help people learn of the behaviors or dispositions that are sinful and self-defeating. It is not normal for people to think like God.

Deception

There are those who have been taught but, directly or indirectly, they have been deceived. The idea of growing up in a dysfunctional home is that people have been exposed to all sorts of false modeling and teaching to the extent that people often grow into thinking that what is truly abnormal is normal. Growing up in certain non-Christian cultures and being exposed to immoral media can deceive an individual into thinking that certain behaviors, values, and beliefs are true when they are not. Therapists can play a critical role helping an individual sort out truth from deception. Some of the deceptions are deep and no longer a part of the person's conscious thinking. A skilled therapist can diagnose and expose those deceptions. Deceptions can take on many shapes, such as negative experiences that have taught wrong perceptions or expectations, misunderstandings of what others have said, poor theology, or simply the lies of the evil one. It is not enough to discover and expose these deceptions; they must be dismantled and replaced with truth and the appropriate behaviors that come out of truth. Good theology makes for good psychology.

Blindness

People have been told but they do not understand or apply that knowledge. There are many ways to become blind. Sin can blind. David knew right from wrong, but in his sin he was blind to the enormity of his sinful behavior. It took Nathan, who counseled David through a metaphor, to make

David see. As soon as he understood what he had done, he repented.

Denial of the Truth

People know the truth but they do not wish to deal with it. This is intentional blindness. Often denial involves a lot of rationalization, or a host of other defensive mechanisms. On the other hand denial can be simply forcing oneself to not think about an issue. Exposing truth denial is critical when working with people struggling with guilt, conviction, or the prompting of the Holy Spirit. A skilled therapist can see through the denial, help the individual take responsibility for the denial, and then help the person face what it was that he or she had worked so hard to avoid.

Hard-Heartedness

Long-term denial leads to the inability to see or hear truth at all. Scripture refers to these people as having a hardened heart, a seared conscious. They run the risk of being turned over to Satan (1 Tim. 1:20) or being turned over to their own reprobate minds (Rom. 2:28–32). A godly therapist may be able to help such a person see their true heart condition.

What Is Involved in Christian Therapy?

A Christian therapist has a thorough understanding of the Scriptures. He or she must know what the Bible says, what it means, and have as a goal for therapy the same goals as the goals God has for His creation as spelled out in Scripture. In addition, the therapist must have a thorough understanding of relevant psychological research, studies, techniques, and information.

Once therapists have met the above criteria, they would do well to answer the following two questions. What is the goal of therapy? And what brings about change in an individual? It is amazing how much one can learn about a therapist by how he or she answers those two questions. In many cases the therapists can't answer them cogently. If the goal of therapy is symptom reduction alone, then the therapist is selling the client short by only dealing with the symptom of a much deeper problem. If the agent that brings about change is the technique or wisdom of the therapist, then the therapy is not taking advantage of all that Christ has to offer. In order for therapy to be Christian it must have as its goal the process of an individual moving toward Christ through salvation and sanctification (Victorious Christian Living). These are the same goals and processes that God uses to make people whole and free. The mature therapist never loses sight of the goal and the source of healing while at the same time gleaning from secular research a thorough understanding of the mental and physical dynamics that can be used in conjunction with the power of God and His Word to bring about healing.

Why Aren't All Christian Therapists Open About Their Faith?

Why are not all Christian therapists active in the work of supporting the counselee toward salvation and the Victorious Christian Life? Why do so many Christian therapists seem to leave their biblical understanding and spiritual goals outside the counseling office?

One reason is the fact that many Christian therapists have had more training in secular counseling theories than they have training in Bible and theology. This may be because of a secular-only training or it could be that the Christian school in which they were trained had professors who looked down on the local church or the Scriptures and have elevated psychology above theology. This may lead to a secular counseling mind-set. It is only natural for counselors or therapists to fall back on the training, studies, and information they know best and in which they have the most familiarity and confidence. In a sense the counseling locomotive pulls the biblical/theological caboose.

Second, the types of clients the therapist sees can help to form the therapeutic style and goals. Most full-time therapists see twenty-five to thirty clients a week. In many of those sessions people are struggling with guilt or conviction. The guilt could be anything from not being good enough to being a moral failure. The counselor hears all of this pain, and in an attempt to help people get out of pain devises a number of strategies to alleviate the pain and guilt that are creating misery for the clients. One might begin to try to convince those patients that they are not so bad. Perhaps everyone has done what they did. Perhaps the guilt they feel is not from God but is self-induced or created by a dysfunctional family. Of course, there are cases in which the above could be true. But after a while the therapist may find himself or herself more and more involved in helping a person escape conviction rather than responding to the conviction. Some therapists have gone so far as to state that at the Cross guilt was dealt with and that "guilt feelings are not from God."[22] One's theology and treatment can become shaped by either the client's or the therapist's psychological needs. At this point the counselor can be very helpful to the depressed mood of the patient but probably is not useful to the actual guilt/conviction that needs to be worked through under the guidance of the Holy Spirit.

Third, many counselors are embarrassed to use biblical or theological terms or principles. Such language does not sound professional. Furthermore it can be complicated and uncomfortable for clients to be confronted. This is often because the therapist lacks conviction about what he or she believes. Perhaps this is why so many Christian therapists appear to struggle with their faith and the churches they attend. I confronted a seasoned Christian therapist on the sin of one of his clients and he responded to me by stating he was "a therapist not a policeman."

Fourth, ethical standards require that the therapeutic relationships not be dual roles.[23] A relationship is a dual role when more than one role is acted out between the client and therapist. This boundary is in place in order to free the client to express himself or herself without receiving any undue influence from the therapist. An extreme, yet not uncommon, example of "dual role" would be a therapist who is having sexual relations with a client during the course of therapy.

But is it biblical to rule out any personal involvement? It is said that the client and therapist must have a professional-only relationship. There is to be little if any relationship outside the counseling office in order not to contaminate the therapeutic process, enabling clients to discover for themselves what they are to believe without the therapist's personal opinions and values interfering. While in therapy, the client is often vulnerable and dependent and therefore is easily influenced by the opinions and values of the therapist. But therapy that is value-free does not exist. Clients are always asking for values. Yet the professional standards most counselors are governed by state that the counselor cannot inject his or her own personal beliefs into the session but must abide by the beliefs of the client. Because of this dilemma many Christian therapists assign emotional therapy to the therapist and spiritual therapy to the pastor.[24]

Fifth, as a Christian you are required to use discipline if sin is to be fully dealt with by an individual. You may be required to take many cases to the ruling body of the church. So much of counseling is done in confidentiality and secret that even Christian therapists are less and less willing to bring issues to the church for discipline.

Last, the therapist may never have experienced the Victorious Christian Life himself or herself and therefore does not know how to help others enter that kind of relationship with God. Bottom line: What does the therapist believe brings health?

Summary

This paper has attempted to demonstrate that God desires that His people experience a life of joy and peace, a life of freedom from enslavement to sin and the effects of sins. He desires that we rest in Him so that He can directly and indirectly be the focus of all our love, hope, and attention. Secular therapy has a similar goal but a different solution. Secular therapy seeks freedom from anxiety (peace) and freedom from depression (joy). It also desires that people understand themselves and find an identity and purpose in life. But for the most part, secular therapists have godless solutions to those goals. While taking the admonitions from secular therapy's detractors seriously, however, there is much to be learned from secular therapy that can be used with (and under the authority of) the power of Christ to open up the "hidden rooms" of a person's heart and expose the contents of those rooms to the truths of Christ.

God did not design us to function and grow very well by ourselves. Through the involvement of talented, gifted, knowledgeable, spiritually and emotionally mature Christian therapists, people can seek to know and understand themselves as they continue to welcome the sanctifying work of the Holy Spirit within them. Many Christian therapists struggle with maintaining the balance of ethical and biblical standards. It is hoped that they will deepen their study and appreciation of God's Word as well as their psychological studies and not be afraid to find appropriate ways to introduce God's truths in a timely and appropriate manner to the client as the client is ready to hear and apply them. Therapy and therapists in the hands of the Holy Spirit can be powerful tools to bring people to Christ and to become like Christ, entering into the Victorious Christian Life.

Notes

1. J. Robertson McQuilkin, *Five Views on Sanctification* (Grand Rapids: Zondervan, 1987), 159.

2. Ibid., 168–69.
3. J. Ehrenwald, *Psychotherapy: Myth and Method* (New York: Grune and Stratton, 1966), 10.
4. David Benner, *Psychotherapy and the Spiritual Quest* (Grand Rapids: Baker, 1988), 28.
5. T. Szasa, *The Myth of Mental Illness* (New York: Harper and Row, 1978), xxiv.
6. E. B. Holifield, *A History of Pastoral Care* (Nashville: Abingdon, 1983), 356.
7. John White, *Putting the Soul Back into Psychology*, (Downers Grove: InterVarsity IVP, 1987), 58.
8. Claudia Wallis, "Faith and Healing," *Time*, 24 June 1996, p. 59.
9. Robert C. Roberts, *Taking the Word to Heart* (Grand Rapids: Eerdmans, 1993), 3.
10. David Benner, *Psychotherapy and the Spiritual Quest* (Grand Rapids: Baker, 1988), 19–26.
11. J. T. McNeill, *A History of the Cure of Souls* (New York: Harper and Row, 1951), 9.
12. M. Luther, *Three Treatises* (Philadelphia: Fortress, 1960), 210.
13. Holifield, *History of Pastoral Care*, 201.
14. David Benner, *Psychology and the Spiritual Quest* (Grand Rapids: Baker, 1988), 28.
15. M. Bobgan and D. Bobgan, *The Psychological Way/The Spiritual Way* (Minneapolis: Bethany Fellowship, 1979), 182.
16. White, *Putting the Soul Back into Psychology*, 32.
17. Roberts, *Taking the Word to Heart*, 269–71.
18. Benner, *Psychotherapy and the Spiritual Quest*, 236.
19. Samuel Slipp, *Object Relations in Family Therapy* (Northvale: Aronson, 1993), 84–89.
20. John Coe, *Is Christ Sufficient? A Response to MacArthur's Indictment Against Christian Psychology*. Presented at the second international congress of Christian counseling in Atlanta, 1992.
21. White, *Putting the Soul Back into Psychology*, 12.
22. Bruce Narramore, *No Condemnation* (Grand Rapids: Academic Books, 1984), 147–48.
23. George Ohlschlager and Peter Mosgofian, *Law for the Christian Counselor* (Dallas: Word, 1992), 174.
24. Benner, *Psychotherapy and the Spiritual Quest*, 158.

PART FOUR

Other Perspectives

Although this volume celebrates the heritage of Columbia International University in teaching a life of freedom and fulfillment in Christ, not all evangelicals agree with that "Victorious Life" approach. In this section we give voice to alternative positions. Not only is this fair to those who differ, it is also fair to the reader. Furthermore, these essays serve to mark out the distinctives of each position, including Victorious Christian Life teaching.

Note that the chief alternative views are presented by leading spokesmen for each position: Kenneth Kantzer on a reformed position, Dennis Kinlaw from the Wesleyan perspective, and Jack Hayford on a charismatic approach. Notice also that there are two chapters dealing with reformed thinking about the Christian life. In the first, Kantzer outlines some of the emphases common to the reformed tradition and also some of the differences with other positions, including Victorious Life teaching. Since not all reformed thinkers agree in the criticisms commonly made, William Larkin, Jr. presents a reformed view that integrates historic Calvinistic theology with Victorious Life theology. It is important to point out the differences among reformed thinkers on the subject because many in the reformed tradition have taught the Victorious Christian Life, including the founder, Charles G. Trumbull, and his associate,

Robert C. McQuilkin. It will quickly become obvious that there is not a unified "reformed view," let alone an official position. Another reason for devoting two chapters to reformed thinking about the matter is that, from the beginning, people from that camp have been the most vocal critics of Victorious Life teaching.

After the four chapters dealing with the three major alternative views, there are two chapters of a different nature. These deal with two influential ideologies that undermine all four of the major views on sanctification. One is inside the faith, the other outside. For all evangelicals, faith in God's empowerment is the key to successful Christian living. But recently there has been a major assault on the traditional understanding of faith, so Elmer Towns analyzes true and false faith. Finally, the overarching formative ideology of our day, commonly called "postmodernism," has spawned relativistic humanism and religious counterparts such as New Ageism. Carl Henry closes this section with a thorough unmasking of our greatest common ideological enemy, postmodernism.

15

About the Author

Kenneth Kantzer once said to a faculty group discussing spiritual gifts, "I don't know what my gift is. All my life when a job needed to be done and I was asked to do it, I just trusted God to enable me." And how God enabled him! One of America's most distinguished theologians, Kantzer has served as chairman of the department of Bible, philosophy, and religious education at Wheaton College, dean and vice president of Trinity Evangelical Divinity School, and president of Trinity College. He was editor-in-chief of *Christianity Today* from 1978 to 1982. Kantzer has contributed to numerous publications, both journals and books. He and his wife, Ruth, have two children, both of whom serve in Christian ministry.

About This Chapter

Although this is a tightly reasoned critique, from a reformed perspective, of certain elements in other views of sanctification, you will not find here any hard-line bashing of those who differ in theology. Rather, you will find an irenic probing for biblical soft spots in the Wesleyan and other traditions, including certain major elements of Victorious Life teaching. Following a clear and forceful presentation of some of the fundamental positive strands of biblical teaching on which all can agree, Kantzer stakes out boundaries he believes many have violated. In it all, however, Kantzer demonstrates affinity for the passion for holiness found in Victorious Life teaching, and he holds out hope for modest success in the quest for God's highest and best. He climaxes with fullness of hope for likeness to Christ in the life to come.

A Reformed View of Sanctification

by Kenneth Kantzer

W hat does the Bible really teach about sanctification in the Christian life? To seek to answer this question is to enter into a whole series of delicate problems where evangelical Christians have often confused the issues by employing different terms to mean the same thing and, in addition, have obscured their essential likeness by stressing the relatively minor differences that separate them. This is not to say there are no differences that are important; and sometimes the debate over what seems on the surface to be a minor issue obscures very important aspects of how to live a holy life. With no hope of settling all these differences in one short article, I shall sketch in brief form what I think to be the most important aspects of biblical teaching on sanctification.

God's Nature

The God of the Bible, who created our universe, including our planet, and sovereignly controls it, is a morally perfect God, who permits humans to sin, but has promised that one day He will renovate our planet and will bring to complete moral perfection all humans who repent of their sin and turn in faith to Jesus Christ.

To speak of God as holy or good needs some further explanation. The holiness of God is really His moral perfection in which He is distinctly and radically separate or different from all that is impure and especially from all wicked beings. The common English word for this applied to humans is simply *good*, but God is *absolutely* good. Unfortunately, the word *good* in common usage usually carries merely the idea of kindliness. The Bible, itself, frequently uses the word *good* to refer to God's kindliness toward His creatures. "Truly God is good to Israel" (Ps. 73:1). But God is good in the larger sense of God's moral perfection as well.

God is also sovereign. "You alone are the LORD. You made the heavens, even the highest heavens, and all their starry host, the earth and all that is on it, the seas and all that is in them. You give life to everything, and the multitudes of heaven worship you" (Neh. 9:6 NIV).

Yet for His own good purposes God permits sin. "What if God, choosing to show his wrath and make his power known, bore with great patience the objects of his wrath—prepared for destruction?" (Rom. 9:22 NIV). And one day God will restore not only our planet, but also humankind. "Creation itself will be liberated from its bondage to decay and brought into the glorious freedom of the children of God. . . . Not only so, but we ourselves, who have the firstfruits of the Spirit, groan inwardly as we wait eagerly for our adoption as sons, the redemption of our bodies" (Rom. 8:21–23 NIV).

The Basis of Sanctification: Regeneration

The basis for sanctification is the new birth or regeneration.[1] Ordinarily in the church today the word *regeneration* is limited to the initial reception of spiritual life by the believer when he or she receives new life in Christ as a child of God. This seems to be its meaning in Titus 3:5–7: "He saved us through the washing of rebirth and renewal by the Holy Spirit, whom he poured out on us generously through Jesus Christ our Savior, so that, having been justified by his grace, we might become heirs having the hope of eternal life" (NIV).

John refers to the same experience: "Yet to all who received him, to those who believed in his name, he gave the right to become children of God—children born not of natural descent, nor of human decision or a husband's will, but born of God" (John 1:12–13 NIV). Again, Paul says, "Therefore, if anyone is in Christ, he is a new creation; the old has gone, the new has come!" (2 Cor. 5:17 NIV). Through His Spirit, Christ brings life, indwells us permanently, and takes on His role as the Lord of our lives.

This new life created by the Holy Spirit enables the believer to act in new and better ways. It creates a new disposition within us and new moral abilities that lead to changed attitudes and actions toward God, toward sin, toward our fellow human beings, and toward ourselves. It creates the "new person" in Christ.

The experience of the new birth and initial sanctification differs from justification in that it represents a work of God in doing something in the believing soul. It sets us apart for God and represents the initial act of transforming us to become truly good. Hence sanctification, like justification, always begins at the moment of faith. There is no saving faith or justification without also a work of moral transformation or sanctification.

Initial Sanctification

The experience of salvation through faith brings a significant moral transformation, our initial sanctification. This is the point of James: "What good is it, my brothers," he asks, "if a man claims to have faith but has no deeds? Can such faith save him?" (2:14 NIV). And in the last verse of the chapter he adds, "As the body without the spirit is dead, so faith without deeds is dead" (NIV). He is not saying that we are saved on the grounds of our good works, but that, if there are no good works, then there is no faith. True faith and justification never stand alone. They are always accompanied by more than a mere positional sanctification. The initial work of sanctification creates a change in the moral quality of the believer.

A similar point is made by the apostle in 1 John 3:9 and 10. The tenses here are very important. If we sin (present tense thus indicating continuous action—if we keep on sinning), we have not been born of God. For the one who has truly been born of God cannot sin (continuous action—keep sinning). So anyone who does not do what is right is not a child of God.

The same theme is also expounded in Galatians 5:16–25. Every person faces one of two ways of life—one is a life motivated and empowered by the Holy Spirit; the other is the natural result of the inclinations of our fallen sinful human nature. After describing the way of life characterized by the sinful heart, the apostle adds immediately: "I warn you, as I did before, that those who live like this will not inherit the kingdom of God" (5:21 NIV). He does not mean that if one envies a single time or is drunk once, or commits other sins that are abhorrent to God, he will necessarily forfeit the kingdom of God. But it is abundantly clear that anyone for whom this is a characteristic way of life will not inherit the kingdom of God. That is, such a person has not been born again and in biblical language is not saved.

What is contemplated in such passages as these is not a long and arduous process in which we begin the Christian life with no initial sanctification. Rather, they teach that when we believe, we are immediately transformed. The change may not always be outwardly observable—especially for those reared in Christian homes or Christian communities. Yet we are a new creation, and this is reflected in our moral life.

Biblical references to our old sinful nature raise a question about the old man (or old self) and the new man (or new self)—the nomenclature employed by Scripture to describe our moral change as believers.[2]

The overwhelming biblical usage seems to indicate that the old sinful self has been destroyed and that in Christ we are new. That is, the old nature or self does not continue to dominate the Christian. True believers are dominated by the Holy Spirit of Christ, who indwells them. The apostle makes abundantly clear that the new believer is not dominated by sin and the old self. "He who sows to his flesh will of the flesh reap corruption, but he who sows to the Spirit will of the Spirit reap everlasting life" (Gal. 6:8). "You have taken off your old self with its practices and have put on the new self" (Col. 3:9–10 NIV).

On the whole it seems best to understand this term *old man* or *old self* as referring to the unregenerate and unsaved person who does not believe and the new self as the new regenerate believing self.[3]

We must remember, however, that the apostle is using somewhat figurative language and must not be pressed to exact preciseness. In the Galatians passage and elsewhere there are references to the "sinful nature" that influences the Christian's life but never dominates the believer.[4] In any case, it is most important to remember that God does not justify or adopt the believer into His family without also radically changing the newly born person morally and spiritually.

No Sinless Perfection in This Life

The Christian life is never free from all sin. This is undoubtedly one of the most controversial issues in Christian thinking regarding sanctification.

Sometimes doctrinal differences become battles over the definition of the word *sin*. It is not easy to bring into harmony all the scriptural writings scattered over many centuries and coming from different backgrounds and situations. Yet I believe that a careful exegesis of the many passages dealing with this topic can be brought into a pattern of consistent teaching and even into a harmony of vocabulary.

Addressing Christians, the apostle John explicitly declares that if we say we have no sin in us, we deceive ourselves. It is our duty as Christians to confess our sin and to turn to our Lord and Savior to deliver us from sin (1 John 1:8–10). This fits in with the prayer our Lord taught His disciples. We are to pray: "Forgive us our sins." When we sin, we are to turn to Christ for His forgiveness and help (Luke 1:2; see also Matt. 6:9–5). The teaching of many other passages confirms that we are blameworthy, that we are in error, and that we have faults that need to be taken care of as Christians. The voluntary offerings of the Old Testament are explicitly stated to be for sin, even sins of ignorance (Lev. 1:3–4, 14, 21; 3:5–6).

Yet the Bible also speaks of Christians as perfect.[5] Perhaps the most revealing passages on this point are Paul's statements in Philippians 3:12 and 15. In verse 15 he notes, "As many [of] us as are perfect" (NASB), thus clearly indicating that some are legitimately referred to by the Greek word often translated perfect; but three verses earlier he stated: "Not as though I am perfect, or I have already attained."

The solution to this verbal paradox is found in a careful interpretation of the Greek word translated "perfect." The word is ambiguous, and only the context helps us interpret each passage accurately. The word *perfect* is too strong a translation to get Paul's full meaning. The Greek word refers to "reaching a goal," and one needs to see the specific goal in the mind of the writer in any given context to determine what he means. In short, the apostle in verse 15 is saying that some Christians are "mature" (have reached a certain moral and spiritual goal—adjective form of the Greek word *teleion*). The same Christians, among whom he numbers himself, are not yet "perfect" (using the same Greek word in its verbal form), but they are headed in the right direction toward the goal promised by Christ. The author obviously has two levels in mind—one of absolute moral perfection (not yet attained), and the other of Christian maturity, which he and others have already attained.

This passage says nothing about sin or blameworthy acts on the part of anyone in either category. From other passages of Scripture, however, we must conclude that perfect Christians, in the sense of being mature, actually do wrong, are blameworthy, and are not free from sin in any ordinary sense of the term. Some day they will be. What we have no right to conclude from this passage is that those who are *not* mature are living as Christians with a pattern of practicing sin. Such an individual would not be considered an immature Christian. He would be an unbeliever.

At a superficial level, one may ask, what is the difference? Most Christians who defend the idea that "mature" or "perfect" Christians never commit sin readily admit that they still do wrong for which they must repent, ask forgiveness, turn to the grace and mercy of God, and seek the healing of a loving but grieved heavenly Father. Yet there are those who hold that there is a second encounter with God that enables a Christian to live completely above sin. There are hidden dangers in this view.

First, and perhaps the most important, is that in all Scripture we find no appeal to a great new crisis of sanctification as the way to overcome sin. It is a mistake to think that this is the solution to our moral and spiritual difficulties as Christians. The biblical remedy for sin in the life of the Christian does not demand a new experience of sanctification. It is rather an old remedy for the Christian. It demands repentance, confession, turning once again to God for His forgiveness, accepting His forgiveness by faith, and choosing to yield ourselves as truly dead to sin, alive to Christ. In short we are to apply the God-given resources of the gospel. We are not to seek a new crisis experience, although turning to the gospel may in itself prove to be a crisislike experience.

Second, perfectionists who believe they have already found full sanctification are not on the daily lookout for problems as Scripture warns us we must be. As a consequence, we may fail to recognize our sin and, therefore, see no need to apply ourselves to the biblical remedy for sin.

Third, when we discover weaknesses and sins that have crept into our Christian life, we do not despair nor do we deny them. Rather we apply the biblical remedy. We repent of our sin and turn to Christ. And we rely on Him and His promises to deliver us from the sins that might otherwise destroy us.

The Christian life, therefore, is one of modest victory, broken at times by grievous sin, and lived daily under the threat of sin that never dare be ignored. Telltale evidences of our sinful and rebellious old nature are never eliminated. Yet we are never dominated by sin. We never live just like the world. The Christian life is lived under the influence of the indwelling Holy Spirit of Christ, in whom we trust and who is our joy and hope.

Final Perfection

While the Christian is never completely freed from sin in this life, Scripture still makes clear that every believer is called by God to perfection. Indeed, God commands the believer to be perfect—as perfect morally as God Himself (Matt. 5:48). Moreover, what He demands of us, He gives us the ability to achieve. We are morally outfitted (the Greek word is *artios*) or completely supplied with the moral and spiritual resources to live an ideal Christian life (2 Tim. 3:17). If we do not reach perfection in this life (and we never do—not even in our best moments), God and His provisions are never at fault. The fault and blame lie 100 percent with us.

Ultimately, so Scripture tells us, every believer will become like God. This will take place in the Resurrection when we see Christ face-to-face. Of course, this likeness to God will not be a metaphysical likeness. We shall never become omnipresent, omnipotent, or omniscient, but we shall be just as pure as God Himself is pure. We shall be absolutely perfect, morally and spiritually, just as God Himself is perfectly holy and perfectly good.

A Continuous Battle

The Christian life is a continuous battle. Romans chapter 7 describes such a battle. This passage is often understood as referring only to the struggles of the unbeliever before becoming a Christian. The Christian is completely delivered from such spiritual battles. Others interpret the passage as a struggle going on within the believer. As I read the passage, there are some things in the chapter that refer specifically to the struggle of the unbeliever. He is without power to do right, and the Scripture tells us that every believer has the power to do right through the resources provided by the indwelling Holy Spirit. Yet the passage also describes accurately many of the experiences of believers and fits in with a large number of other passages of Scripture exhorting the Christian to battle against sin.

A better way to understand the passage, therefore, is to recognize it as a general, yet very vivid, description of the struggle that occurs at both levels. Even the Christian believer is not free from such struggles. The most important thing to note is the solution that the apostle offers. The struggling unbeliever is to turn to Christ, who has the power and the will to forgive us, to redeem us, and to make us holy. Struggling believers are not encouraged to seek a different sort of experience. Rather we are referred to exactly the same resource for hope of moral victory as the unbeliever. We are to ask for forgiveness as our Lord commanded us. We must confess our sin, recognize what our Savior has done for us, yield ourselves to Him as our Lord, and turn to Him for resources and for freedom from sins that creep into our lives. No doubt a battle remains. It is a battle in which we must engage all our life long. It is a battle in which at every point along the way we fall short of our goal of absolute perfection. Our love, as Augustine taught us long ago, is never as perfect as God's love. But what a difference in the kind of battle it is! As a believer it is a battle in which we have God indwelling us by His Spirit, transforming us bit by bit, guiding us, disciplining us, comforting us, leading us gently along the way, promising us the full resources we need to overcome all sin in that battle. It is a battle in which we fail and fall into sin, but it is also a battle in which we never fail completely so that our life becomes a pattern of failure. We are never without some victory. We are not slaves to sin. We are not married to sin, but we are sometimes unfaithful to our Lord. We must resist sin and battle continuously against it.

The danger in failing to see that this battle takes place is serious. If we think we never need to battle, we do not need to prepare ourselves with the resources that God has placed at our disposal to enable us to battle against sin successively.

Only One Kind of Christian

With respect to the Christian faith, the Bible only knows two classes of people and one class of Christians. It speaks of the born again and the once born, of regenerate and unregenerate, of saved and unsaved, of those in Christ and those outside of Christ, of the old self (old man) and the new self (new man), of those who practice sin and those who do not practice sin.

Yet, as we have noted, the Scriptures also note important differences in this single class within Christianity. The "old nature" still affects us so as to lead to un-Christianlike attitudes and actions.

Some have suggested that all the statements setting forth only one class of Christians must be taken as generalizations.

It must be understood that there are exceptions even when they are not listed. True, they would say, in general a Christian is a Christian, one category. But, it is held, those passages are not dealing with the question of any possible distinction among Christians. It is true that the biblical authors sometimes make generalizations without explicitly indicating certain valid exceptions.[6] But the problem with this understanding is the very explicit way in which the categories (old man and new man, practice sin and not practice sin) are set forth emphatically in such mutually exclusive terms.

Perhaps the two passages that most clearly focus on the issue are 1 John 3 and 1 Corinthians 3. The present tense employed in the 1 John 3 passage indicates continuous action and does not rule out the occurrence of sin in the life of the believer. That way the passage retains the single category of Christians who are truly saved or born again, but the meaning is that they do not practice sin rather than that they do not ever sin at all.

A clearly related passage is 1 Corinthians 3, which is often used to prove that there are after all really two classes of Christians—the carnal who walk like ordinary men after the flesh and the spiritual who walk under the direction and power of the Holy Spirit. Yet if this passage is interpreted as referring to a class of Christians who ordinarily and continuously walk as non-Christians—whose practice is just like the unsaved—then it flatly contradicts 1 John 3 and many other explicit passages by Paul himself. The passage certainly must be understood as referring to attitudes and actions that are, in fact, like those of unbelievers; and Paul is calling those carnal who do such things. When they do so, they are acting like unsaved people. Yet Paul does not mean that such believers are living exactly like ordinary unregenerate humanity. He is not saying that these people are practicing a carnal way of life. If we interpret the passage carefully, therefore, it is quite consistent with 1 John 3:2; Galatians 5; and Romans 5–7. Those who *practice* a carnal way of life are unbelievers, but believers may fall into carnal attitudes and actions of the unregenerate even when that is not their regular practice.

Why is it important to understand that there is only one class of Christians? Why not simply say that the Bible has three classes—one unsaved, and two saved classes—the carnal and the spiritual? For one thing, to have two classes of Christians makes the biblical commands to exercise church discipline difficult or impossible to apply. If Christians walk exactly like non-Christians, then the only way we could distinguish Christians from non-Christians would be by their profession of faith, not by their life. Yet Scripture makes clear that we are to exercise discipline on the basis of the walk of professing believers.[7] We are to bar the unbeliever from the Lord's table and to cut that person off from the assembly of God's people, but the fallen believer is to be treated lovingly and considerately as a brother in need.

Perhaps the most important reason for stressing the single class among Christians is the scriptural emphasis upon the oneness of the body of Christ. We are brothers and sisters—part of one family in the deepest sense. If one member suffers, we all suffer together. Each is to bear the burden of the other. This unity in Christ dare not be broken or endangered. If some Christians, the perfect or the mature or the sanctified, view themselves as a separate and distinct class from other less gifted or less pure Christians, it would be difficult for this not to affect their attitude and actions toward other Christians; and Scripture itself certainly gives no warrant for dividing Christians, whatever differences may exist between them, into two separate classes of people.

Many Patterns of Sanctification

Holy Scripture allows for many patterns of sanctification. In the actual experience of believers, there may be one or many crises. Likewise, there may be one or many lapses into grievous sin when Christians fall far below their spiritual and moral attainments of the past. Yet whether we have one crisis or many, whether we have one fall or many, or whether we have a continuous smooth and steady growth from the original work of sanctification at the new birth until the moment we meet Christ, all from a scriptural point of view are parts of a larger pattern of growth.

Scripture never suggests that any particular pattern is ideal (other than absolute perfection). And within the broad patterns of growth from initial sanctification (the experience of every true Christian and of every believer) to perfection (when we are translated into the next world and meet Christ face-to-face), no pattern is "normal." God has chosen to lead His children along by many paths, and what is right for one is not right for the other. To seek to impose a specific pattern of sanctification upon all Christians is not supported by Scripture. More important, it limits the wondrous work of the Holy Spirit who chooses to sanctify us according to His infinite wisdom and according to what He knows is specifically and individually best for each particular child of God.

Motives for Holy Living

The Christian's motives for leading a holy life are many and varied. First of all, he or she is to be good simply because that is right. As humans, God formed us with a conscience that senses a difference between what is right and what is wrong and has built into our very being a sense of obligation to do what is right.

The second and most lofty motive for holy living is the desire to be good because we love God and that is what He wishes and has commanded us to do. We love Him just because of who and what He is. He is pure love and loves us with an infinite love that draws out from us a corresponding love for Him. "We love because he first loved us" (1 John 4:19 NIV, see also all of chapters 4 and 5 and 2 Cor. 5:14).

The third motive is gratitude for all that God has done for us. Particularly, we should be grateful for His mercies when we realize that He loved us so much that He chose to give up the full exercise of all His prerogatives as deity and came down into our midst as a lowly creature, to live among us as sinners and finally die for us in order to redeem us to Himself and restore us fallen human creatures to the fellowship of God Himself.

Fourth, we are motivated by a desire for peace of mind and heart and conscience. If for no other reason, we do what is right because we do not suffer so much from smitings of conscience when we do what is right. This, in fact, is often a painful but very effective motivation to do what is right and refrain from doing wrong.

Fifth, and on a lower scale, we are motivated to be holy by the knowledge that God has chosen to reward those who truly obey Him (2 Cor. 7:1). God gives us life out of the goodness of His heart and on the basis of the work of Christ, not because we have earned it by what we ourselves do, yet in His grace He chooses to reward us for our obedience—an obedience that He Himself has created in us.

Sixth and finally, the lowest level of motivation for the Christian is fear of punishment or, rather, discipline. Scripture makes clear that not all evil that befalls a Christian is punishment because of sin. Christ bore on Himself the punishment that we deserved—all of it. But when evil, pain, suffering, even death befall the Christian, God has permitted it on purpose. Sometimes that purpose is punishment for sin. Always it is His way of sanctifying us. The Christian believer knows this and takes the warnings about discipline seriously. Thus we are motivated to do certain things and to avoid other things because we wish to avoid the divine discipline that will come if we do wrong and need the corrective disciplinary hand of God.

Summary

In summary, then, the biblical doctrine of sanctification flows out of the biblical doctrine of God. It is based on His love and concern for human beings and desire to make them, in spite of their sin, into the kind of being with whom He can have fellowship and joy together eternally in heaven. He never regenerates or begins the work of justification in any believer without also beginning the gradual work of sanctification. There is no such thing as a morally unchanged believer in Christ. That change continues a lifetime, but never brings perfection, whatever words we use to describe the moral goals we do reach. Yet it always brings a life raised to a moral and spiritual plane quite distinct from the world.

Unfortunately, an individual life on this plane may or may not seem obviously different from the lives of some who are not believers. We finite humans can only observe the external aspects of a human life. The new life in Christ, which is always present in the believer (though not always obvious) is achieved by the power of God in every believer. And that work continues through the Christian's whole life with all sorts of crises, slips into the old life, and yet gradual and real growth. Finally at death and entrance into the immediate presence of God, we are brought by His grace to the consummation of our life. We become like God, perfectly holy, perfectly good, prepared to live eternally in fellowship with a holy God.

Notes

1. Calvin, followed by many of the early reformers, used the word *regeneration* in a very broad sense so that it becomes the equivalent of sanctification rather than a description of the initial life that comes through Christ. As Calvin sees it, it represents the whole of the rejuvenation of the person by the Holy Spirit beginning with faith and taking a lifetime to reach its completion. The Scripture itself certainly uses the term in this broad sense as Matthew 19:28 shows. Its usage in Titus is nearer to the customary usage in the church today. See Calvin, *Institutes*, book 3, chapter 3.
2. For example, see Ephesians 4:20–24 with its contrast between the old self and the new self. See also Romans 6:6 and Colossians 3:9.

3. An excellent discussion of this by Anthony Hoekema is to be found in *Five Views on Sanctification* (Grand Rapids: Zondervan, 1987), 80–81; and an even more full treatment in the work of John Murray, *Collected Writings of John Murray*, 2 vols. (Carlisle, Pa.: Banner of Truth, 1977), 293.
4. See Galatians 5:13, 16, and 17. Here the sinful nature clearly refers to an influence that still remains to plague the life of one who is a believer.
5. See the "perfection" ascribed to Noah in Genesis 6:9 and 9:20 and to Abraham in Genesis 7:1.
6. For example, in the biblical condemnations of divorce, legitimate grounds for divorce are not always listed.
7. See, for example, 1 Corinthians chapter 5, and the instructions as to how to deal with a professing Christian who is living in grievous sin.

16

About the Author

William J. Larkin, Jr. is a professor of New Testament and Greek at Columbia Biblical Seminary and Graduate School of Missions and has been on that faculty since 1975. An ordained Presbyterian minister, Larkin had some pastoral experience prior to his doctoral studies, is regularly in pulpit supply, and has lectured in many theological schools overseas. His *Culture and Biblical Hermeneutics: Interpreting and Applying the Authoritative Word in a Relativistic Age* (Baker, 1989; University Press of America, 1993) was a landmark contribution to the ongoing debate concerning the impact of culture on the interpretation of Scripture. Most of his writing, however, has been in the field of New Testament studies, such as his recent volume in the InterVarsity Press New Testament Commentary series, *Acts* (1995). Larkin and his wife, Edna, have two children.

About This Chapter

This essay should put to rest the oft-repeated canard that a person fully committed to the reformed position cannot adhere to Victorious Life teaching. With thorough analysis of both positions and with lucid logic, Larkin identifies the two sticking points for many in the reformed tradition and with complete fidelity to that tradition offers a way of reconciliation. Those who are troubled by a perceived incompatibility that makes them wary either of the reformed tradition as it relates to sanctification or of Victorious Life teaching, could find this chapter a landmark contribution.

An Integrated View of Victory and Covenant Theology

by William J. Larkin, Jr.

G iven the strength and persistence of criticism by reformed thinkers,[1] the development of a reformed approach to the Victorious Christian Life teaching might at first sight appear impossible. Indeed, Clarence Loucks, after his thorough study of Victorious Life teaching concludes that "in its attempt to synthesize Calvinist and Wesleyan ideas in its doctrine of holiness, the Victorious Life movement has succeeded only in developing a theological mixture that is both unfamiliar and unacceptable to proponents of these two traditional theologies."[2] Some critics see Victorious Christian Life teaching as so logically incoherent,[3] such a distortion of biblical truth,[4] and so harmful emotionally and spiritually,[5] that they would strongly discourage any attempt to articulate it, even with an infusion of insights from a reformed perspective.

Geoffrey Bromiley's assessment from an earlier day gives us hope that such a task is worth pursuing. Bromiley said, "That there is no basic discrepancy between the Reformed and evangelical doctrine and the message of Keswick is all to the good. But we have to recognize that the general call for a conscious act of surrender does give rise to a difference of emphasis, and even opens the way to false and dangerous misconceptions."[6] But it is a chastened hope since many misunderstandings surround the teaching. The task, then, is negative and positive. We must face and answer the criticisms reformed thinkers have presented. And from a reformed perspective and in reformed language we must set out the five pillars of Victorious Christian Living—Sin, Divine Provision, Consecration, Spirit-filled Living, Service. If the criticisms can be answered either in terms of uncovering misunderstandings or achieving mutual correction, then the way will be cleared for an articulation of a reformed approach to the Victorious Christian Life.

Several factors in the history of the debate must be kept in mind if we are to make progress in reconciling the apparent differences between reformed and Victorious Christian Living teaching. First, the debate has proceeded somewhat fitfully. Reformed thinkers after Warfield evidence little or no awareness that W. H. Griffith Thomas responded cogently and in some detail to the Princeton theologian's criticisms.[7] So Loucks observes, "Perhaps it is not an overstatement to suggest that virtually every theological attack on the victorious life in the twentieth century is little more than a footnote on Warfield's criticisms."[8] Similarly, although Bromiley[9] engages J. I. Packer's criticisms, Packer's reiteration of them thirty years later does not reflect very much interaction with Bromiley.[10] The Victorious Christian Life Movement's avowedly practical, nonintellectual approach produced few theologians who would have an appetite for engaging in such dialogue. Steven Barabas, historian of the movement, catches this spirit when he says, "The Convention is not interested in academic discussions of theology and ethics, or even in adding to the store of Bible knowledge of those who attend, but simply and only in helping men to be holy."[11]

Second, at least two critics of the movement betray personal emotional and spiritual hurt from the teaching, while a

third, Warfield, is often caustic in his remarks.[12] Weisiger
rightly counsels, "Our descriptions of sanctification call for
humility and charity. Temperament and type of experience,
plus denominational conditioning, affect our understanding
of Scripture and our formulations of doctrine."[13]

Third, the two schools of thought do converge in a number of ways. There are reformed roots to the theological articulation of Victorious Christian Living in North America, for
Robert C. McQuilkin, whom his son labels the theologian of
the movement, was of Irish Presbyterian lineage. Where
reformed and Keswick thought have formally interacted, as in
the case of Hoekema and Robertson McQuilkin, remaining
differences have been reduced to two from the eleven Loucks
catalogs for Warfield and those after him.[14] With a general
knowledge of the debate's history and a commitment to get
beyond the "personal atmospherics" that can tend to cloud
our understanding, we will look at the remaining reformed
objections. We purpose to be "reformed" in all affirmations,
i.e., reforming, correcting, all statements from whatever
source according to the Word of God.

The two areas about which there is not yet a meeting of
the minds are the nature of sin, especially, in the life of a
Christian who is living victoriously, and the Victorious Life's
understanding of the relationship of justification to sanctification.[15] The second area manifests itself in the specific question: Is there a qualitative distinction between the lives of
defeated and victorious Christians?

Hoekema objected to the traditional Victorious
Christian Living definition: "uniform victory over known sin."
He found the distinction between known and unknown sin
and the claim of victory problematic when compared with biblical teaching on the demands of a perfect divine moral standard, the difficulty in recognizing sin (Ps. 19:12; 1 Cor. 4:4);
the failure to do anything from perfectly pure motives, and
the defilement of even our righteous deeds (Isa. 64:6).[16]

Robertson McQuilkin actually rejected the traditional definition, having sharpened the earlier "uniform victory over known sin" to "consistent victory over intentional sin," though Hoekema didn't respond to his extended exposition of the implications of that definition. McQuilkin's definition can be seen again in the article elsewhere in this volume[17] where he makes explicit the distinction between intentional and unintentional sin. Victorious living is a Spirit-filled Christian consistently choosing not to commit intentional sins. This speaks to most of Hoekema's concerns, though the description of victory would probably still give him pause. Hoekema needs to be reminded that McQuilkin affirms this within a nonperfectionist framework and to address the question: How should the truth of Romans 6:14 be expressed in experiential terms?

An additional difficulty in this general area surfaces when J. I. Packer strongly contends, "The belief that full deliverance from all known sin is enjoyed by consecrated, Spirit-filled Christians using the faith technique makes it impossible to read Romans 7:14–25 in the natural way."[18] The *New Geneva Study Bible* rejects the Victorious Life teaching's usual option for interpreting the "I": "a Christian in an unnatural and unhealthy spiritual condition, one failing to draw on the indwelling Spirit's resources." It opts for "Paul is describing himself and Christians generally, who, although in Christ and free from the condemnation of the law, do not yet perfectly fulfill the requirements of the law."[19] Robert C. McQuilkin, however, fits neither Packer's nor the *New Geneva Study Bible*'s expectations. He would agree with the *New Geneva Study Bible*. "It is not, therefore, wrong to say that the struggle described in the seventh chapter of Romans is the experience of the Christian." And he would say, against Packer, that there is a note of victory even in chapter seven: "I thank God—through Jesus Christ our Lord!" (Rom. 7:25). A natural reading of the chapter is not incompatible with Victorious Life teaching.[20]

The second main area to be resolved is whether there is a qualitative distinction among Christians. Hoekema says no and McQuilkin says yes.[21] McQuilkin makes this the final sticking point between the two positions.

> In summary it might be said that there is no basic conflict between Hoekema's presentation of Reformed teaching on sanctification and the Keswick approach. But for those Calvinists who deny the existence of an unacceptable, qualitatively distinct way of life experienced by some Christians, a way that can and must be corrected by a renewal of the original faith-commitment to God, a conflict does exist.[22]

Behind this disagreement are issues like the inseparability of justification and sanctification, the harmful emotional and spiritual side effects that can come through the acceptance of such stratification, the relationship between process and crisis in the sanctification process, and whether human beings do decisively impede the sanctification process. There is also the concern about the proportion of Christians who at any one time are in a defeated versus a victorious mode. McQuilkin says many, if not most, while Hoekema is not so sure.

Each proponent has a legitimate concern. Victorious Life teaching wants to make sure that Christians of the reformed persuasion do not lapse into a contentment with their spiritual condition by viewing differences in sanctification progress as a matter of degrees, grounded in God's sovereign initiative, but not properly balanced by a concern for human responsibility. Reformed thinking desires to make sure that the qualitative difference is not an ontological one, creating two classes of regenerate individuals, and potentially sundering the necessary link between justification and sanctification. McQuilkin needs to be reassured that reformed thought does take seriously the relationship between regenerate condition and holy, righteous behavior. John Owen in his work *On Temptation and the Mortification of Sin in Believers,* may help here. He notes that there are a great number of "professors" of the faith who have "miserably unmortified hearts," as evidenced by their sinful lives. In fact, he wonders out loud whether they are regenerate, having any "saving light" in them.[23] Thus Victorious Life thinking should explicitly consider the option that many "professors" with no matching life are not Christians. Reformed thinking for its part should, as Kenneth Prior has done, investigate more closely the role of crisis experiences in the sanctification process.[24]

It is hoped that this foray into reconciling remaining differences has cleared the way for considering a "Reformed Approach to Victorious Christian Living." The five basic steps of a Victorious Life Conference will provide the framework. Three fundamental changes must be made, however, if the exposition is to be most compatible with reformed thinking. First, although Victorious Christian Life teaching certainly stands in the reformation tradition of God's initiative in providing salvation by grace alone that must be received by faith alone, its purpose to serve as a spiritual clinic for the regenerate meant that its starting point was an analysis of man's problem: "Sin," followed by the solution: "God's Provision." A reformed approach would want to formalize the logic of grace, which always begins with God. Second, the third day needs to be retitled "Repentance/Consecration." The element of yieldedness or consecration will not be lost, but it will be subsumed under a larger category, which allows us to deal with those "defeated" professing Christians who need to come to Christ for the first time. It will also highlight the fact that the decision made by the "defeated" true believer is a return to what has been his from regeneration. Finally, day four will be retitled the "Spirit-Filled Life and Christian Responsibility" in order to highlight the active role the Christian must play in his sanctification.

Day One: "God's Provision—Grace in Present Salvation." At regeneration the Christian is given a new heart and spirit that are further sanctified "really and personally" through the virtue of Christ's death and resurrection, with which he or she has been united (Gal. 2:20; Col. 3:2–3; 1 Peter 2:24; Eph. 5:30; Rom. 6:3–4). All this occurs by God's Word and Spirit dwelling in the Christian (John 17:17; Eph. 5:26; 2 Thess. 2:13; 2 Cor. 3:18; Rom. 8:13).[25]

Several implications for a Christian's dealing with sin in his or her life follow. First, Christ's past becomes our past. Positionally, we have died to sin just as Jesus did (Rom. 6:10–11). We are no longer liable to experience the condemnation/penalty for our sins (Rom. 8:1; 5:1). Second, our present knows liberation from the necessary dominion of sin because of Christ's past (Rom. 6:6, 14). John Murray exults, "By the grace of God there is this radical change that it [sin] does not exercise the dominion. The self-condemnations which it evokes are the index of this fact. It is this destruction of the power of sin that makes possible a realized biblical ethic."[26] Third, that new heart and new spirit within us are actively, constantly, permanently, universally, i.e., through all aspects of ourselves, and progressively making us more and more like Christ (Jer. 31:33; Rom. 8:6; John 4:14; 2 Cor. 3:18). This Spirit-induced sanctification process more and more weakens our remaining corruption, the indwelling sin, and the appetites it seeks to ignite and so tempt us to think, speak, and act in ungodly ways. At the same time the Spirit is strengthening and enabling us to manifest more and more the gracious life of Christ (Col. 3:5; Rom. 8:13; 2 Cor. 13:8). Because this sanctifying defeat of sin in a Christian's life is permanent and constant, it could, in one sense, be considered "automatic," completely independent of the Christian's involvement. But given other teaching in Scripture, this is not the case. To show the vital role the Christian has in sanctification, the "indicatives" declaring God's provision are always matched by "imperatives" pointing out human responsibility (Rom. 6:10–11, 12–14; Gal. 5:24–25). But even there the strength to fulfill that responsibility always comes from God (Rom. 8:13; Phil. 2:12–13; 2 Peter 1:5–8). The first step to victory is to know the nature of the victory in which Christians already stand (Rom. 5:1–2).

Day Two: "Sin." Sin does have a continuing presence and power in the life of the Christian. In order to encourage each other on to victory, we must understand what can bring us defeat. John Calvin graphically declared, "There remains in a regenerate man a smoldering cinder of evil, from which desires continually leap forth to allure and spur to commit sin . . . [it is] sin when man is tickled by any desire at all against the law of God. Indeed, we label 'sin' that very depravity which begets in us desires of this sort"[27] (cf. James 1:14–15). This sin creates an ongoing life of conflict, but not necessarily of defeat. Romans 7:20–23 portrays the struggle.

The temptations a Christian faces about dealing with the presence of sin (habitual principle and desires, potential commitment of wrong thoughts, words, deeds) in his life do reduce to a lack of faith or a lack of surrender/obedience. He may be tempted to frustration, even despair of the conflict he constantly faces, viewing even the struggle a defeat or thinking that he cannot consistently gain the victory when facing temptation (Rom. 7:24; 2 Cor. 4:7–11—positions Paul chooses not to take). Or most earnest to fulfill his part or lured away by a shortcut dependence on some human technique or experience, he can be tempted to drift away from the life of faith: the conscious reliance on the Spirit to provide the only strength that will win the victory (Gal. 3:3). His drift might be in the direction of disobedience: succumbing to temptations and even to a period of active rebellion against God's law (cf. 1 Peter 4:1–3; 2 Peter 1:9). The indwelling sin and the ungodly use of appetites they spark, even though both are being weakened by the sanctification process, do have power to allure, and if the Christian is not vigilant, sin is the result.

Day Three: "Repentance/Consecration." If we would move away from a life of defeat, either through unbelief or lack of obedience, we must repent and return to the full exercise of the graces and privileges as those who are experiencing present salvation in which sin has no dominion over us. Lest Satan delude us into thinking that the struggle against sin will always, or at least most of the time, lead to defeat, we must carefully consider the biblical motives for making such a radical break with sin. First, there is the matter of our eternal destiny. Romans 8:13 says that "life," eternal life, results for those who "by the Spirit . . . are putting to death the deeds of the body" (NASB). Not living a life of victory with the Spirit's help removes from us a well-founded assurance that salvation in the future will be ours. Second, our vigor, power, comfort, and peace in the Christian life depend on consistently living a life of victory. Sin is our active foe. As John Owen urges us, "Be killing sin or it will be killing you" (Rom. 8:6; 1 Thess. 3:8).[28]

Since some profess faith in Christ, but their lifestyle makes it indeterminate whether the dominion of sin has been broken in their lives (Matt. 7:20–21), this call to repentance will be a call to salvation (Luke 24:46–47). For the truly regenerate whose defeat stems from unbelief, it will be a call to return to the faith relationship in the covenant of grace. Those who have chosen to see the continual struggle against sin as in reality a life of defeat and have given up in frustration, cynicism, or despair[29] must embrace again, or maybe for the first time, that this "indicative" is actually true of them. "Sin shall not have dominion over you." Then they must commit themselves to live in the light of that fact. For those whose unbelief has shown itself in a self-effort that led only to defeat, there must be an owning of the truth that it is only by the power of the Spirit that sin may be put to death (Rom. 8:13). This will lead to a life of humble dependence on God to do the work of present salvation "with them and through" them (Phil. 2:12–13).

Repentance for the disobedient through drift or active rebellion means to return to a life of covenant obedience under the lordship of Christ. It must seize the "imperative" end of the "indicative/imperative" paradigm and with integrity and renewed commitment endeavor with the Spirit's aid to make true in experience the "indicative" they are claiming. "If we live in the Spirit, let us also walk in the Spirit" (Gal. 5:25).

Day Four: "Spirit-Filled Life and Christian Responsibility." Once the decisive repentance returns the Christian to the stance of faith and obedience, what must he learn of the "how" of this life of victory? First, with reference to ability, it is only by the power of the Spirit that one can live in victory (Phil. 2:12–13). The Christian must be active in his struggle against sin, but as the *Westminster Confession of Faith* asserts, "[It is] through the continual supply of strength from the sanctifying Spirit of Christ, [that] the regenerate part doth overcome" (Rom. 6:14; 1 John 5:4; Eph. 4:15–16).[30]

Second, as to process, a life of victory involves "mortification" and "vivification." In the phraseology of John Owen, derived from the imagery of Romans 8:13 and Colossians 3:5, mortification is by the Spirit to take away indwelling sin's power, life, vigor, and strength so that it cannot produce its effects. This happens as we take part with grace in its principle, actings, and fruits against the principle, actings, and fruit of sin.[31] Vivification is mortification viewed in positive terms: to be "more and more quickened and strengthened in all saving graces" (Col. 1:11; Eph. 3:16–19).[32] It is "the desire to live in a holy and devoted manner, a desire arising from the rebirth; as if it were said that a man dies to himself that he may begin to live to God" (Rom. 6:11; 1 Peter 2:24).[33]

Third, although the Spirit supplies the grace for achieving victory, "we must diligently seek and wait for these supplies in the ways and means whereby they are communicated."[34] This means the proper use of the means of grace. In prayer, we both tell God about our struggle against sin and ask His help (Ps. 55:2; Rom. 8:26–27). Meditating on and reading and hearing the Word encourage us in the great "indicatives" of our present salvation and the "imperatives" of our duty (John 17:7; 2 Tim. 3:15–17; Rom. 6:1–14). Worship, the sacraments, and church fellowship strengthen us in grace through the mutual encouragement that the body provides (Rom. 6:1–4; 1 Cor. 10:16; Rom. 15:1–3; Eph. 4:16; Col. 3:16; 1 Cor. 12:7). God's providences, especially trials and afflictions, are aimed at the grand goal of conforming us to the image of His Son (Rom. 8:28–29). They help us mortify deep-seated pride as they force us to cast ourselves back on the Lord for grace (2 Cor. 12:7–10).

Day Five: "Service." If the life of victory is to make us more Christlike, then service and mission will be central to the victorious Christian, as they were to his Lord (Luke 19:10; 22:24–27; Mark 10:45; John 4:34). Indeed, Jesus commissioned His disciples using the analogy of His own commission (John 20:21). A life of victory frees us to serve others and share the good news of salvation—past, present, and future— to the ends of the earth (Luke 24:44–48).

In sum, we have suggested that if we take the Hoekema-McQuilkin dialogue, together with McQuilkin's essay in this volume, we may reduce the remaining differences between the reformed and Victorious Christian Life to two areas: the nature of sin in the Victorious Life and the relation of justification and sanctification, or more precisely, the nature of the spiritual distinction between defeated and victorious Christians. We found that Robertson McQuilkin's further clarification, moving from the traditional Victorious Life distinction of known and unknown sin to intentional and nonintentional sin did speak to many of Hoekema's concerns about the rightness of claiming that the Victorious Life is consistently free from "known sin." The description of victory as freedom from intentional sin would still cause difficulty to reformed thinkers. They need to be reminded that this is affirmed within a nonperfectionist framework as a capacity, not a "track record." The challenge for all is the description in experiential terms of the great truth of Romans 6:14. As for the interpretation of Romans 7, Robert C. McQuilkin showed long ago that it can be affirmed of a Christian and even point to a life of victory, though out of intense struggle.

The relation of justification and sanctification can be further clarified when the precise nature of the "qualitative distinction" between defeated and victorious Christian is further expounded. Hoekema and McQuilkin could come closer together in their positions if the former would investigate more thoroughly how crisis experiences of repentance/consecration may fit within the process of sanctification and the latter would emphasize more that some who are living defeated lives may not be regenerate at all.

In sum, what is the common ground between the traditions that might produce "A Reformed Approach to the Victorious Christian Life"? By virtue of union with Christ, Christians receive the sanctifying benefits of Christ's death and resurrection, among which is the breaking of the necessary power of sin in a life. Sin, indeed, shall not have dominion over the Christian because he is under grace. The remaining sin in the believer tempts him or her to live a defeated life. In unbelief, the Christian in the midst of the struggle against sin ceases fighting toward victory or continues on in self-effort. In disobedience, the believer manifests his defeat through drift or open rebellion. Only a crisis experience of repentance/consecration will return the Christian to a proper covenant relationship of faith and obedience. And for "professors" of the faith living defeated lives, this will be a salvation experience. The Spirit-filled life of victory will be lived totally in God's strength, pursuing a lifestyle that is dead to sin and alive to God, availing itself of the means of grace, by which the supplies of strength from the Spirit come.

Notes

1. Benjamin B. Warfield, "The Victorious Life," in *Perfectionism* (Grand Rapids: Baker, 1991), 2:561–611; John Murray, review of *So Great Salvation*, by Steven Barabas, *Westminster Theological Journal* 16 (1953): 79–84; James I. Packer, "'Keswick' and the Reformed Doctrine of Sanctification," *Evangelical Quarterly* 27 (1955): 153–67; *Keep in Step with the Spirit* (Old Tappan, N.J.: Revell, 1984), 145–64; Anthony A. Hoekema, "Response to 'The Keswick Perspective,'" in *Five Views of Sanctification*, Melvin E. Dieter et al. (Grand Rapids: Zondervan, 1987), 187–90. Recent exponents of the reformed approach to sanctification criticize aspects of the teaching without naming it. See, for example, Kenneth F. W. Prior, *The Way to Holiness* (Chicago: InterVarsity, 1967), 65–71; Sinclair B. Ferguson, "The Reformed View," in *Christian Spirituality: Five Views of Sanctification*, ed. Donald L. Alexander (Downers Grove, Ill.: InterVarsity, 1988), 60–63; R. C. Sproul, general editor, *New Geneva Study Bible* (Nashville: Thomas Nelson, 1995), see notes on 6:1–14; 7:14–25, and "Sanctification" note, 1806.
2. Clarence M. Loucks, "The Theological Foundations of the Victorious Life: An Evaluation of the Theology of the Victorious Christian Life in the Light of the Present," Ph.D. diss. Fuller (Ann Arbor, Mich.: UMI, 1984), 223. Cary Weisiger draws a similar conclusion. "I know of no synthesis that effects a complete reconciliation between the teaching of the Reformers and their successors and the teaching of Wesley and his successors" ("The Reformed Doctrine of Sanctification," booklet IX in *Fundamentals of the Faith* series [Washington, D. C.: *Christianity Today*, n.d.], 7).
3. Warfield, "The Victorious Life," 2:584.
4. Packer, *Keep in Step*, 159.
5. Ibid., 158; Douglas Frank, *Less Than Conquerors: How Evangelicals Entered the Twentieth Century* (Grand Rapids: Eerdmans, 1986), 164.
6. Geoffrey W. Bromiley, "Holiness and the Keswick Movement," *Evangelical Quarterly* 24 (1952): 231. Note the similar assessment by Robertson McQuilkin from the Keswick perspective. ". . . there is no basic conflict between Hoekema's presentation of Reformed teaching on sanctification and the Keswick approach" ("Response to 'The Reformed Perspective,'" in *Five Views of Sanctification*, Melvin E. Dieter et al. [Grand Rapids: Zondervan, 1987], 99).
7. W. H. Griffith Thomas, "The Victorious Life (I–II)" *Bibliotheca Sacra* 76 (1919): 267–88; 455–67.
8. Loucks, *Theological Foundations*, 200.
9. Geoffrey W. Bromiley, "Keswick's Teaching Concerning Sanctification," *The Life of Faith* 79 (1955): 673, 687, 700, 722.
10. Packer, *Keep in Step*, 150–64.
11. Barabas, *So Great Salvation*, 108.
12. Packer says, "A burned child, however, dreads the fire, and hatred of the cruel and tormenting unrealities of overheated holiness teaching remains in his heart to this day. Now I was that student" (*Keep in Step*, 158). Frank is not so explicit but the tone of his chapter seems to also reflect such an engagement (*Less than Conquerors*, chapter 4). Warfield will remark, "If we wish to observe the lengths the notion may be carried, that the 'old man' in us is unaffected by the intruding Spirit, we have only to turn to Mr. Robert C. McQuilkin's somewhat incoherent tract on 'God's Way of Victory over Sin.' . . . How, in the name of all that is rational, can I retain a power to resist Him when I retain no body or mind or soul or spirit of my own . . . ?" ("Victorious Life" in *Perfection*, 2:584, 600).

13. Weisiger, *Reformed Doctrine of Sanctification*, 23.
14. Anthony Hoekema, "Response," 187–90; J. Robertson McQuilkin, "Response," 98–99.
15. Ibid.
16. Anthony Hoekema, "Response," 187–88.
17. Robertson McQuilkin, "Imperfections," 55.
18. James Packer, *Keep in Step*, 161.
19. *New Geneva Study Bible*, 1778.
20. Robert C. McQuilkin, *The Message of Romans: An Exposition* (Grand Rapids: Zondervan, 1947), 87. John Murray also concurs that Romans 7 is not necessarily about defeat ("Review," 82–83; cf. Sinclair Ferguson, "Reformed View," 62–63).
21. Anthony Hoekema, "Response," 188–90; J. Robertson McQuilkin, "Response," 99.
22. J. Robertson McQuilkin, "Response," 99.
23. John Owen, *On Temptation and the Mortification of Sin in Believers* (Philadelphia: Presbyterian Board of Publication, n.d.), 163.
24. Kenneth Prior, *Way of Holiness*, chapter 10.
25. Much of the phrasing of this definition is taken from *Westminster Confession of Faith* 13:1 (*The Confession of Faith: Together with the Larger Catechism and the Shorter Catechism with Scripture Proofs*, 3d ed. [Atlanta: Committee for Christian Education and Publications—PCA, 1990]).
26. John Murray, *Principles of Conduct: Aspects of Biblical Ethics* (Grand Rapids: Eerdmans, 1957), 220–21.
27. John Calvin, *Institutes of the Christian Religion*, 2 vols. (Philadelphia: Westminster, 1977), 3:3:10.
28. John Owen, *On Temptation*, 154.
29. If Douglas Frank is representative of the boomer generation among evangelicals, when he labels Victorious Life teaching "religion" over against a paradoxical Christian life, lived simultaneously under the judgment and mercy of God, where as a people of despair we know "his victory in some way involves our own brokenness and defeat," then there are many in this category (*Less Than Conquerors*, 166).
30. *Westminster Confession*, 13:3.
31. John Owen, *On Temptation*, 151; Sinclair Ferguson, *John Owen on the Christian Life* (Edinburgh: Banner of Truth, 1987), 72.
32. *Westminster Confession*, 13:1.
33. John Calvin, *Institutes*, 3:3:3.
34. John Owen, *The Holy Spirit: His Gifts and Power* (Grand Rapids: Kregel, 1954), 314.

About the Author

Dennis Kinlaw is perhaps best known as longtime president of Asbury College, but he has a record of distinguished service in other arenas as well. He has taught in the field of Old Testament at Asbury Theological Seminary, preached in evangelistic campaigns around the world, and contributed to many journals and books including his book, *Preaching in the Spirit.* That title catches the essence of the man—preaching and life in the Spirit. Although a leader in the Wesleyan movement, Kinlaw is highly respected in the broader evangelical world, serving, for example, as senior editor and board member of *Christianity Today* magazine. He and his wife, Elsie Katherine, have five children.

About This Chapter

Here is a remarkable essay. Invited to give the Wesleyan alternative to Victorious Life teaching—with freedom to critique it—Dennis Kinlaw instead gives a moving testimony of how he—a lifetime committed Wesleyan—found fullness of life in Christ through the teaching of the Victorious Christian life.

Indeed there are differences between the two traditions. For example, though Victorious Life teaching assumes the practical need most Christians have for an encounter with God subsequent to initial conversion, it doesn't hold with the Wesleyan tradition that such an encounter is theologically necessary. Again, though Wesleyans hold out hope for an experience of "perfect love," Victorious Life teaching, at least after the early years, has vigorously denied the possibility of any kind of perfection in this life. But Kinlaw has chosen rather to wed the two traditions in the context of his own experience, demonstrating both victorious Christian living at its best and perfect love as well. You will find not only the story of Kinlaw's pilgrimage from defeat to victory, but an intriguing analysis of that same pilgrimage of the disciples as recorded in the Gospel according to Mark.

Victorious Christian Living from a Wesleyan Perspective

by Dennis F. Kinlaw

It was during the difficult days of the Second World War. I was a college student and had developed a close friendship with some classmates whose parents were missionaries in the Orient. When Japan overran China, these missionaries were seized and placed in Japanese prisoner-of-war camps. Because of my closeness to their sons, these missionaries became a concern of mine.

It was an exciting day when we learned that they had been released and were returning to America. It was even more exciting when these valiant soldiers of Christ showed up on campus to see their children. Because their sons were my friends I had the privilege of getting to know them. The impact was such that its influence lingers still.

Coming from a typical American church, I had never known anyone who had suffered for Christ. There is still a clear picture in my mind of the toothpicklike legs of the mother of my friends whose diet had been a daily bowl of rice, much of which had been quite alive before it was cooked.

The surprise to me was their spirit. There was no sense in them of having been heroic. Nor was there a trace of self-pity. There was simply the joyous expression of gratitude for the privilege of having been on the battle line for Christ.

There was something else about them that impressed me. They used a language that was not natural for one coming from my background. The nouns were relatively familiar; it was the adjectives and adverbs that struck the new note.

They did not speak just of "surrender." They spoke of total surrender. Nor did they speak simply of "consecration." They urged on us a complete consecration. Their language included expressions like being "filled with the Spirit," "the baptism of the Spirit," "entire sanctification," "death to self," and "being crucified with Christ."

Slowly I became aware that from their point of view there were Christians and then there were Christians, that some Christians were quite different from others. It was in such a context that I became acquainted with the expression, "the Victorious Christian Life."

The problem for me was not that I could not understand their language. Rather it was the discomfort that swept me when I realized that they knew a relationship with Christ that I did not enjoy. The thought of such put a deep fear inside me. I recognized that these were Christians who knew something of God's inner cleansing and empowering that I did not know. Their witness threatened me. A hunger began within that has continued through the decades since. I got as close to those missionaries as I could get and found that each one spoke of an experience after conversion where God brought him or her into a knowledge of a grace and a victory that manifested itself in a difference from me in their language, their life, and their knowledge of Christ.

The experience raised for me a thousand questions. Was there something lacking in my conversion? The change had been definite enough. It had been like that between night and day. I had known at the time of my conversion the clear witness of the Spirit that my sins were forgiven and that I was a new creature in Christ. My joy in Him was so full that I lovingly and naively assured Him that night by my bed that I would never sin against Him again. That vow was quickly broken, but the sense of belonging to Christ and of the new life in Him had never left. But now I knew there ought to be something more. There came to me a sense of sinfulness I had not known before becoming a Christian. It was not a conviction for sins as much as it was for my sinfulness. I knew my heart was not wholly Christ's, that I still had a finger on my life, that my commitment had a conditional character to it. I knew that a measure of self-will remained that contained a concealed rebellion about it. My new friends assured me that I was not unusual, that they too had been where I was, but that Christ had delivered them from that inner reserve and had set them free to follow Him wholly and unconditionally. Their lives confirmed their testimony.

That raised the question for me as to whether their witness was biblical.

It was necessary then for me to turn to Scripture to see if what they told me was to be substantiated there. The search convinced me that the Bible confirms their claim. There are Christians and there are Christians. *Christ died to do more for us than most of us have been willing to let Him do.* The salvation provided on the Cross is greater and fuller than many of us permit ourselves to know. There is a life of holiness and victory possible through His blood for any who will properly and earnestly seek it.

As I studied and prayed, I was pleasantly surprised to find that what these missionaries described was not alien either to my own Methodist heritage nor was it unsubstantiated in Scripture. The "two-stage" story can be found in both. Let me share first a bit of biblical data that has become precious to me. It is seen in the gospel as it is given in the book of Mark and as it was experienced by the disciples of Jesus.

Mark's Gospel is easily divided into three sections. The first is the story of the public ministry of Jesus from John's presentation of Him to Israel up to Peter's confession that

Jesus is the Christ in chapter 8. The second is the story of the Lord's journey from Caesarea Philippi to Jerusalem. There we see Jesus traveling with His Twelve in a deep and intimate companionship as He tells them what will happen in Jerusalem (chapters 9–10). The third section, chapters 11–16, gives us the story of Christ's last week in the Holy City, His death and His resurrection. It is the first two sections that are our primary interest here. They tell us how the disciples came to faith but how glaring deficiencies remained after they had come to believe. Those deficiencies bear a profound resemblance to needs found in most of us who today call ourselves "born-again" Christians. These deficiencies found a remedy in the subsequent experience of the disciples, a cure that many of us who believe in Jesus desperately need today. In fact, the lives of the disciples reflect the two-stage pattern of Christian experience spoken of earlier.

There is a brilliance in the way Mark makes his case in the first eight chapters as to who Jesus is. The argument is done by story, not proposition. The stories flow one after another, and Jesus is the central figure in each one. Every unit tells of some remarkable act or word of Christ and presents itself in such a way that the question is inevitably raised: "Who can this unusual person be?" In most, the question is implicit. In some, it becomes quite explicit. But, in all, the interrogation lurks: "Who is this One who moves among us?"

When Jesus teaches, it is with an authority that distinguishes Him from all other teachers. He speaks convincingly, yet He Himself has not been taught. He has powers that are inexplicable. He commands evil spirits and they obey. He lays hands on the sick and they are healed. He touches blind eyes and persons who have never seen, see. He cleanses lepers, restores paralytics, and raises the dead. He multiplies bread and fish, stills a storm, and claims to do what only God can do. He claims to forgive sin. He refuses to be bound by the legal restrictions of Judaism as to diet or holy days. In fact, He claims to be superior to such prescriptions. He is Lord even of the Sabbath. Yet He is neither arrogant nor self-aggrandizing. All is done in such a way that everyone is forced to question His identity.

Mark lets us know that most everyone had an answer except the disciples. His family thinks He is beside Himself and should be taken home (3:21). The Jewish leaders say that He is in league with the devil, that His power comes from Beelzebub (3:22). The people of Nazareth want to believe that since He came from Nazareth and is one of them, He is really an inconsequential nobody (6:1–6). King Herod, plagued with guilt after the death of John the Baptist, is quite convinced that Jesus is John the Baptist come back to haunt him (6:14). The devils know Him for who He is but Jesus muzzles them (1:23–26; 3:11–12). All have an answer except the Twelve.

After seven and a half chapters, Jesus is ready to raise the question with His Twelve. He takes them north to Caesarea Philippi. Here they are untroubled by the crowds. He has His own alone. He can force the question with them. Peter rises to the occasion. He affirms that they have come to believe that He is the Christ of God, the Messiah. They have come to faith. They believe that He is the One for whom Israel has been waiting. They affirm that He is the One for whom they have been looking.

Immediately a change takes place in His relationship to them. There is now a deeper intimacy. There is a much closer identification. They are His and He is theirs. His deepest secrets, formerly only allusively given, are now freely and openly shared. He speaks of His destiny, of His passion. He includes the three leaders of the apostolic band, Peter, James, and John, in His conversation on the mountain with Moses and Elijah. There they hear the divine voice, speaking from heaven, say: "This is My beloved Son. Hear Him." What was faith in Caesarea Philippi now becomes knowledge on the mountain. They know, at least these three, that He is the Christ. The men of this little band are His chosen ones, His elect.

Jesus obviously sees them as belonging to Him. From the other Gospels we learn that He calls them friends, not servants (John 15:14–15). He tells His Father that they are not of the world just as He is not (John 15:19; 17:14–16). He says that His Father loves them because they love Him, Jesus, and because they believe He came forth from God (John 16:27). He says that those who receive them receive Him and the Father, but that those who reject them lose both Him and His Father (Matt. 10:40; Luke 10:16). They are living before Calvary, but it is difficult not to believe that these men who had left vocations, families, friends, and homes to follow Jesus and to love Him are not proleptic beneficiaries of that atonement yet to come in the annals of time but which had already transpired in the bosom of the eternal God. If Abraham was among the redeemed, certainly these are in the same category. They believe in the God of Abraham and that Jesus is His Christ. And as they make their way toward Jerusalem they go anticipating the manifestation of the Son of God.

As we have noted, a change takes place after the confession at Caesarea Philippi. There is a deeper intimacy between Christ and the Twelve. There is also a dramatic change in the subject of most of the stories. Now the stories are not about Christ; they are about His disciples. And what a disappointment. Not once does a disciple look good from the confession at Caesarea Philippi until after the Resurrection.

As they descend from the Mount of Transfiguration, He speaks of His resurrection. This is beyond their ken. At the foot of the mountain they find a distraught father who has brought his son, who has a mute spirit that often convulses him, to Jesus' disciples. But these disciples who, on other occasions, had power over such spirits (6:7; Luke 10:17) have dissipated that grace and are unable to help this needy one.

Jesus must upbraid them (9:19). That story begins the disappointing revelations of chapters 9 and 10. They have learned who Jesus is. Now they begin to learn who they are, and the picture is not a pretty one.

As they journey southward toward Jerusalem Jesus begins openly to share with them the nature of His mission as the Christ. He has come not to reign now but to suffer and die. He explains to them that in Jerusalem He will be arrested, not crowned. He will be killed but on the third day He will rise. Mark's comment on their response is simple: "They did not understand this statement, and they were afraid to ask" (9:32 NASB).

Now Mark picks up a theme introduced in Caesarea Philippi. It is the theme of the incomprehensibility of the Cross even for believers. You will remember that, after Peter confessed Jesus as the Christ, Jesus spoke for the first time openly and explicitly about the Cross. Peter turned to the Christ whom he had just confessed and rebuked Him (8:32). Then Jesus turned to His disciple and spoke the strongest language used anywhere in the Gospels about another person: "Out of my way, Satan! Peter, your thoughts are not God's thoughts, but man's! (8:33 J.B. PHILLIPS).

Their hearts are His but they cannot think His thoughts. Thus Mark introduces the concept developed more fully by Paul of the carnal, fleshly mind (for example, Rom. 8:5ff.; 1 Cor. 3:1ff.; Gal. 5:16–26) as opposed to the mind of Christ (Phil. 2:1–21). They know who Christ is, believe in Him, love Him, have left all to follow Him, but their inner beings have not yet been freed to think His thoughts and freely choose His ways. Some of the old is still with them.

When they come to Capernaum that evening, He inquires about a conversation the Twelve had from which they obviously had excluded Him. With embarrassment they report that they had argued about who would hold what position in the government of the messianic kingdom, which they knew

He was going to establish since He was the Christ. He now begins to instruct them more fully in the fact that His ways are not their ways. His kingdom will not come by power but by meekness and self-sacrifice.

John informs Him that they had done one good thing that day. They had found a man casting out devils in Christ's name. They had rebuked the one who ministered in Christ's name because he was not one of their band. The arrogance of rebuking one for using a power to meet human need, a power the Twelve had once had but had now dissipated, seems to have been completely missed by John. He was blind to the irony.

Jesus speaks to them about children (9:37, 42). It is not the mighty of the earth who represent best His kingdom; it is the child (cf. Matt. 18:1ff.). The disciples must turn their value systems upside down if they are to think His thoughts and be part of His kingdom. It was after these discussions that some parents brought their children to Jesus for His blessing. The disciples rebuke the parents because in their minds they think He is too important and that *their* business is too great for Jesus to bother with children (10:13–16). It hardly seems an accident that the story that follows is of the rich young ruler whose false values cause him to miss the kingdom. Disciples, brainwashed by a fallen world, are still thinking and wishing in the categories of this fallen world.

Jesus speaks again of what is to happen to Him when He gets to Jerusalem. The response is that James and John request the posts at His right and left in the kingdom they are sure He will establish. The other disciples hear of the request of James and John and they are angry. They too have their minds on place and position. They cannot think His thoughts. He thinks cross while they think crowns. They are still carnal. Again He tells them that the Son of man has not come to be served but to serve and to give His life as a ransom. The problem is not now to find what they can do to serve Him. There is a deep need in their own hearts to which they are oblivious but which must be faced.

One can almost hear Peter's response to these strange comments of Jesus about the sufferings, the Cross, and the Resurrection. "There He goes again. He obviously has this little litany He feels obligated to recite to us. I don't have the vaguest idea as to what He is talking about. But, if He feels better saying it, let Him say it." They love Him, believe in Him, but cannot think His thoughts nor understand His ways. They are still carnal.

One fascinating aspect of Mark's presentation of this story is the fact that this sad account of the blindness and obtuseness in the disciples is sandwiched between accounts of two miracles. The first in 8:22–26 is the story of the blind man in Bethsaida whom Jesus had to touch twice before he could see clearly. The second is the story of Bartimaeus in Jericho (10:46–52) to whom Jesus restored sight. Is this Mark's way of telling us that Jesus had no problem with physical blindness, that it is the blindness of His own disciples as well as the sins of the world that necessitate the Cross? The reality is that this blindness and self-interestedness were unrelieved until Pentecost.

In light of chapters 8–10 it should be no surprise to us that the disciples' performance is less than exemplary during that final week in Jerusalem. They are looking for the fulfillment of Israel's hopes (13:4) but not by way of a cross. Reflective of this is the indignation of some at the waste of spikenard on Jesus' head, which He sees as preparation for His burial (14:8). As He prays in agony in Gethsemane for strength to face the next day, His best, Peter, James, and John, sleep unsuspectingly. When Peter realizes that his Master has been arrested, he is so afraid for himself that he cannot admit to a servant girl in the court of the high priest that he is in any way identified with Jesus. As if to underscore his message about the Twelve, Mark mentions only the women as following

Christ, though at a distance during those final hours (15:40–41). He tells us that Mary Magdalene and Mary, the mother of Joses, observed where Jesus' body was buried. Is Mark telling us that, if it were not for the women, the disciples would not have known where to go on Sunday morning to find His tomb?

The good thing about all of this story is that Mark does not give the final chapter. We must turn to Acts for that. And what a delightful contrast! The eleven are now different men. They have been dramatically changed. There is a power in them not seen in those last six months with Christ. Peter and John heal the lame man at the gate of the temple (Acts 3:1ff.) and the disciples are used in miraculous ways to bless the needy (Acts 2:43; 8:6–8; 9:36ff.).

Something has also happened to their understanding. The Cross is now no tragedy. It is their glory, their message, and their method. They realize that Christ's sufferings and death had all been preindicated by the prophets and were the predetermined divine plan for the redemption of the world (Acts 3:17–18; 10:39–43). But more, their fear is gone. The same disciples who "forsook Him and fled" (Mark 14:50) when Jesus was arrested, now stare down the very officials who murdered their Master and say: "Whether it is right in the sight of God to listen to you more than to God, you judge. For we cannot but speak the things which we have seen and heard" (Acts 4:19–20). The rulers are astounded at their boldness and their perception.

Perhaps the most dramatic evidence of the change is not directly alluded to by Luke. It is everywhere obvious though in the text. The lust for place and position is gone. Self-interest no longer dominates their thoughts. The glory of Christ and the establishment of His kingdom are their passion. Self-sacrifice, not the protection of their own interests, has become for them a privilege, a way of life. Luke tells us that they could now rejoice that they were counted worthy to suffer shame for

Christ's name. The stuff of martyrdom now moves within their hearts.

They had learned who He was and had given themselves to Him. As they walked with Him, they found out who they were, the depths of their own self-interest, and their incapacity to free themselves from its hindering claims. It was only when they had seen the Cross and had been filled with the Spirit that they found God's intended freedom.

It is clear from Scripture that God wants to fully possess and control our hearts. John Bunyan illustrates this in his classic *The Holy City*. When Immanuel had driven Diabolus and all his forces out of the city of Man-soul, Diabolus presented a petition to Immanuel. He requested that he might maintain just a small part of the city. This request Immanuel rejected. Then Diabolus begged to have at least a small room within the walls. Immanuel's response was firm: "He should have no place in it at all, no, not to rest the sole of his foot." Every person who has experienced the regenerating power of Christ knows that this is what ought to be.

The reality though is another matter. Note the following bit of poetry.

> Make me a captive, Lord
> And then I shall be free;
> Force me to render up my sword,
> And I shall conqueror be.
> I sink in life's alarms
> When by myself I stand;
> Imprison me within Thine arms
> And strong shall be my hand.

This matchless prayer was not written by a sinner seeking forgiveness. It was written by George Matheson when he was a forty-eight-year-old Scottish clergyman known for his piety. The cry of Matheson's soul was that there was still the strong potential for rebellion within his regenerated heart. It may be significant for our purposes to note that this hymn was written some eight or more years after Matheson had given the church the timeless "O Love That Wilt Not Let Me Go."

And note this expression of anguish from a young follower of Christ struggling to be fully Christian.

> I saw the humility of Jesus, and my pride; the meekness of Jesus, and my temper; the lowliness of Jesus, and my ambition; the purity of Jesus, and my unclean heart; the faithfulness of Jesus, and the deceitfulness of my heart; the unselfishness of Jesus, and my selfishness; the trust and faith of Jesus, and my doubts and unbelief; the holiness of Jesus, and my unholiness; I got my eyes off everything but Jesus and myself, and I came to loathe myself.[1]

This was not the cry of a sinner seeking conversion. This was the testimony of Samuel Brengle, a young believer who had walked with Christ long enough that, like the disciples in Mark 8–10, he was able to see himself and the depth of sinfulness that remained within after conversion.

All of this precipitated for me the battle of a lifetime. I found that Matheson and Brengle spoke for me. I knew that there was still within me a resistance that kept me from belonging wholly to the One whom I loved. I had never felt so sinful and so unclean even before I found Christ. How could I ever find freedom from the reserve within that still resisted the Holy Spirit?

It was then I began to discover that all of salvation is by grace. We are as helpless to sanctify ourselves as we are to regenerate our own souls. There is a grace that can deal with sin and guilt. There is a grace in Christ that can also deal with the unsurrendered self. In brokenness I pleaded for that grace.

It was not an easy moment. I discovered that the ego within will not surrender of itself. It must be crucified. So I prayed, "Lord, can You break the knuckles of these hands with which I am holding on to a corner of me for me?" His response was, "Yes, may I?" In terror and desperation I said, "Please!"

The result was that He did just that. His Spirit came and flooded my inner being. With that filling came a release and a cleansing. I felt a freedom I had not known before. That freedom was the freedom now to surrender to the One I loved. And in that surrender came fulfillment. The love that I had known in measure now filled and possessed me. I remembered that word of Christ that Peter could not grasp when it was spoken to him: "Whoever desires to come after Me, let him deny himself, and take up his cross, and follow Me. For whoever desires to save his life will lose it, but whoever loses his life for My sake and the gospel's will save it" (Mark 8:34–35). And I loved it. For in discovering the truth of which Christ there spoke, I knew that I had found the key to victorious Christian living. The days since have joyously confirmed it.

Recently I was reminded of a quotation I could not forget. It was a prayer with God's response.

"Father, I have a problem.
It's me!"
"Child, I have an answer.
It's ME!"

Thank God there is in Christ not only an answer for the problem of my sins, there is also an answer to the problem of me. That great salvation is the promise of victory to those who will receive it.

Note

1. Clarence W. Hall, *Samuel Logan Brengle: Portrait of a Prophet* (Atlanta, Ga.: The Salvation Army Supplies and Purchasing Dept., 1933).

About the Author

Jack Hayford is senior pastor of The Church On The Way, the First Foursquare Church of Van Nuys, California. While dean of students at LIFE Bible College in 1969, he was given the "temporary" assignment of pastoring eighteen people, an embryonic church that now numbers more than eight thousand. A recognized leader in the pentecostal/charismatic movement, Hayford is known throughout the larger evangelical world as a bridge builder, ministering in major congresses and conventions of all varieties. He is able to build those bridges because of his fidelity to Scripture and irenic spirit. Hayford has authored more than two dozen books and nearly five hundred songs and hymns, several of them—like "Majesty"—award-winning. On radio and television Hayford ministers over more than fifteen hundred stations and cable systems. He and his wife, Anna, have four children and nine grandchildren.

About This Chapter

In the vivid prose for which he is noted, Jack Hayford does a remarkable thing—he speaks powerfully to both charismatic and noncharismatic simultaneously, without directly addressing either and without speaking down to anyone. In his "Seven Points of Pursuit," when he speaks of "a heart alive with expressive worship," "a tongue aglow with prayer and praise," and "a posture acknowledging the invisible war," many a noncharismatic congregation needs to listen. But when he speaks of "a mind attuned to . . . the Word," "a walk advancing through holiness of life," and "an eye and an ear alert to a global harvest," many charismatics should take careful note. Occasionally pentecostal distinctives come through, but in clearly outlining the central themes of victorious Christian living from a charismatic perspective, the major effect of this chapter is to set afire any heart that is in thirsty pursuit of God.

Victorious Christian Living from a Charismatic Perspective

by Jack Hayford

The shepherd had paused at the stream for about twenty minutes now, allowing his sheep to be refreshed as he prepared to lead them down the long mountain slope, returning from summer's pastures to winter's at a lower elevation. Suddenly, the thick brush immediately to his right—where the hillside descended precipitously toward the valley—was bristling with movement, and from the distance a high-pitched howl floated up the gorge. Then, more scrambling than running, and clawing for footing without any of its usual grace, an antelope pushed through and out from the bushes—its eyes showing panic and one side of its body badly scratched from recent battle.

Having gained steadfast footing, the magnificent creature stood to its full height, its chest heaving as it gasped for air to service the need of its wildly beating heart. Stressed by its struggle to escape the predator below and strained by its climb to safety, it turned its head this way and that to discern its security at this brookside setting. As it did, the shepherd slowly moved backward—away from the antelope—seeking to assure it that a place of peace had been found. And he smiled, as the beast now ambled slowly to the water's edge, furtively looked about once more, and then bowed its head to begin drinking deeply of the quietly bubbling stream.

It would be later that day, as the sheep found their resting place for the night and as the fire that had warmed his meal shone forth its guardian flames against night prowlers who would disturb his flock, that the shepherd took a guitar-like instrument from the protective bag that had been slung over his shoulder. The sheep pricked up their ears as they heard the familiar strumming, and after several minutes of contemplation even as he played, he began to sing:

> As the deer pants for the water brooks,
> So pants my soul for You, O God.
> My soul thirsts for God, for the living God. (Ps. 42:1–2)

The Seeker's Song

Though imagination has created the scene for David's heartfelt cry to the Lord, the spirit of his quest is unexaggerated. There is no one who is honest about the pressures of twenty-first-century living who would pretend that the soul isn't under violent attack. The adversary of all humankind is stalking souls by means of deception, roaring through circumstances to induce fear, and ripping and shredding human lives as too many succumb to his assault. But there is a people who have not been overcome, a host of saints who have sought higher ground—to elude the enemy—and who have found secure refuge and a place to refresh the soul with living water.

So, David's song is the expression of millions today who are seeking a new dimension of fullness in Christ, who are opening to the Holy Spirit's assistance in finding triumphant life through the truth of God's Word and in the warmth of His presence. No thoughtful members of this multitude of seekers have launched their pursuit of such victorious living for so shallow a reason as a private quest for mere novelty or vain experience. Most are wise enough to know that the human soul can never be truly satisfied by emotion or sensation.

Still, in every sector of the body of Christ today, a breed of Christian is appearing who is gripped by a passion for fullness—who is unsatisfied to test the possibilities of anything less than what he or she sees to be the full potential of Holy-Spirit-filled living. At times, their passion may be misread by some, just as it is misrepresented by the few who suggest these seekers are "just interested in experiences" rather than desirous of a Bible-based, Christ-centered life.

But as the following outline reveals, the heartbeat of their passion is clearly rooted in Scripture. Thus, the true fruit of such passion will never produce an air of presumed superiority to others of different Christian tradition. Indeed, the pentecostal or charismatic believer's definition of "victory" will foremost be testified to as one of triumph over the flesh or the works of the devil, never as one of competition with others who love the Savior. So what constitutes that complete definition? Consider the following.

Seven Points of Pursuit

To begin, the components of victorious living must never be comprised of humanistic values. Nor are they transient values evolving with the passage of time, as though Christian victory is ever the product of clever nuances rather than abiding principles. If we are to pursue any goal with passion, the goal should first be proven one of biblical substance, and be accompanied by evidence that this value has always been a part of the lifestyle of God's people. Accordingly, the victorious living pursued with passion by any of this circle will be found to include: (1) worship, (2) the Word, (3) prayer, (4) holy living, (5) loving service, (6) spiritual warfare, and (7) evangelism. Let's look at these as passion pursues them, through:

- a heart alive with expressive worship.
- a mind attuned to the Spirit and the Word.
- a tongue aglow with prayer and praise.
- a walk advancing through holiness of life.
- a hand available to fellowship and ministry.
- a posture acknowledging the invisible war.
- an eye and an ear alert to a global harvest.

As I explore this outline, I ask you, dear reader, to allow me to do it from a subjective point of view, as a classical pentecostal or charismatic, as just another brother in Christ who has no point to make, other than his few discoveries garnered through daily seeking to live and exemplify "victorious living."

1. A Heart Alive with Expressive Worship

First, the fountainhead of all victorious living is found at one place alone: at the throne of God. It is from there that the Almighty's rule emanates, and it is where His Son, Jesus Christ, is now seated in triumph at His right hand. These two facts undergird all triumphant living: (1) that we have been restored to a relationship with our Creator, (2) through the accomplished victory of our Redeemer (Rev. 1:4–6).

It is these facts that provide both the grounds for and the glory in our worship of the Lord. Our worship is alive because our Redeemer is—and our praise finds triumphant expressiveness because joy and rejoicing are the obvious and logical responses to this fact. Jesus' exaltation produces our exultation, as our high praises declare His high triumph over sin, death, and hell (1 Peter 2:5, 9; Ps. 149:1–6).

We make much of triumphant worship, and it is an established priority of our lifestyle—as individuals and as congregations (Ps. 47:1–2). We worship the Father, Son, and Holy Spirit—taking note of the *majesty* of God's attributes (1 Chron. 29:10–13), the *marvels* of His grace (Eph. 2:4–10), and the *miracles* available through His presence (John 14:13–14). We not only worship *at* His throne, but with worship we welcome the presence *of* His throne's rule in our midst. For Psalm 22:3 testifies to the readiness of God to invade the presence of His people's praise with visitations of His grace and glory. Victory distills when He is near—and our worship not only acknowledges this fact, but we humble ourselves to experience, *now,* the transforming and delivering power of the God we praise (Ps. 63:1–5).

2. A Mind Attuned to the Spirit and the Word

Just as the throne of God is prioritized with our worship, His Word (and His Spirit's message to us through it) is central to our attention. As with all vital Christian traditions, the Bible is central to the authority governing the believer's life and living. I have hardly ever met a pentecostal/charismatic who would not testify that his experience in the Holy Spirit was especially meaningful above all other reasons, because the Word of God became more vibrantly alive and practically dynamic in his living through that experience and its maintenance.

Victorious living depends on the nourishing and the nurturing we receive from God's Word—both the food it gives for growth and the faith it stimulates for our living. But we approach the Scriptures less as an intellectual resource than as a spiritual book to be spiritually discerned (1 Cor. 2:10–13). This brings us to a distinct point of dependence upon the Holy Spirit, who we believe not only "breathed" the Word of the Scriptures (2 Tim. 2:16–17), but who also "breathes upon" those same eternal and changeless words of the Word to speak in our midst today (Rev. 2:29).

This does *not* mean that we "add to" anything of the completed pages of the Bible, but that we *do* allow the Holy Spirit to move among us in ways that bring an immediate prophetic quality to them—speaking into our moment if we'll tune to heaven's wavelength (1 Cor. 14:26). We do this because such examples as Paul's words to Timothy indicate that living and serving victoriously require a continued sensitivity to the "words" the Holy Spirit speaks to our heart, as we build our life on *the* Word (1 Tim. 1:18–19).

Jesus emphasized that "hearing" the Word of God is more than simply a matter of being under the sound of preaching or teaching, or even having read or memorized the Word (as vital as all those disciplines certainly are). He pointed to the fact that human hearts "hear" (i.e., "receive" God's Word) to different degrees, and the degree of a person's "hearing" determines the degree of that person's fruitfulness (Mark 4:13-20). So we keep our minds attuned to heaven's broadcast band, knowing the Word is made alive by the presence of the Holy Spirit, allowing the One who authored the Holy Scriptures to write them into our hearts (Jer. 31:33; 2 Cor. 3:1–3).

3. A Tongue Aglow with Prayer and Praise

The first time the Holy Spirit ever moved upon the church of our Lord Jesus, He produced supernatural praises to God. The "tongues" of Pentecost were understood by listeners, not as a gospel message (which Peter preached later), but as a supernatural sign of God's presence as people exalted God with praise following their having waited in His presence with prayer (Acts 2:1–11). So it is, a pentecostal/charismatic employs the practice of speaking with tongues, not as an exercise of prideful display or public interruptiveness, but as a practical and private means of prayer and praise (1 Cor. 14:2, 39, 40).

The Word of God invites us to pray at two dimensions: Paul models this, saying, "I will pray with the spirit, and I will also pray with the understanding" (1 Cor. 14:15). Praying with "the understanding" employs one's native language, which we might describe as prayer in our "mother tongue." While praying "with the spirit," which extends beyond the mind's ability, might be described as prayer in our "Father tongue."

Such supernaturally assisted prayer is neither self-serving nor gratuitous exercise—neither practiced as a surrender to an emotional binge nor as a tokenistic show of supposed spiritual advancement. To the contrary, prayer "in the Spirit" requires a constant humility with gratitude for such a resource, and recommends a perceptive application to my prayer practice, seeing:

(1) I am directed to pray "in the Holy Spirit" as a means of building up my defenses against the darkness of the day or the drifting patterns of the neglectful (Jude 20); and,

(2) I am commanded to pray "always with all prayer and supplication in the Spirit," in recognition that this is the means by which others will be blessed by my intercession and also that the gospel will advance through Christian ministries (Eph. 6:18–20).

4. A Walk Advancing Through Holiness of Life

If God's Word reveals anything, it declares His desire that His people live as ones who are born of His paternity and behave as citizens of His kingdom: "Be holy, for I am holy" (1 Peter 1:13–16). There is no substitute for practical godliness. I cannot honestly make any experiential claim to "being filled," "worshiping in the Spirit," or "speaking in tongues" as a replacement for plain, daily godly living. Neither can I substitute any degree of "studying the Word," "discipling group activity," or "doctrinal purity" as my definition for a holy life.

The Bible announces the believer's pathway of victorious living as "overcoming the world" (1 John 5:4–5). This specifically calls us to a life that is motivated and measured by different values than those that guide the worldling, the person yet outside the life Jesus brings to us (Col. 3:1–17). That "world" is governed and manipulated by the "world spirit" (Eph. 2:1–3; 1 John 2:15–17); whereas we are called to draw on a new life power—the energy of the Holy Spirit, whose power alone can enable us to a godly lifestyle (Eph. 5:8–18).

Holy living is essentially manifest in (1) the way I relate to my family members (Eph. 5:21–6:4), (2) the moral integrity I maintain in obedience to God's Word and ways (Eph.

4:17–32), (3) the attitude I reveal to my neighbors, to my work associates (Eph. 6:5–9), (4) the unselfishness that characterizes my care toward others (Rom. 12:9–21), and (5) the prayerful and citizenlike behavior I show toward leaders— both in the church and in society (1 Tim. 2:1–3).

It is also important to remember that true "victorious living" will produce holy living that is warm and real, not merely a pious pretense—a mere set of learned behavioral patterns of religious robotry. Holy living is in our progressive growth in the loving qualities, gentle grace, and generous ways of our Lord Jesus Christ (Rom. 14:14; Gal. 2:20). *He* is the definition of "holy living," not a list of churchly requirements. And accordingly, I am more likely to become a godly "overcomer" by drawing near to Jesus, than in attempting to perfect a set of "proof patterns" attempting to verify some superior status as a "better than others" Christian.

In the last analysis, true holiness will be manifest in true humility, which, first, will be lovingly receptive toward all people (seeing this is God's way, Rom. 5:8). It will also keep me from comparisons with others (2 Cor. 10:12), while maintaining my own walk with God and refusing to take it upon myself to "improve" the behavior of others by issuing my selfrighteous demands.

5. A Hand Available to Fellowship and Ministry

There is no pathway of victory that can be walked alone. Nor is there anything of valid "victorious living" that doesn't include relationship with and service to others. Vibrant Christian living keeps its hand outreached—(1) available to join with others in loving unity (Eph. 4:1–4), and (2) available to touch with a servant-spirited compassion all who are lost, unclean, or sinful (1 Cor. 5:9, 10; Jude 22–23). Jesus earmarked these grand priorities, saying, "A new commandment I give to you, that you love one another; as I have loved you" (John 13:34); and "He who is greatest among you, let him be . . . as he who serves" (Luke 22:26).

Love for one another and a spirit of gracious service toward the needy and the lost have always been hallmarks of the "victory life" and are prized values among most pentecostals/charismatics. Because a passionate pursuit of life in the Spirit of Jesus calls us to "seek peace and pursue it" among believers rather than nitpicking at our differences (1 Peter. 3:10–11). And that same passion will relentlessly keep a tenderhearted love for the lost—however bent, perverse, or sinful their ways (Luke 19:1–10).

Strangely enough, successful invasions of bitter separatism or judgmental criticism into the Christian community are usually born of a supposed quest for preserving purity and righteousness. But separatism and judgmentalism are tragic misapplications of biblical purity and discernment. So, the Spirit-filled pathway calls us to take caution, lest we tolerate anything of a "separatist" pride, which results in evicting the love Jesus commands us to have. It will keep me from ever demeaning or disdaining any believer in Jesus whose practices differ from mine, or whose doctrine may not be as "perfect" as I perceive mine to be. I'll also learn to avoid destructive judgmentalism (Luke 9:53–56), the spirit that enshrines anger toward such groups as abortionists, homosexuals, or unrighteous governmental leaders, and fails to express the loving compassion in passionate intercession—what their true situation should call from me.

So it is, biblical "victorious living" will find that "the narrow way" we have chosen to walk in Christ was never to give place to narrow-mindedness. A large heart, with a reaching hand, is always in tune with the Spirit of truth—who is more interested in revealing love that stoops to serve than a mind or tongue that exalts its superior morality or wisdom.

6. A Posture Acknowledging the Invisible War

Spiritual warfare is a large item on the agenda of the pentecostal/charismatic, and it is rooted in words of Jesus: "I will give you the keys of the kingdom of heaven," and "the gates of Hades shall not prevail . . ." (Matt. 16:19, 18). In this passage, the Savior announced His intent to "build My church," and He clearly links the church's victory over darkness to each believer's participation in that promise. The "keys" are ours to employ to see dark powers broken.

The apostle Paul also saw the church's expansion as directly linked to spiritual warfare. The classic passage in Ephesians 6:10–20 does more than simply *describe* the fact of our struggle against invisible powers (vv. 10–12) and *define* how we are to gird for battle against them (vv. 13–17). It also *directs* the action we're to take (vv. 18–20)—showing that prayer warriors hold the keys to "open doors" for the gospel's spread. This is the use Jesus had in mind for the "keys" of the kingdom to gain victory over the "gates of hell" (i.e., its sinister strategies, dark realms of dominion, and strongholds of bondage upon peoples and nations).

The realm of the demonic—of principalities, powers, world rulers of the darkness and wicked spirits in the spirit-realm (Eph. 6:12)—has been subjected to our Lord Jesus Christ (Eph. 1:15–23). In the wake of His cross, resurrection, and exaltation, the church has been commissioned to extend His victory. What was finished at the Cross (Col. 2:14, 15) continues to move toward its fullness in triumph as kingdom liberation reaches to every human and nation. Believing that this directive is not a call to mystical supernaturalism, but to practical action that "does business" in the invisible realm, we move into prayer and ministry . . . and with the following final objective.

7. An Eye and an Ear Alert to a Global Harvest

Just as the believer's *foundational* purpose is to glorify God in worship, so his *final* purpose in life is to spread the light of the gospel to everyone he can. The whole point of Christ's baptizing us with the Holy Spirit is that the message of His life and love may reach to the ends of the earth (Acts 1:5–8). It is a passionate issue—Jesus made it so.

- Jesus is the One who said "the harvest is great" and laborers are needed (Matt. 9:37–38).
- Jesus is the One who said to passionately pursue the harvest, because "it is ripe" now (John 4:35).
- Jesus is the One who said there is a limit to our opportunity for harvest, because "the night is coming when no one can work" (John 9:4).
- Jesus is the One who has set forth the awesome terror of the options—salvation or condemnation, eternal life in heaven or eternal perishing in hell (John 3:16, 36).

This same passion motivated the apostle Paul: "For the love of Christ controls us, having concluded this, that one died for all, therefore all [outside Him] died" (2 Cor. 5:14 NASB). And it is with this conviction, that eternal issues are at stake when evangelism is either neglected or advanced, that we open our eyes to a global vision and our ears to the Holy Spirit's directives. We gauge our faithfulness to the gospel by our faithfulness to spread it. And we seek to minister the fullness of Christ's person and power in every way—the saving life of Jesus, the healing power of Jesus, and the delivering mightiness of Jesus. The full gospel offers freedom to the full human being, as Jesus said,

> The Spirit of the LORD is upon Me,
> Because He has anointed Me
> To preach the gospel to the poor;
> He has sent Me to heal the brokenhearted,
> To proclaim liberty to the captives
> And recovery of sight to the blind,
> To set at liberty those who are oppressed;
> To proclaim the acceptable year of the LORD. (Luke 4:18–19)

The victorious life we live in Christ is born of His power as He *forgives* us and spread by His power as He *fills* us. And as this pattern is propagated by our openness to His Spirit, He will continue to replicate His life and His ministry through ordinary believers touched by His extraordinary grace—by His power and for His glory!

About the Author

Elmer Towns is one of evangelicalism's most prolific authors, having written fifty books and more than two thousand articles, both scholarly and popular. Several of his books have been bestsellers, and one, *The Names of the Holy Spirit*, was the 1995 recipient of the Gold Medallion Award of the Christian Booksellers Association, named Book of the Year. Towns has been in academia most of his life, serving as president of Winnipeg Bible College for five years and as cofounder with Jerry Falwell of Liberty University. Today he is dean of the School of Religion at Liberty. He and his wife, Ruth, have three children and four grandchildren.

About This Chapter

The key to living free and fulfilled is faith, but there are many views of what faith is. This chapter examines faith in detail, identifying biblical strands of teaching about faith and also noting the various schools of thought about what faith really is and what it can be expected to accomplish. The author maintains a clinical detachment; through identifying views that violate Bible teaching, his emphasis is on pointing toward some of the fundamental teachings of Scripture about faith, themes on which all can agree. Though there is reference to faith for living a victorious life, the focus of the chapter is more on faith to see God do mighty works. This is as it should be because both the "say it faith" movement and the "power encounter" movement focus more on ministry than on living godly lives. And those are the movements that have impacted the evangelical view of faith. Elmer Towns is well suited to address this issue, having researched and written a number of volumes on the theme of faith.

Alternative Views of Faith

by Elmer Towns

I was "born again" on July 25, 1950, and entered Columbia Bible College seven weeks later. There were many factors that unmistakably changed my life, but none of the transforming experiences were as influential as the faith for answers to prayer by faculty and students. The president, Robert C. McQuilkin, had announced a faith goal of $332,000 for the completion of the new women's dorm for Thanksgiving 1950. As a student, I constantly prayed for that goal, and it was more than a casual or repetitious prayer; the faith goal became three things to my life. First, it was an enormous burden that we *must* have this answer to prayer. Second, it was a captivating goal that included new students like myself who were not included in the planning or construction of the new women's dorm. The faith goal captivated me. Third, it was a faith-stretching goal because I had trouble trusting God for room and board, much less $332,000.

Electricity went through the crowd when Dr. McQuilkin announced that we had reached the financial goal. What I thought was empirically impossible (because of my little faith), became a stimulus to me. As I reflect on that experience, I am certain I learned that God was much bigger than my need of room and board, that: (1) God was big enough to supply a three-story, modern-constructed building, (2) faith could provide money, (3) the people of Columbia Bible

College could touch God with their faith, and (4) I was not a man of faith, but it would be a challenge to learn more about faith and to experience faith to move mountains.

Going through Bible college, I saw God miraculously provide funds for fellow students so they could finish their training. I saw God provide for the monthly faculty salaries. I also saw the same miraculous supply for those going to the mission field. In a small way I experienced God's financial provision, although I worked a secular job both in Bible college and graduate school.

As a pastor, my faith was severely tested, I wanted to know I could trust God for the salvation of the lost . . . to touch young people to surrender to full-time service, and to raise money for programs, buildings, and the support of missionaries. As a pastor, I had limited success in growing churches, constructing buildings, and the implementation of new programs. Although I learned much about faith, and saw God honor a few feeble steps of faith, I could hear the Lord say so often, "O you of little faith" (Matt. 14:31).

Then I became a college president, and I remembered the example of Robert C. McQuilkin. I remembered the example of $332,000 for the new women's dormitory plus the monthly provision of finances for faculty salaries. Winnipeg Bible College, Winnipeg, Canada, was a "faith institution" that believed in a policy of "full information without solicitation." This means I wrote prayer letters to share the financial needs of the school with our prayer warriors, but we did not have a stewardship department, a person to raise funds, or any programs to provide finances for growth. As a college president, I felt the pressure of being a spiritual leader, that is, a man of faith to provide for the college's needs. However, each time I had to call the faculty into the office on Friday afternoon and tell them that there was not enough money for salaries, I felt my lack of faith. In those Friday afternoon experiences, each faculty would tell how much they desperately needed to make it through the week, and we would divide up whatever money was in the college treasury. Rather than feeling the victory of Robert McQuilkin, who often said, "Thanks be to God who always leads us in triumph in Christ" (2 Cor. 2:14), I often felt defeated. I knew I was not a man of great faith.

Both as a pastor and college president, I searched desperately for faith and struggled to grow my faith. On several occasions I prayed all night for the needs of Winnipeg Bible College, begging God for money. In these experiences, I would pray so intently that I came to the place where I talked myself into confidence, absolutely knowing that the money would be there the next day. When I went to the post office box, the money was not there. Then I rationalized that God had answered the prayer, the money had been mailed, but had not arrived at our mailbox yet. Over the next three or four days the money did not come in. Again, these experiences undermined my experience in faith, rather than built up my faith.

Wrong Assumptions About Faith

Now that I look back on my growing experiences, I understand why my "faith expressions" did not always bring about an answer.[1] I saw that even a sincere person could express his faith in a wrong way or have a wrong view of faith. In the first place, I was viewing faith more as a human ability or a human skill, as one views his ability to speak in public or his skills to study the Bible. I had come to believe that the ability to get things by faith depends on the ability of the one who exercises faith. I had missed the fact that one's faith is measured by one's source of faith, that is, God Himself.

Second, I looked at faith as a muscle to grow and become stronger. Faith was measured in one's ability to hang on to God. When, in fact, the nature of faith is not in doing more for God, but surrendering and letting Him do more through you. A third mistake was blind faith, that is, blinded to the total plan and purpose of God as revealed in Scripture. I had to learn the lesson of how faith and works were interrelated, as taught by James: "Faith by itself, if it does not have works, is dead" (James 2:17). A farmer can have deep faith that God will give him an abundant harvest, but he must plow the field, plant the seed, and work diligently to harvest it. Also, the farmer must have the best skills, the best soil, and the best tools to produce the greatest harvest.

My failures as a Bible college president were faith failures. I was wrongly trusting God because I was wrongly claiming His promises, even though I was sincere in heart. I went to the board of directors and told them our great dreams were not being realized because, "you do not have because you do not ask" (James 4:2). Even though I took that verse out of context in applying it to asking for funds, I did mention that James points out the problem of spiritual pride and that perhaps God was not answering our prayer because, "you ask and do not receive, because you ask amiss, that you may spend it on your pleasures" (James 4:3). As president, I had to make sure that the exercise of my faith was not for material gain or for ego, but for the glory of God. However, when faith was properly understood, Winnipeg Bible College went on to become accredited by the American Association of Bible Colleges, and chartered by the Province of Manitoba, and moved into its most productive days of training young people for the mission field.

Wrong Assumptions by the Faith Teachers

There has grown up another movement to trust God by faith, called a faith movement. This movement, also called a Word of Faith movement, claims to be an innovation, previously unknown and unused by historic Protestant Christianity. The father of this faith movement was Essek William Kenyon, born in 1867, whose view can be summarized in the statement,

"What I confess, I possess," a view often used by many prosperity preachers.[2] One of the modern-day proponents is Frederick K. C. Price, who says, "If you have bicycle faith, all you're gonna get is a bicycle."[3] Yet Price goes on to let people know that if you have his type of faith, that is, Rolls Royce faith, you, like him, can drive a Rolls Royce.

One verse faith teachers often quote is Mark 11:22: "So Jesus answered and said to them, 'Have faith in God.'" Most of this movement will translate this verse to read, "Have the faith of God." They are teaching that your faith is insufficient to accomplish great things, but "God is a faith God"[4] and if you get "the faith of God," you get power, or enablement, that others don't have. Since God can do anything, you now have God's faith, so you can do anything. Probably the best-known current followers of this movement are Kenneth Copeland, Kenneth Hagin, Benny Hinn, and Frederick K. C. Price. They would teach (1) that God is a faith being, (2) that there is a God kind of faith available to people today, and (3) that God's power is released by the "word of faith" so that they can literally bring into existence whatever they request.

As a result, faith teachers can accomplish the miraculous: they can drive out devils of sickness and affliction, heal all manner of illness including AIDS, raise the dead, pronounce judgement on their enemies even to death, bring into existence vast amounts of money including yachts and cars, plus other divine interventions. All this is the result of their word of faith.

Kenneth Copeland teaches that the faith formula can actually penetrate what he calls the Holy of Holies by (1) seeing or visualizing whatever you need, whether physical or financial, (2) staking your claim on Scripture, and (3) speaking it into existence.[5]

While Mark 11:22 is not the only verse used by faith teachers to make faith claims, the Greek of Mark 11:22, *Echete, pistin, theou,* is an "objective genitive" according to

A. T. Robertson, which simply means that the noun (in this case, *theou*), is the object of the action. Robertson states, "It is not the faith that God has, but the faith of which God is the object."[6]

Faith teachers desire what people of all ages desire, power with God and power over other people. They have (1) made faith the source of power, not God, (2) made their words the source of power, not God's Word, (3) made themselves the source of God's power, hence elevating themselves over God's purpose in our lives of suffering, poverty, trials, and sickness. Obviously, no one wants to suffer physically or financially, but God's purpose is our maturity, "to be like Jesus," and for that sometimes pain and suffering is needed. The chief end of man is not to avoid difficulty, but to glorify God (by worship) and enjoy Him forever (by obedience).

Toward a Biblical Understanding of Faith

We cannot arrive at a biblical understanding of faith by simply pointing out the abuses of our faith. Nor can we learn to exercise great faith by analyzing the weaknesses of others. To know and acquire great faith, we must come back to the Word of God. In this section, we will analyze six expressions of faith found in the Word of God. Note, there is only one kind of faith, but it is expressed in six ways.

1. Doctrinal Faith

Throughout the New Testament "the faith" and "doctrine" are used interchangeably. When faith has an article preceding it as in "the faith," it means "the statement of faith." Therefore, to correctly understand faith, or correctly apply faith to "move mountains," we must have a complete and accurate understanding of doctrinal faith, or the teaching of the Bible.

The apostle Paul certainly recognized the importance of correct doctrine. He constantly opposed those who sought to change the faith. Perhaps he was concerned about accurate doctrine because of his own experience. When, as Saul of Tarsus, he was persecuting the church, he thought his doctrine was accurate and that he was serving God. But he was wrong. When he met Christ on the Damascus road, he gained a living faith that changed what he believed (content) and how he lived. Because he understood the abuses of wrong doctrine, Paul talked about those who had departed from the faith (1 Tim. 4:1) and denied the faith (1 Tim. 5:8). At the end of his life, the apostle was able to say, "I have kept the faith" (2 Tim. 4:7). Jude challenged his readers to "contend earnestly for the faith" (Jude 3).

If we want to have a growing biblical faith, we need to ground it on a complete, comprehensive, and correct knowledge of God. A certain woman once heard someone compliment her great faith. "I have not a great faith," she responded, "I have a little faith in a great God."

Doctrinal faith is both the beginning and the test of our Christianity. If our statement of faith is wrong, then our personal faith is misplaced. We must begin with a correct statement of faith, and we must build both saving faith and "mountain moving" faith on that.

2. Saving Faith

A person becomes a Christian by faith. "For by grace you have been saved through faith" (Eph. 2:8). When the Philippian jailor cried out "What must I do to be saved?" he was exhorted to exercise belief, the verb expression of faith. "Believe on the Lord Jesus Christ, and you will be saved, you and your household" (Acts 16:31). Obviously, we must have saving faith based on correct doctrinal faith before we can exercise "mountain moving" faith.

3. Justifying Faith

Whereas saving faith is an experiential encounter with Jesus Christ, justifying faith is nonexperiential. When we place our faith in Jesus Christ, we are justified, that is, we are declared righteous. Note, we are not *made* righteous, for we

are still sinners, sinners saved by grace, and we stand before God in the righteousness of His Son, Jesus Christ. Justification is not something that we feel with our senses, but something that happens to our record in heaven. God is the One who performs the act of justification (Rom. 8:34). Man is the one who receives the action and is justified (Rom. 5:1). Justification is the judicial act of God whereby He justly declares righteous all those who believe in Jesus Christ. Paul declares, "From faith to faith" (Rom. 1:17), which means from the experience of saving faith into the position of being justified by faith, "*ek pisteos eis pistin*." How does this influence "mountain moving" faith? Because we are His legal children we can go to God knowing we have access to Him. It is an act of faith when we act on our new relationship to God as His child. He will hear us when we request things according to His will.

4. Indwelling Faith

The Bible teaches that a person cannot overcome sin and sinful habits by himself. Faith is the secret of the victorious Christian life. "This is the victory that has overcome the world—our faith" (1 John 5:4). Even beyond triumphant living, a person can walk in moment-by-moment communion with God. A medieval monk described this victory as "practicing the presence of God." This life of victory and fellowship is made available by the indwelling of Jesus Christ (John 14:21). When a person becomes a Christian, Christ comes into his or her life (John 1:12). The believer has union and communion with Christ (John 15:5; 14:20). Not only does Christ dwell within the believer, the power of Christ is available to him. Paul testified, "Christ lives in me; and the life which I now live in the flesh I live by faith in the Son of God" (Gal. 2:20). The secret of victorious living is allowing the life of Jesus Christ to flow through us. Believers must surrender their fears and rebellion to Christ. In so doing, they find a new indwelling faith to overcome their problems. Paul described this "new faith" that comes from Christ, "the promise by faith in Jesus Christ [that] might be given to those who believe" (Gal. 3:22). Therefore, to get "mountain moving" faith, we do not have to "hold on tighter," but we must surrender to the One who indwells us. We let go.

5. Living by Faith

This is also called daily faith. Paul explained this faith expression: "We walk by faith, not by sight" (2 Cor. 5:7). He also commanded, "The just shall live by faith" (Rom. 1:17). When a Christian is living by faith, he is obeying the principles of God's Word in every area of life. He puts his faith in God for victory over sin, for joy, for fruit, wisdom, illumination of the Word, and for God's leading in his daily life. Beyond these spiritual qualities, those who walk by faith must trust God for physical protection, food, clothing, and a roof over their heads. Those who go beyond daily necessities and trust God with "mountain moving" faith, obviously, must be living by faith, that is, obeying the principles of the Bible.

6. The Spiritual Gift of Faith

Among the many and varied spiritual gifts of the Holy Spirit to the body of Christ corporately and believers individually is this ability to serve Him by faith. God supernaturally gives us the ability to serve Him by exercising faith (Rom. 12:7). This is more than the gift of salvation. This is called a "serving gift" or an ability whereby a person serves God by exercising faith.[7] Because not everyone gets the same results when exercising their gifts, so not everyone gets the same results when they exercise their gift of faith. Paul explained that gifts differ: "Having then gifts differing according to the grace that is given to us" (Rom. 12:6). God has given some greater faith to enable them effectively to carry out their ministry in a greater way.

George Mueller had great answers to prayer; perhaps his secret was the gift of faith (Mueller denied he had this gift). The outstanding thing about his life was his faith in God to provide the needs of the orphanage in Bristol, England. Once the dining-room tables were empty, there was no food in the kitchen, and more than two thousand hungry orphans waited for dinner. Mueller exercised faith and thanked God for the meal that was not there. Then the driver of a broken wagon knocked at the door to tell he had a wagon full of food that could not be delivered. Mueller had an ability to trust God that most do not have.

An Analysis of the Gift of Faith

I was still intrigued by how certain men and women were able to move mountains. This became my doctrinal project at Fuller Theological Seminary, Pasadena, California, "An Analysis of the Gift of Faith in Church Growth." I saw in certain people an ability to "move mountains" that others didn't have . . . contemporaries such as Bill Bright, Billy Graham, Jerry Falwell, Robert C. McQuilkin, and other great men in history such as John Wesley, Martin Luther, and John Calvin. I wanted to know, did they have a gift from God to trust Him for greater things? Did they have a gift of faith that was greater than that of most believers? Could others get this gift of faith? How could the gift grow? In my doctrinal project I determined that there were three basic interpretations of the spiritual gift of faith. First, the *instrumental view,* which appeared to be the traditional or historical view. Second, the modern-day evangelical view, which is the *insight view*. Third, the *intervention view* held primarily by pentecostals and the third-wave (i.e., those who believe signs and wonders are operative today) plus other modern-day entrepreneurial leaders with dynamically growing works (evangelicals), who are not primarily pentecostal/charismatic in persuasion.

1. The Gift of Faith as an Instrument

The gift of faith is interpreted to be the ability of the Christian to use the instrument of Christianity to carry out the work of God in the world. In Ephesians 6:10–18, Paul describes the Christian who fights the enemy with faith and other instruments. The instruments he uses are truth (v. 14), righteousness (the knowledge of imputed perfection, v. 14), the gospel (v. 15), the helmet of salvation (v. 17), and the sword that is the Word of God (v. 17).

Howard Carter, a Pentecostal, follows this definition: "The gift of faith can be defined as faith imparted by the Spirit of God for protection in times of danger, or for divine provision, or it may include the ability to impart blessing."[8] This definition does not include insight or the intervention of God. The purpose of the gift of faith includes the ministries that God has already promised, such as protection, provision, and blessing. Later, Carter describes the gift of faith with more intentionality. "This remarkable gift brings into operation the powers of the world to come; it causes God to work for you."[9]

John of St. Thomas, a Roman Catholic, suggested a traditional view in his discussion of the gift of faith: "Faith believes in God . . . without involving itself in inquiry or judgment concerning matters of faith. It performs no operation other than that of believing."[10] Accordingly, instrumental faith would be available to all believers, not just a few gifted individuals who build large churches or accomplish great projects for God.

Also, the instrumental view would make faith a response to or an ability to use the Word of God. This says nothing about the gift of faith uniquely giving a vision of service, or solving a crisis or unique problems. The instrumental view is more conformable to a historic Protestant view; i.e., God does not necessarily do miracles today, but works through the means of grace and according to His laws. Miracles or signs are viewed as a demonstration of authority to validate the message from God; hence, there is no longer a need for miracles because the content of revelation is complete (Jude 3). This also implies that God does not supernaturally intervene in the ongoing affairs of life, but rather He works through the means of grace (the instruments, including faith) that He has already supplied. Therefore, the interventional gift of faith (the third view) is believed by some as having properties similar to a miracle, hence not applicable to this age of grace.

2. The Gift of Faith as Insight

The gift of faith is the Holy Spirit giving the Christian the ability to see (envision) what God desires to perform or is able to perform regarding a project. After the Christian perceives what can be accomplished, he dedicates himself to its accomplishment. Perhaps the best-known definition of this view was suggested by Peter Wagner, who states: "The gift of faith is the special ability that God gives to some members of the Body of Christ to discern with extraordinary confidence the will and purposes of God for the future of His work."[11]

The emphasis of this definition is in the Christian's ability to see what God can do in a given situation; hence, it is implied that the Christian must see God's nature and purpose, and that is understood only through His Word. Kinghorn supports this second insight approach by stating, "The gift of faith is given to some Christians as a special ability to see the adequacy of God and to tap it for particular situations."[12] To this definition, Flynn adds that the gift of faith not only sees potentials but overcomes obstacles. "The gift of faith is a Spirit-given ability to see something that God wants done and to sustain unwavering confidence that God will do it, regardless of seemingly insurmountable obstacles."[13]

The insight view recognizes that God is the source of all Christian work, but the person who exercises faith senses his or her responsibility to carry out the project. This view places a high degree of responsibility and accountability on man. God is active in giving vision, but man is passive in receiving the vision; then he allows God to work through him to accomplish this project. This view implies that the work of God is accomplishing a project, but that He accomplishes it through the vision of His servant. It also implies that the work of God is accomplished in relationship to the ability of the worker—including man's knowledge, wisdom, motivational powers, and leadership ability. Of course, God gave these abilities to men, but God gave them through secondary means (training, reading, etc.). Faith energizes those means.

3. The Gift of Faith as Intervention

The gift of faith is the ability to move God to intervene divinely in a crisis that is facing a project, or change the expected order of events so that the work of God goes forward. This view holds that the gift of faith is active and the person is responsible, but God is the source of the gift and the source of accomplishment. Traditionally called the gift of miracles,[14] it features divine intervention in a miraculous way.

The leader usually has divine certainty that God will intervene (perhaps because of insight); hence, he makes an expression of faith. Gee explains:

> The spiritual gift of faith is a special quality of faith, sometimes called by our older theologians the "faith of miracles." It would seem to come upon certain of God's servants in times of special crisis or opportunity in such mighty power that they are lifted right out of the realm of even natural and ordinary faith in God—and have a divine certainty put within their soul that triumphs over everything. It is a magnificent fit and is probably exercised frequently with far-reaching results.[15]

Underwood's definition is not as long, but implies the same elements: "This is extraordinary wonder-working faith for a particular occasion."[16]

Harold Horton clearly indicates that the initiation of moving the mountain begins with man exercising the gift of faith. "The Gift of faith is a supernatural endowment of the Spirit whereby that which is offered or desired by man, or spoken by God, shall eventually come to pass."[17]

So, the third view of interventional faith is an ability given by the Holy Spirit whereby a person changes the events in a normal ministry, so that the work of God goes forward. The third view does not negate the two previous views, however, but incorporates them. The interventional view will use instrumental and insight faith to initiate interventional faith.

Principles to Take Away

1. Great Faith

Jesus offered the possibility of much greater results by faith than any of us have conceived and any of us have ever realized. He rebuked His disciples for "little faith" (Matt. 14:31) and exhorted them, "If you have faith as a mustard seed, you will say to this mountain, 'Move from here to there,' and it will move" (Matt. 17:20). Just because many have not fully exercised faith (average believers) and because others have a wrong basis for faith (modern faith teachers), no one should back away from the proper biblical exercise of faith. It is still possible for someone to exercise greater faith in God than anyone else in history, and to accomplish more for God than anyone else in history, and to influence the world more than anyone else in history. The possibility is there. Dwight L. Moody is credited with the statement, "The world has yet to see what can be accomplished by a person who is totally dedicated to God."

2. Great Gift

There seem to be certain individuals who have a greater "gift" of faith than the average believer. Some like Bill Bright, Billy Graham, James Dobson, and Henrietta Mears do exploits. But no one should back away from faith, thinking he is not equally gifted nor given the spiritual gift of faith. The Bible exhorts, "earnestly desire the best gifts" (1 Cor. 12:31) and "stir up the gift of God which is in you" (2 Tim. 1:6). Apparently Timothy got his gift as others applied their spiritual gift of preaching. "Do not neglect the gift that is in you, which was given to you by prophecy" (1 Tim. 4:14). Just as I was enormously challenged to more faith at Columbia Bible College, so we all can grow in our expression of faith by the example and ministry of those with a greater gift than ours.

3. Expression of Faith

At the very heart of faith is belief in God that should lead to our expression of faith. Sometimes those with the greatest faith have the greatest expressions in prayer requests, vision statements, construction plans, and financial goals. This does not mean they have surrendered to the faith teachers and "name it" in order to "claim it." While the faith teachers and historic Christianity are so very close because both appear to exercise "say it faith," in fact the two positions represent two different paradigms of faith. The faith teachers have an unlimited view of man's ability and faith's ability, and by implication, a limited role of deity in the faith process. The historic Christian position has a sovereign view of God, and since man is limited, along with the limitations of his thoughts and words, so man's expression of faith can never be omnipotent. We should never "command" God or "demand" anything by faith. We should say, "If the Lord wills, we shall live and do this or that" (James 4:15).

4. The Law of Faith

When Paul used the statement, "The law of faith" (Rom. 3:27), he was not telling us to have faith in the law, or that faith has a higher legal system to save us than the old law of Moses. Paul was telling us that there are principles and laws by which to express faith in God. When we follow the principles of faith we will get results, and we will fail when we violate these principles. Some of these principles that lead to success are: (1) we know and apply the Scriptures when exercising faith; (2) we submit to God's will, not demanding or commanding God to do our will; (3) we recognize our human limitations and the influence of lust on our desires; (4) God blesses our faith most when we seek to carry out His biblical commandments and when we seek His glory, not our own.

Conclusion

The more we study the inexhaustible depths of faith and reach for the loftiest expressions of faith; the more we search for new truths of faith, and experiment with innovative keys of faith; the more we idolize the giants of faith, or follow after what man would teach us about faith—the more we come back to faith's simple ingredients (for there is profundity in simplicity): "only believe" (Mark 5:36).

Notes

1. In response to my desire to understand faith I wrote three books about three areas of faith-expression. The first was *What the Faith Is All About* (Wheaton, Ill.: Tyndale, 1983), a study of doctrinal faith. The second was *Say It Faith* (Wheaton, Ill.: Tyndale, 1983), a study of how people could get greater faith. If I understood what the Faith Movement would do with the phrase "name it, claim it" I would never have used the title *Say It Faith*. The third was *Stepping Out on Faith* (Wheaton, Ill.: Tyndale, 1984), a study of the gift of faith and an analysis of the faith of ten men who planted churches.
2. E. W. Kenyon, *The Hidden Man*, 5th ed. (Lynwood, Wash.: Kenyon's Gospel Publishing Society, 1970), 98.
3. Frederick K. C. Price, *Praise the Lord* program on TBN (21 September 1990).
4. Charles Capps, *God's Creative Power* (Tulsa, Okla.: Harrison House, 1976), 2–3.
5. Kenneth Copeland, "Inner Image of the Covenant" (Fort Worth, Tex.: Kenneth Copeland Ministries, 1985) audiotape #01-4406, side 2. The summary of this argument is taken from Hank Hannegraaff., *Christianity in Crisis* (Eugene, Oreg.: Harvest House, 1993), 80. This volume has a complete analysis of the teachings of the Faith Movement and an outstanding refutation.
6. A. T. Robertson and W. Hershey Davis, *A New Short Grammar of the Greek New Testament*, 10th ed. (Grand Rapids: Baker, 1933, 1979), 227–28.
7. Some evangelicals call this an enabling gift (along with the gifts of knowledge, wisdom, and discernment) that is used to supplement the serving gifts. While I recognize this current identification, I feel Paul has a greater meaning because in the context of spiritual gifts he says, "Though I have all faith, so that I could remove mountains" (1 Cor. 13:2).
8. Howard Carter, *Spiritual Gifts and Their Operation* (Springfield, Mo.: Gospel Publishing House, 1968), 37.
9. Ibid., 42.
10. John of St. Thomas, *The Gift of the Holy Spirit* (London: Sheed and Ward, 1951), 243.
11. C. Peter Wagner, *Your Spiritual Gifts Can Help Your Church Grow* (Glendale, Calif.: Regal Books, 1979), 158.
12. Kenneth Cain Kinghorn, *Gifts of the Spirit* (Nashville: Abingdon 1976), 65.
13. Leslie B. Flynn, *Nineteen Gifts of the Spirit* (Wheaton, Ill.: Victor Books, 1974), 141.

14. Donald Gee, *Concerning Spiritual Gifts* (Springfield, Mo.: Gospel Publishing House, 1972), 43.
15. Ibid., 43.
16. B. E. Underwood, *The Gifts of the Spirit* (Franklin Springs, Ga.: Advocate Press, 1967), 31.
17. Harold Horton, *The Gifts of the Spirit* (Nottingham, England: Assembly of God Publishing House, 1934), 31.

About the Author

Throughout the last half of the twentieth century, Carl F. H. Henry has been considered by many the dean of evangelical theologians. Beginning with *Remaking the Modern Mind,* which shattered the complacency of evangelicals in 1948, to the massive, six-volume *God, Revelation, and Authority,* Henry has penned fifty volumes, many of them influential well beyond the evangelical world. A "founding father" of Fuller Theological Seminary, he has taught and lectured in many seminaries throughout the world. Henry also was founding and longtime editor of *Christianity Today.*

About This Chapter

In this section on "Alternative Views" we have heard from leading spokesmen for various evangelical positions on sanctification. In this chapter we look beyond the evangelical world to the largest context: what the dominant worldview has to say about the possibility of living a supernatural life. Modernism is said to be bankrupt, but postmodern thinking is even more opposed to the biblical, supernatural view of life. Henry gives a masterful summary statement of the contrast. The chapter is tight, heavy theological discourse, so why does it appear in this volume? Because postmodern thinking has penetrated if not permeated the thinking of Christian laypeople, as Henry points out, but it has also infiltrated the ranks of our theologians as well. It would not do to act as if this most powerful of contemporary ideological enemies did not exist. Henry shines a clear spotlight on that enemy.

The Victorious Life and the Postmodern Mind

by Carl F. H. Henry

The defection from moral absolutes has led to horrific ethical inversion not only in secular society but even among some professing church leaders. Gene Edward Veith, Jr. gives this staggering illustration:

> The killing of a child in the womb used to be considered a horrible, almost unspeakable evil. Today abortion is not just legal. It has been transformed into something good, a constitutional right. People once considered killing the handicapped, the sick and the aged an unthinkable atrocity. Today they see euthanasia as an act of compassion.[1]

The emergence of the term *postmodern* serves notice that the so-called "modern era" has had its day. Its reigning presuppositions—including exaggerated divine immanence, the sovereignty of human reason, the omnicompetence of science, the fluid nature of the self, and evolutionary progress toward utopia—are being rapidly abandoned. Unlimited faith in the scientific method as the supreme source of truth is crumbling. In its place a specifically postmodern alternative now calls for our generational loyalties.

The evangelical claim that Christianity is the one true religion is widely rejected today on the ground that one who affirms religious exclusivity in a pluralistic society is per se intolerant. Postmodernism has no role for objective truth.

The emerging contrast between the modern and the postmodern view, and their mutual departure from apostolic and medieval Christianity, evoke Princeton theologian Diogenes Allen's pointed comment that an immense intellectual revolution is under way, one "perhaps as great as that which marked off the modern world from the Middle Ages."[2]

Allen sees in the end of the modern era an opportunity for a resurgence of Christian orthodoxy now that Enlightenment confidence in human reason and in science is giving way. Thomas Oden too insists that Christianity has new credibility because the modernist assault is now seen to lack force. Others contend that postmodernism already so deeply penetrates the universities and the intellectual culture generally that the prospect is bleak for such a development. Veith senses the new opportunity, but he warns that postmodernism resolutely pursues its relativistic alternative.

David Harvey centers postmodernism's complaint against modernism in the latter's assumption (along with Christianity) of objective truth, universal meaning, and moral absolutes.[3] Veith quotes Ihab Hassan's summary of antitheses (here abridged):

> Modernists believe in determinacy; postmodernists believe in indeterminacy. . . . Modernism emphasizes purpose and design, postmodernism emphasizes play and chance. . . . Modernism seeks the logos, the underlying meaning of the universe expressed in language. Postmodernism . . . embraces silence, rejecting both meaning and the Word.[4]

Whereas postmodernism portrays the self as having neither an authentic individual identity nor a universally shared identity, Christianity much more profoundly discusses the human condition through its clear focus on the spiritually and morally divided self. It does so, moreover, with a critical eye both on the exuberant humanism of modernity and the anti-humanism of postmodernity. It affirms that man is distinct from animals because of what God the Creator and moral Judge has done and is doing. We are by divine creation embodied souls, with a destiny in eternity. Yet we are tragically implicated in the sin of Adam and are mutinous moral rebels on our own account. Christians can confront the postmodern deconstructionist analysis of society ventured in terms of power, money, and sex with an even more comprehensive contradiction, challenging the deconstructionist idolatries through the category of sin.

The very possibility of a centered self is ruled out by destructive postmodernism. That is the case both with regard to the divine Self, which vanishes altogether for "death of God" radicals, and for the centered human self—whether centered in God or in the world or in some intermediate moral realm. Reality is reduced to fluctuating relationships. For existentialism the human self exists only in decision; the notion of a universally shared human essence gives way. Once this bizarre leap is taken, the classic doctrines no longer make sense that Jesus Christ is the Second Adam, that the incarnate Logos assumed the essential nature of humankind, and that believers will ultimately be conformed to the divine Redeemer's image.

When Christianity confronted ancient Greek culture with the good news of salvation in Christ, its revelatory morality deplored infanticide, prostitution, and homosexuality, whereas today pagan society not only condones but even encourages these vices. Postmodernism not only denies that truth exists, but it undergirds its program of relativism by a program of literary criticism that strips away objective meaning and absolute truth. The very possibility of an ideal human life is intellectually precluded by the drift of modernity from supernatural revelation and its replacement instead by secular humanism and finally by raw naturalism. The God-centered life is eclipsed by the world-centered self, and this is considered virtuous. With the transition to postmodernism, no centeredness whatever is admissible.

The postmodernist insistence that social relationships are a mask for power need hardly be taken as evidence that there is no authentic self-identity or that there is no universal humanity, or that specifically human values are illusory. Orthodoxy should be able to use postmodernists' weapons to deconstruct deconstructionism and to present an evangelical apologetic. Only by a return to the transcendent Logos might modernity or postmodernity recover absolutes.

Tragedy is compounded when, instead of seizing a possible opportunity to turn postmodernism against itself, the very mind-set of postmodernists, as Veith laments, "is gaining a foothold *within* evangelical churches."[5] The subordination of truth to feeling is seen, for example, in the deliberate avoidance of preaching on hell, simply because people don't "like" to hear about it. The cults offer the masses what they want. The question of evidence or of tests of truth becomes irrelevant. The pulpiteer who makes his auditors feel good about themselves and gives them what they order becomes their spiritual authority. Tolerance is their prime virtue; diversity signals a reminder that we must not be critical of others' beliefs, even if they deplore ours and banish logic.

A generation that shuns conceptual thought—including theology and moral principles—and is moved emotionally by images and pictures, and that flees rational argumentation and the laws of logic, but opts instead for liturgy and mystical experience, is wholly vulnerable to the postmodern flight from the biblical heritage. To be an intelligent disciple of Christ today requires more than emotional verve; it demands a commitment to truth and right.

The ancient Roman persecutors of the Christians rightly sensed that the real threat of Christianity to other religions lay in its claim to be the one true religion. Their proclamation of "one Lord" made the Roman emperor spiritually redundant. The Roman response was to nominate Christians for the death penalty. Almost nobody would die for Christ today: nothing is considered worth dying for—not even the murder of an innocent, let alone a choice between the gods. Pluralism is a mark of modern sophistication, and tolerance of false gods is depicted as Christian sensitivity.

For the Christian the contentions of the culture, whether those of the intellectual elite or those of the popular masses, can never be determinative of right and wrong. It is interesting that in our twentieth century the evangelical discussion of life—which in the Bible brings into focus physical life, spiritual life, and eternal life (in stark contrast to death)—not infrequently has explored the theme of "the victorious life." The Hebrew and Greek equivalents of the terms *victory* and *triumph* do not occur frequently in the Bible, and where they do, their interest is in God's triumph or victory. Even the psalmist exhorts the Hebrews to direct the voice of triumph to God (Ps. 47:1). So too in the New Testament, the focus is on victory that the Lord achieves in and through us ("Thanks be to God who always leads us in triumph" [2 Cor. 2:14]; "Thanks be to God, who gives us the victory" [1 Cor. 15:57]).

Yet two passages in the writings of John the evangelist speak in terms that suggest, even if somewhat dimly, the theme of the believers' triumphant overcoming. They are 1 John 5:4: "This is the victory that has overcome the world" and Revelation 15:2: "I saw . . . those who have the victory over the beast, over his image."

The immediate context of the passage in 1 John declares that what it means to love God is to keep His commandments, and that God's commands are not oppressive. Love of God is not merely an exhilarating emotion, nor is obedience to the divine commands a deplorable legalism. The law might indeed oppress us if we sought by conformity to it—that is, by works of righteousness—to fulfill it as the ground of our salvation, since fulfill it in our present sinful condition we simply cannot. Yet God's law is good, and the godly man or woman will seek to live by it.

What John next emphasizes in this passage is that "whatever is born of God overcomes the world." The reference may well be not to persons alone, that is, to the people of God, but basically to God's commandments, by which the world will ultimately be judged.

The victory that conquers the world is our *faith*—not our inner enthusiasm but the intelligible content of God's revelation, the message of divine law and grace. As believer after believer resists and conquers worldly temptations, the evil world is subdued spiritually by those who believe that Jesus is the Son of God. The Christian life is here set in the world-and-life-view context of the triumphant sovereign, our creator, redeemer, and judge.

The message in Revelation 15 speaks of "those who have the victory over the beast." In view of their faithful testimony, in the face even of martyrdom, the saints are in the Apocalypse repeatedly depicted as triumphing over the beast. "The beast" is metaphorically used in the Apocalypse to designate the enemies of God and of the people of God (cf. Dan. 7; Rev. 13:17). The confessors of Christ emerge triumphantly from supreme tribulation as divine judgment hurls its final blows against a spiritually defiant race.

Here again the spiritual victory is preeminently God's, and only secondarily, through their devotion to Him, that of God's people. There is no place here for an honor roll of variously graded saints, as if any human being possesses in himself/herself distinctive levels of virtuous achievement and contribution. It is God who wins the victory, and in and through His divine activity alone may we speak significantly of a believer's victorious life.

In 1 Corinthians 15:57 we hear the triumphant shout of victory not alone over sin but also over death as its consequence:

"Thanks be to God, who gives us the victory through our Lord Jesus Christ." The passage anticipates 2 Corinthians 2:14: "Thanks be to God who always leads us in triumph in Christ, and through us diffuses the fragrance of His knowledge in every place." As Murray Harris comments, "Christ undertook a battle not rightly his; we share in the triumph not rightly ours."[6]

We in Christ and Christ in us is therefore a succinct summary of the Christian life. To be sure, the ground of our acceptance as sinners in the presence of the Holy Lord is the substitutionary life, death, and resurrection of the sinless Redeemer, and personal faith is the instrumentality by which divine forgiveness becomes ours. There is great confusion today among those who attach God's justification of the sinner in ambiguous ways to human works. There is no doubt that Catholics and Evangelicals today verbally affirm justification by grace through faith. But repeatedly a rider is appended that the Protestant reformers would have condemned, by attaching to this formula the necessity of some works. *Sole fide* is thereby subtly modified. When sanctification is blended into justification as a condition of forgiveness, confusion results both in New Testament doctrine and in Christian experience.

The apostle Paul writes that "God willed to make known what are the riches of the glory of this mystery among the Gentiles: which is Christ in you, the hope of glory" (Col. 1:27). The grand and glorious themes of revealed religion here gain an inner, subjective linkage: the long-hidden mystery, now revealed, is that the eternal Christ takes up residence in the life of God's people. The theme "Christ in you" has larger prominence in the Epistles than many interpreters suggest.

The New Testament portrays the Christian life at times by the imagery either of a walk (Rom. 6:4; 8:1; 13:13; 1 Cor. 7:17; Gal. 5:16, 25; Col. 2:6, etc.), or of a race (1 Cor. 9:24; Heb. 12:1; Gal. 2:2; 5:7; Phil. 2:16). These characterizations serve well to illustrate both understandings and misunderstandings of the victorious life. That the life of the true believer is oriented primarily to the supernatural realm, and no longer primarily to the secular realm, is indisputable. Augustine's comment was truly on target: "Thou hast made us for Thyself O Lord, and our hearts are ever restless until they find their rest in Thee." Yet in this life we participate in a cosmic struggle between God and Satan, good and evil, truth and falsehood. The climax of the Christian life awaits the future when at the Lord's return we shall all be fully conformed to the image of Jesus Christ.

What then of the present interim? What of growth in grace and in our knowledge and obedience to the Lord? Are we engaged only in a time of spiritual *waiting*? Is the victorious life simply a holding fast, a beginning each day where we began the day before, seeking to keep Satan at a distance while we await the climactic day of the Lord's return in final and universal conquest of evil? What then becomes of sanctification? Is there no merit to the theme of progressive salvation, or of progressive sanctification? Does the Christian life begin and end with an emphasis only on the new birth?

If the idea of moral and spiritual standstill is inadequate, what then of the alternative view of a radical experience of transformation that lifts one to ethical perfection or at least holds out the possibility of freedom from all known sin? Is the Christian life a *race* that leaves behind entirely the unregenerate world? Surely the Christian ought never to feel "at home" in a world that lies "in wickedness" (1 John 5:19 KJV). No excuse will readily exonerate the disposition even of some—and more than we might hope—evangelicals today to strike unnecessary compromises with the surrounding culture. Yet is sinless perfection really a biblical option—unless one speaks of the eschatological future, or redefines sin and sinlessness in the present, or focuses on the incarnate Logos?

The Protestant reformers held that even regenerate humanity sins daily in thought, word, and deed—in short, that we will not as Christians live a single day on earth without a necessary dependence on the shed blood of Christ our Mediator. The victorious life does not, in this view, involve a revolutionary leap of total sanctification enabling one to run a sinless race that wholly marginalizes sin and evaporates all need for daily forgiveness. Was it not Jesus who in the Lord's Prayer instructed His disciples to pray daily: "Forgive us our trespasses"?

If the Christian life is not merely a waiting period, and is also not a once-for-all eradication of evil in this life, is it not for all a *walk* that leaves the world behind in intention and in noticeable measure, one that draws motivation and power from fellowship with the risen Lord? Its animating energy is the Holy Spirit, the source of new birth and sustainer of a new and ongoing moral and spiritual life. This walk may have its detours. The regenerate self soon learns that not everything that once seemed acceptable is truly proper. Even the Christian conscience needs at times to be corrected by the Bible. Indeed, the hallmarks of a Christian walk are faithful attendance to Scripture reading and prayer, earnest pursuit of the Christian virtues ("the fruit of the Spirit" [Gal. 5:22]), fellowship with other believers, and outreach to others in sharing the gospel.

In walking, one sometimes encounters unexpected barriers to progress. But there is nonetheless more progress than in simply standing still; ongoing immobility suggests the absence of life. Yet even in a momentarily confused walk at sunset, the risen Lord may suddenly and unexpectedly join us along our Emmaus roads and newly set our flickering hearts aflame. It is life we are concerned about, and if we walk with Christ, the journey will be inevitably victorious.

By the postmodernist every such affirmation of objective truth, of universal good or evil, of a transcendent authority, and of an objectively given word is swept aside. Reality is for each of us declared to be simply what we make it. Pluralism is the name of the game of life; to challenge it is to be intolerant and to fly in the face of the relativity and flux to which everything supposedly reduces.

Here the alleged "death of God" has run its speculative course. God, creation, Jesus Christ, redemption, the Holy Spirit, judgment, justification and sanctification, and eschatology belong to an outdated language game. Absolute truth is a fiction, objective meaning a myth; history is merely our postulation of the past.

Since Christian theology declares that the Holy Spirit uses truth as a means of conviction, we can see that postmodernism maximizes the revolt against the great tradition and heritage of the West. Truth becomes a nonentity, and the holy Scriptures a bit of poetry waiting for our interpretation. It is the deep sorrow of our century that what began as an effort to win the world for Christ in a single generation (let alone in the entire twentieth century) has ended on a note so spiritually devastating.

Yet the evangelical movement has resources to rescue the realities of life from their secular distortion and to restore them again to a more profound conception and content. But strong currents exist within the churches that impede such a recovery. The churches are often too much influenced by the very forces they would confront and alter.

The charismatic renewal and therapeutic counseling have monopolized much of the discussion and understanding of sanctification. Both these movements modify, although in very different ways, the Christian church's historic understanding of the normal Christian life, or of what has in recent times been called the Spirit-filled life. The therapeutic alternative tends in many cases to strip the understanding of sanctification of any and all supernatural elements and to regard as psychologically harmful the curtailment of sexual libertinism and calls for the crucifixion of the natural self. The charismatic movement often pursues the opposite extreme, and calls for an intensified break with the world and a transcendentally ordered life that moves apostolic gifts into the present age.

To be sure, one still finds in secular academe references to Christ and to the Spirit. But such terms are invested with a meaning quite alien to the biblical inheritance. One need only turn, for example, to William A. Beardslee's essay on "Christ in the Postmodern Age: Reflections Inspired by Jean-Francois Lyotard" in Griffin, Beardslee and Holland, *Varieties of Postmodern Theology* (1989). Here we are told that today one can no longer speak of Christ or of the Spirit as have Christians in the past, but that new ways of understanding such expressions are required. For Beardslee the "new" way is process philosophy, although others promote equally unsatisfactory alternatives. Creativity as projected by A. N. Whitehead becomes the ongoing activity of the Spirit. While the Spirit is associated with Christ, readers are told that "in a pluralistic world, we do not claim the exclusive presence of the Spirit in Christ that Christians have sometimes affirmed" (p. 75). "Even those who are drawn by the Spirit to the cluster of meaning that we call Christ might cast about for another way of speaking about this meaning" (p. 76). *Meaning* here becomes a vagabond term. Beardslee acknowledges that the Crucifixion and Resurrection that climax "the story of Jesus" still serve to open up new dimensions of life (p. 77). But this ambiguous confession hardly is equivalent to affirming the Nicene Creed!

Postmodernism is an earth-crafted ideology, one that has no real option but to turn back the clock. The future Judge of men and nations has already been publicly identified by His resurrection from the dead. Firmly anchored in both eternity and time, the Christian life view ongoingly offers triumphant living, while its speculative rivals merely eke out another half-day in the history of thought.

Notes

1. Gene Edward Veith, *Postmodern Times, A Christian Guide to Contemporary Thought and Culture* (Wheaton, Ill.: Crossway Books), 17.
2. Diogenes Allen, *Christian Belief in the Modern World* (Louisville, Ky.: Westminster/John Knox Press, 1989), 2.
3. David Harvey, *The Condition of Postmodernity* (Cambridge: Basil Blackwell, 1989).
4. Quoted from "The Culture of Postmodernism," *Theory, Culture and Society* 2 (Wheaton, Ill.: Crossway Books, 1985): 123ff., by Veith, *Postmodern Times*, 43f.
5. Veith, *Postmodern Times*, 193.
6. Murray Harris, *The Expositor's Bible Commentary*, ed. Frank E. Gaebelein, vol. 10, 332.

PART FIVE

Conclusions

We have celebrated seventy-five years of God's faithfulness at Columbia International University by focusing on the central theme of the school from its beginning: Victorious Christian Living, becoming free and fulfilled. And staying that way! In doing this we have heard from leaders of the movement and from leaders of alternative perspectives as well. We have watched in grateful astonishment as people whose names we know, and some we have met in these pages for the first time, have demonstrated the outworking of the teaching in all aspects of life. We have traced history and wrestled with theology under the tutelage of recognized scholars. How, then, do we conclude? What better way than to take one last look at the past and then turn to exult in the end of it all: the return of our Lord in glory.

James Hatch gives us an overview of the unity and diversity that have characterized Columbia under four very different leaders, and Terry Hulbert reflects on the close connection between Victorious Living and the Second Coming. These two chapters are longer than some because of the subject matter and also to bring our Festschrift to a fitting conclusion.

21

About the Author

James M. Hatch served a pastorate in Mississippi following graduation from seminary, then went to the University of Chicago for graduate work. Upon completing the program there he joined the faculty of (then) Columbia Bible College, and his entire career has been devoted to that ministry. Teaching in the fields of social studies and the Bible, Hatch quickly gained a reputation as a peerless teacher. He powerfully influenced the minds and hearts of succeeding generations. Many regret that Hatch's brilliant integration of the behavioral sciences with biblically revealed truth, all under the authority of Scripture, is attested to only by hundreds of grateful graduates—he never yielded to the constant demands that he write. This essay may be his first venture into writing! "Buck" Hatch and his wife of more than half a century, Mittie, have three living sons, eleven grandchildren, and two great-grandchildren.

About This Chapter

This isn't the dry history of an institution; it's the engaging story of four men. Here you'll find an overview of the lives and teaching on the Victorious Life of the four presidents of Columbia International University, written by the one best qualified to do it. Buck Hatch not only served under the first three presidents, knowing each intimately, his profound understanding of Victorious Life teaching coupled with his brilliant analytical mind enable him to focus on the commonalities of the leaders but also, for the first time, to identify the distinctives of each. The stories are told with historical and theological precision, but the author's warm affection for each shines through.

Victorious Life Teaching from Robert C. McQuilkin to Johnny V. Miller

by James M. Hatch

A ny consideration of a biblical doctrine must be done in the light of Scripture. This study must be based on the actual statements of Scripture and the implications of these statements. Yet, on a deeper level, this study should be done also in the light of the way the Bible handles doctrinal matters. Rather than just present "doctrine" as such, the Bible always gives it in close connection with what God actually is doing on the earth. Since God's great "activity" in Scripture is the redemption of the world, all the doctrines or teachings given by God are deeply related to that redemptive purpose. This doctrine of redemption constitutes the guideline for those who are to be the channels through whom He works redemption. This gives direction to them, especially in the manner of life they must exhibit. Thus the doctrine of sanctification—so central to God's redemptive purpose—is always ultimately related to God's worldwide program of redemption in what we have come to call "missions."

As we look at the teaching of the Victorious Life as taught by the leaders of Columbia International University, it must be seen in connection with the work of God in redeeming the world. These two themes, holiness of life and world evangelism, are inseparable as they both flow from the same source, God's redemptive work, and even a casual contact with CIU will show that victorious Christian living and missions have been its hallmark through the years. We turn now to see how these two areas of God's grace were exemplified and taught by its four presidents.

From the vantage point of one whose life and ministry were vitally changed through all these men, this is more than an academic pursuit. Having taken seminary training under the first president and having taught under the administration of the first three, my reflections will be very personal as we look at "Victorious Life Teaching from Robert C. McQuilkin to Johnny V. Miller."

Robert C. McQuilkin, 1923–1952

It seems to be God's way that He begins a work, not on a large scale, but in a very small "seed," usually in the heart of one man. Thus when He began His work of redemption recorded in Scripture, He began in the heart of Abraham. To him God said, "I will make of you a great nation." In a similar way God began the work of CIU in the heart of Robert C. McQuilkin. Long before there were a multibuilding campus and hundreds of students, God planted the seed of CIU in the heart of a young businessman. The story of his life is the story of Columbia International University in its basic emphases.

In Robert McQuilkin, God found a man of unusual natural abilities. His was a keen, inquiring, open mind, never satisfied with superficial answers. He was of a joyful, friendly, outgoing temperament. Thus, as he began his adult life, he found success in business and also in his church activities. To this gifted man, God gave the twin seeds that were to characterize CIU.

This implantation began when his searching mind examined the teaching of the Bible as to the manner of life that should characterize the Christian. This life was to be one of joy, peace, and delight in the Word of God, of some real measure of deliverance from besetting sin, and of supernatural results from Christian service. As a young Christian, he sensed none of these in his own life. To this sense of need the Lord brought choice servants to share from the Bible and their own experience what God could do in transforming a life.

In keeping with his general makeup, he did not respond lightly. He carefully considered the issue of surrender, the first condition of a life of victory, and with the same care he looked at the matter of faith, the second condition. After careful consideration and with a hungry heart, he took two steps: surrender and faith. As a result, God entered his life and made a deep and lasting change in every area. Thus the message of the Victorious Life became his passion—he had seen this in the Bible, had tasted it in his experience, and longed that other believers should enter into the same experience.

The two conditions for the Victorious Life, which had been so significant in his own experience, were strong parts of his preaching. He pleaded with others to meet the condition that had been so significant to him. They too must feel, "for the first time consciously in my life, there were just two persons in the universe—my Lord and I, and nothing mattered except the will of that other Person."[1] This was full surrender. Then he wanted others to join him in thanking "God apart from all feelings and upon the basis of His Word, that His grace is sufficient, that Christ is actually living in my heart, and that He is meeting all (my) needs."[2] That is the faith that is the victory.

With this seed of holiness of life in place, God also implanted the seed of world missions. This drove him and his wife to seek the will of God regarding their own missionary service as God seemed to be opening the doors for ministry in Africa. But suddenly the door closed—the ship on which they were to sail sank in the harbor! At the same time, however, the door opened for a preaching ministry in Victorious Life Conferences across the nation. About the dual vision, he later writes, "The Victorious Life message, as you know, from the beginning has been linked with the missionary message, and for several years we have been looking forward to a 'world tour' to carry the message of Victory in Christ to the mission fields. I am praying that God may give me the privilege of going 'into all the world' in this way since He has made it clear I am not to take my family for settled missionary work in Africa."[3]

Instead, God had another plan in mind for the one in whom He had planted so deeply the double seed. He put in his heart the vision for a school with the Victorious Life message at its center. So in 1923 God opened the door to lead the fledgling Southern Bible Institute in Columbia, South Carolina, with a twin vision: victorious living and world missions.

For twenty-eight years McQuilkin built Columbia Bible College on that foundation. As an energetic and gifted administrator, he led CBC from only two rooms in the Colonia Hotel to a two-block campus with hundreds of students. As a model teacher, he led many to a balanced study of the Bible and to a personal understanding and appropriation of the life of Christ. In keeping with his gifts and temperament, his teaching was biblical, logical, and systematized. He was deeply aware of the need of so many believers for a new kind of life. The basis of that awareness was what he referred to as the "standard of the Christian life." Whether from the Old Testament's, "The Lord is my Shepherd"—so I have no unmet needs—or the New Testament picture of "He always leadeth in triumph," McQuilkin made very clear the kind of life God expects.

Next, after this high standard and resulting sense of need, came the good news for the believer: the provision God has already made for this kind of life is more than adequate. The full, finished work of the Cross, the power of the Holy Spirit, and the fact of the union of the believer with Christ were given as the "hope of glory."

Next comes the response required from the believer to appropriate this life. As might be expected from his own experiences, the two responses of surrender and faith were a very important part of his teaching. In his preaching, he was almost "evangelistic" in his plea for the needy believer who had heard of God's provision to take these necessary steps. Finally, McQuilkin did include in his teaching those things necessary for continuance and growth in this new life. Though he emphasized the "crisis" of a decision to yield and trust more than the process of growth in godliness, he did teach the necessity of the daily use of the Word, prayer, and Christian fellowship.

Anyone who knew Robert McQuilkin personally cannot be satisfied looking at him merely as a teacher of the doctrine of sanctification. For him, it was never just a doctrine, as wonderful as it may be, but rather it was his very life and he wanted that for others. His son said at his funeral, "I feel that the greatest characteristic of his life was this, that he lived the message that he preached. . . . So wonderfully did God the Holy Spirit work this fruit in his life that I have never known him once to fail his Lord in lip or in action. . . . I know that he has made mistakes and that . . . he was a sinner. But I who knew him well have never known him once to fail his Lord in the slightest way."[4] This is the Victorious Life in Robert C. McQuilkin.

Thus through the life and ministry of Robert C. McQuilkin, God built an educational institution that would be marked by that which characterized its founder, glorifying God by following Him in victorious living and world evangelization.

G. Allen Fleece, 1952–1966

In the biblical record of God's redemptive work, when Moses, who set the eternal guidelines for all by the Law he gave, had completed that foundational work, God said to Joshua, "Moses My servant is dead. Now therefore, arise, go over this Jordan, you and all this people, to the land which I am giving to them. . . . As I was with Moses, so I will be with you" (Josh. 1:2, 5). In the summer of 1952, Robert C. McQuilkin died and the mantle of God's work at Columbia Bible College fell on G. Allen Fleece, one of McQuilkin's disciple partners who understood, practiced, and powerfully proclaimed the dual message of Spirit-filled Christian living and world evangelization. This had become his own message in the pastorate, as a Bible teacher at Moody Bible Institute, and then at Columbia and in a broad conference ministry.

Though very different in natural gifts and experience, Fleece was well suited for the next phase of God's work at CBC. There was the need to solidify and develop the team that McQuilkin had gathered and especially to transpose it into a new "land where it could develop to its full potential." This called for a leader with the kind of radical biblical faith, that having been tested, would prove that all things are possible with God. God found such a leader in G. Allen Fleece, who led in building a new campus through God's miracle provision, time after time.

Anyone sitting under the powerful expository preaching of Fleece could feel the passion of his heart, and that passion was the twofold message laid as the foundation of the ministry by Robert C. McQuilkin. As to world missions, he did not see this as just one possible aspect of a church's activity. As he said in one of his messages, "Missions is an integral part of the life God seeks to impart to us."[5] He is reputed to have taught that every Scripture passage correctly interpreted has a missionary application. He put this imprint on CBC's graduate school, calling it the "Graduate School of Missions."

As to his presentation of the Victorious Life message, he was not given to logical systematizing of the doctrine. His strong gift was to give careful expositions of biblical texts. It was a wonder to see him unfold Bible passages so they became "profitable for training in righteousness." One could almost say, in the light of Fleece's profound expositions, that every Scripture, correctly interpreted, has teaching about the Victorious Life. These expositions came to the hearer where he was, so he could understand it in terms he could translate into life.

The unique way Fleece perceived and proclaimed the Victorious Life was, in the broad issues, the same as that of McQuilkin. First, he sensed the need of many Christians for something qualitatively different. His deep conviction was, as he said in one message, "The difference between Christians is not a matter of degree. There are degrees of the manifestation of the fruit of the Spirit. There is growth in grace. But 'growth' is not the word to explain the basic difference. We do not grow into grace, we grow after stepping into future development."[6] God, who began this good work through McQuilkin, was now moving it on through G. Allen Fleece.

J. Robertson McQuilkin, 1968–1990

When the Lord led Fleece to resign as president in 1966, the board of trustees began immediately its search for the next leader. But by the beginning of the next school year, there was still no one in sight. In fact, for two years "there was no king in the land." During this time the Lord held on to His work and perhaps showed something of the fact that in reality He is the real King.

During this time of searching, the name of Robertson McQuilkin continued to be placed before the committee by various ones. This was resisted by the committee, fearing that some may have just wanted one with the name of the school's founder. As the second year wore on and this name continued to appear, a member of the search committee flew to Japan to see the one who had the "name." He found that he was not a clone of his father but rather had hammered out his own biblical approach to life and ministry. After flying him to Columbia for intensive interaction with the board, there was a clear conviction that God was putting His finger on Robertson McQuilkin to be the third president of Columbia Bible College.

As is usually the case with God's chosen instruments, Robertson McQuilkin was different from the previous two in basic personality. His was an active and analytical mind, not willing to settle for any conclusion until it had been carefully scrutinized against the Word of God and the input of the body of believers. Though he listened to and invited the opinions of others, he was a man of strong convictions. His style of leadership was more of the "team" approach. He faced the awesome task of leading this adolescent institution, now in its new land, into the maturity of a new era. God gave him an unusual ability to lead through some radical changes without disruption or destroying the unique essence of the institution.

In this third leader of CBC there appeared very strongly the "double seeds" that had become the hallmark of the institution. As to the seed of world missions, this had become his ministry. After beginning as a teacher at the Bible College under his father, he was led to head up a struggling Christian high school in Asheville, North Carolina. God used his leadership to bring that school to life and to become a strong force in the kingdom of God. And yet while there, he felt a continuing powerful call to the mission field. All those who knew of his ministry at Ben Lippen School thought he should remain there where he had been so used of God. Only his godly mother felt otherwise. In following God's concern for the world, he went to Japan as a church planter. He was greatly used there to fulfill the Great Commission.

When the call to CBC came, he would not consider it without the input of the elders of the church of Japan. With their strong support, he came. But even at CBC it often came out that he considered this an interim position to his service in Japan. This vision of world missions was infused deeper into CBC and into the church of the United States in ways that cannot be explored here.

As to the primary "seed" of the Victorious Life, this was his first love. He was more theologically analytical than expository in his presentations and continued to hammer out a hermeneutical understanding of the teaching of the Bible on holiness of life. The broad teachings were the same as his two predecessors, and yet there were emphases that were unique to him. He saw the whole and didn't "ride" any particular aspect of teaching on sanctification.

McQuilkin seemed to be stronger on the "process" than the "crisis." His teaching on the Victorious Life was very strong and helpful on the continuation of "the Life." There was much more emphasis on the use of the "means of grace." He did emphasize prayer and use of the Scripture, church fellowship and outreach, but these were all in the context of an intimate and continuing personal relationship with the Lord. Then to these he added suffering. "Suffering may be God's great shortcut to spiritual growth."[7]

Even with these particular emphases, McQuilkin was clear on the main points of the heritage of the message of the Victorious Life. As to the "standard," he held first the clear teaching of the Bible. In McQuilkin's view, the normal Christian life is a life filled with joy, concern for others more than one's own interests, victory over temptation, power in effectively serving God, and a constant, loving relationship with the risen Savior.[8] This is the kind of life God expects and can provide for all believers.

As to the need of many believers, McQuilkin felt deeply that there is among believers a qualitative difference. Some don't need more of what they have but something new. Then they could experience the "normal Christian life." "Some Christians have a life pattern of defeat, whereas others have a life pattern of spiritual success."[9]

As to the glorious provisions of the gospel, here again, McQuilkin was strong. According to him, it is not some new or additional experience. Rather it is to understand and by faith appropriate what was given at salvation. He writes, "I know of no exception to the consistent teaching of the New Testament authors that the solution for the defeated, failing, sinning Christian is to return to what took place at salvation. They were brought from death to life, they were joined to Christ, they were possessed by the Spirit."[10]

McQuilkin resisted many of the illustrations that seem to present the Christian almost as a pipe that is passive, through which the indwelling Christ flows. "The beauty of God's victory in our humanity is that He does it, not by-passing or replacing us. Rather He renews the new person after the likeness of God."[11]

As to the conditions for entering into and maintaining this new life, surrender and trust, these are clearly taught also. Yet Robert C. McQuilkin probably "preached" these more strongly and seemed to keep them separate. Robertson McQuilkin is very clear on these, though he tends to combine surrender and trust as two facets of a single requirement, faith. As he dealt with these, however, he was clear that according to Scripture both are necessary, though surrender was the critical turning point. Feelings of trust would always need to grow.

As to the process, McQuilkin was perhaps clearer than his predecessors, strongly emphasizing the necessity of the "means of grace." Yet his strong point seems to be something deeper. It is not just a matter of doing these things, but something much more wonderful. As he expresses it, "Success in continuing the Christian life, like success in the beginning of it, does not depend on the mastery of some complex doctrinal system or upon the achievement of some esoteric additional experience, but upon a relationship with a person. And that relationship is so simple that a child may understand and experience it."[12] According to this, a believer in this ultimate relationship with his Lord sees the Bible as the means of His speaking to him, prayer as an intimate way of talking to Him, and "church" as a joyful union with others who love Him.

It is beyond the scope of this essay to refer to the many accomplishments of Robertson McQuilkin in his leadership at CIU, and yet it is fitting to note that he continued to gather and train a team in living and serving in newness of life. He did this not only in his chapel messages but also in special meetings with faculty and staff. On one occasion he lead the team to examine each course to see how it could really incorporate the Bible data on holiness of life. About this team, he wrote in a personal letter to me, "I am aware of the unique privilege of living among people most of whom actually do live a consistent Spirit-filled Christian life. The moral lapses are near zero but the positive victories seem so normal. It is not a vain hope that a whole ministry can be so imbued with the Biblical teaching of the normal Christian life that it makes a difference."

Perhaps the greatest manifestation of the Victorious Life was the role McQuilkin was to play at the occasion of his resignation as president. It was not from the sense of a mission fulfilled nor a call to another work; rather it was a joyful willingness to give up his ministry to care for his wife of many years. As she gradually deteriorated from the ravages of Alzheimer's disease, he realized he could not continue in both responsibilities. So he chose to care for her as she had cared for him. So through the months that followed, Robertson McQuilkin took up the career of cooking, housekeeping, and caregiving with joy and no sense of sacrifice. This is the Victorious Life in its glory!

Johnny V. Miller, 1991–Present

For its fourth president, the finger of God pointed to one who was different in background, experience, and gifts from any of the first three. Raised in a migrant family with the influence of a Christian mother, and later the love of a godly wife, Johnny Miller began his walk into the will of God. As a Christian, he went through a time of deep doubt and rebellion. Turning from all that was Christian, he tried to cover the emptiness with worldly things. When this failed to satisfy and thoughts of suicide were finally rejected, God brought him back to Himself through the biblical teaching of a Spirit-filled pastor.

Through the long road of seminary and graduate training, God surprised His servant by making him an effective church planter in Texas. Out of this pastoral experience, God led Miller to teach at Columbia Bible College. After four years there, the strong love of the pastorate led him back to his first love. But again the call came to institutional teaching, this time to Columbia Biblical Seminary. It was there that the board of trustees, following a thorough, worldwide search for McQuilkin's successor, chose Johnny V. Miller as president.

In this, the fourth and current president of Columbia International University, one sees very clearly the "double seed" that continues to be the genius of CIU. These are seen in his personal "mission statement": "My purpose is to glorify God through Christlike living and by motivating people to fulfill the Great Commission."

As to foreign missions, he was fed missionary biographies by his mother as a young person, and he and his wife were planning on missionary service even from high school days. After his formal training, they went to Sweden to become career missionaries. Because of visa problems,

however, this long-range plan was disrupted. When next sensing a call toward Africa, the illness of his father, for whom he
was responsible, blocked the plan. The missionary burden,
nevertheless, has continued as the heart of his life and ministry.

Planted alongside this missionary passion is the other
"seed," Miller's understanding, appropriation, and proclamation of the life that God has for all of His people. Miller's
teaching of the Victorious Life message has the flavor of his
own person. As a scholarly, careful student of the Word and as
a gifted pastor/teacher, it was only natural that biblical exposition would be the medium he used to proclaim the message.

As would be expected, certain aspects of the teaching of
the Victorious Life would receive Miller's special emphasis.
He is deeply aware of the need of many Christians and of the
church as a whole for something different in their manner of
life. All too often he sees Christians whose "faith" does not
require a transformed life. To him the only answer is a biblical
faith that brings the power of God.

Perhaps more than any of the former leaders at
Columbia International University, Miller seems to be more
deeply aware of the pains, hurts, and struggles that many
Christians experience as they face living for God. This comes
first from his understanding of Scripture. He sees great struggles, fears, and weaknesses in Paul, the greatest exponent of
the "Victorious Life." He sees this also in Moses ("Who am
I?"), Jeremiah ("I cannot speak"), and many others. This
awareness of struggles may have come also from his personal
experience and from his pastoral work. In the latter, in a large
church planted by God through him, of the eight hundred
families, two hundred were in some way involved with alcoholism. Later, in a seminary class at CIU, 30 percent of the
students were from alcoholic families. Then he realized his
own fears and insecurities regarding the awesome challenge
of planting a church in an affluent community were not

incompatible with the Victorious Life in and through him. A large, vibrant, Spirit-filled church in that very situation is a testimony to the power of God in and through a weak vessel.

As to the "means of grace" for the continuation of the Victorious Life and growth in it, these are very clear in Miller's life and teaching. As to the use of the Bible in his life, this seems to be the great hunger and drive of his life. This would, at times, lead to some frustration when administrative duties seem to keep him from the kind of searching the Scripture he would desire. As to prayer, according to his testimony, this is not something he "has to do"; it is the delight of his life to meet with his best friend and to ask from the One who is able to do what no human can do. The church fellowship has been such a great part of his gift and experience that the necessity of that "means" goes without saying.

Thus Johnny V. Miller continues to lead this mature institution forward according to the two great "seeds" of its founding fathers. It is still God's working supernaturally in a believer's life to bring about holy living and effective involvement in world missions.

In this very limited look at the "Victorious Life" teaching at Columbia International University from Robert C. McQuilkin to Johnny Miller, we have seen these four as "vessels of gold and silver . . . set aside for noble purposes . . . made holy, useful to the Master, and prepared to do any good work." Scores of graduates of this institution join me in rising up to call them blessed, and more important, to "continue in what they have learned and become convinced of because they know those from whom they learned it" (2 Tim. 2:20–21; 3:14).

Notes

1. Robert C. McQuilkin, *Victory in Christ* (Columbia, S.C.: Columbia Bible College, n.d.), 18.
2. Ibid., 19.
3. Alleene Spivey Hehl, *This Is the Victory* (privately published by the author by Wentworth Printing Corporation, West Columbia, S.C., 1973,) 23–24.

4. *CBC Victory Message* (Fall 1952), 14.
5. G. Allen Fleece, audiotape #56034, CBC tape library.
6. "The Hand of God on Job," audiotape, CBC tape library.
7. J. Robertson McQuilkin, *Five Views on Sanctification* (Grand Rapids: Zondervan, 1987), 181.
8. For a full statement of these characteristics, see *Five Views on Sanctification*, 151.
9. Ibid., 160.
10. Ibid., 166.
11. Ibid., 179.
12. Ibid., 166.

About the Author

Terry Hulbert presided as dean of Columbia Biblical Seminary and Graduate School of Missions during its period of great growth from fewer than one hundred students to more than four hundred (1972–88). It became a major center of influence in the world of missions during that time. Subsequently, Hulbert served the entire institution as vice president for Academic Affairs of Columbia International University. He began his academic career teaching at Northwestern College in Minneapolis, served as pastor of several churches, founded the Theological College of Central Africa in Zambia, and, before coming to Columbia, was director of the mission agency under which he served, the Africa Evangelical Fellowship in the United States. Hulbert and his wife, Jean, have one daughter who serves with her husband in the United Arab Emirates.

About This Chapter

What a grand climax to a volume on victory in Christ—the victory of Christ! Here the life of victory is linked to the second coming of Christ as perhaps nowhere else in the literature of either the Second Coming or of victorious Christian living. The excitement of that intimate connection will grip you with a new passion for holiness as you review the overwhelming New Testament emphasis on the link between the two themes. Not occasional or incidental. Pervasive! And yet, so many preachers on prophecy are little noted for emphasis on Spirit-filled living and so many preachers of holiness refer little to the second coming of Christ. But indeed there is coming a day when we will be free and fulfilled, free to be all we were designed to be and filled to all the fullness of God. Hallelujah! In the meantime, then, how shall we live? Terry Hulbert points the way.

The Victorious Christian Life and Christ's Return

by Terry C. Hulbert

Our Lord's return is now seventy-five years nearer than when Columbia International University opened its doors! The passion of our first president and our "founding mothers"[1] to live and teach the Victorious Christian Life was born of their hope for Christ's appearing. Five years before CIU was born, Robert C. McQuilkin wrote: "Is the hope of his coming a real hope for you that makes it the incentive to be ready and makes it a real event to watch for with expectation, as for the return of a loved one? . . . The Victorious Life truth is vitally linked with the hope of his coming."[2] Linkage between Spirit-controlled living and Jesus' return defined CIU three-quarters of a century ago. More than seven decades closer to that great moment, how much more should it motivate our generation!

Our Focus

When we think about Christ's coming we ask questions: When will He return? Do events in the Middle East point to His return in our lifetime? Will He come once to judge the world, sending the lost to eternal punishment and the saved to eternal bliss? Or will He come before (or after) the Tribulation to take away His church in a "rapture"? Are there "signs of the times" that we should be reading and interpreting?

These questions have challenged Bible students for centuries, but the most important question often goes unasked and unanswered. Given the certainty of Christ's return, Francis Schaeffer asked, "How shall we then live?" When we see Christ, our eschatological questions will be irrelevant, but how we have lived will become eternally important.

What had Jesus Himself emphasized when He spoke about His return? What was the burden of Paul and John and Peter as they wrote of this great event? What can we learn from the writings of these apostles and from Jesus Himself about the relationship between His return and how it should affect our daily lives? On that night before He went to the cross, Jesus linked His promised return with how His followers should live, "Wash one another's feet . . . love one another . . . abide in me . . . go and bear fruit." A half-century later the apostle John recalled this connection as he wrote, "And now, little children, abide in Him, so that when He appears, we may have confidence and not shrink away from Him in shame at His coming" (1 John 2:28 NASB). R. C. McQuilkin expressed it this way, "If we are not enjoying the Victorious Christian Life, which is just another way of saying 'abiding life,' we are not ready for his coming. And if we are not ready for his coming, we are not ready for his presence in our midst now."[3]

We often limit being ready for Christ's return to salvation. Will He find us saved, qualified to be with Him for eternity? Many Scriptures do warn about the danger of not believing on Him before His return, since that moment fixes forever our eternal destiny. The same question also relates to the moment of our death, whether sudden or expected. Daily we are edging toward that final moment that will mark forever the meaning of our lives. But believers must ask and answer that other crucial question, "How then should we live?" Answer: Victoriously, ready every moment for His return!

This linkage between the Victorious Christian Life and the coming of our Lord has defined the dynamic of Columbia International University for three quarters of a century.

Our Authority

In the Gospels Jesus' warnings of judgment relate primarily to the nation Israel, although the principles taught have broader applications. For instance, one prediction of His sudden return is climaxed by this scenario: "There will be two women grinding at the same place; one will be taken, and the other will be left" (Luke 17:22–37; Matt. 25:36–25:13 NASB). In Luke 19:11–27 Jesus adds the element of the believer's accountability illustrated by the stewardship expected in the investments of various amounts of *minas* entrusted to servants in the absence of their king. The parable of the virgins in Matthew 25:14–46 also features accountability in anticipation of Christ's return. Although these passages emphasize salvation and stewardship, they do not reflect the provision of Spirit-empowered living that followed Pentecost.

In the Epistles we find at least ten exhortations that directly connect victorious Christian living to the return of Christ. Rather than assurance of salvation, they emphasize the expectation that when He appears, He will find us "blameless," living in daily victory over sin.

1. Philippians 1:6

For I am confident of this very thing, that He who began a good work in you will perfect it until the day of Christ Jesus. (NASB)

God's progressive perfecting of believers prepares them for the "day of Christ." His coming not only climaxes this process but it also constitutes the purpose for which God is doing this work of grace. Our spiritual growth relates directly to our anticipation of Christ's return.

The words "day of Christ" also remind us of the judgment-seat-of-Christ event predicted in 1 Corinthians 3:13.

Here Paul again connects the quality of the believer's life and ministry to "the day" of Christ's return: "Each man's work will become evident; for the day will show it, because it is to be revealed with fire; and the fire itself will test the quality of each man's work" (NASB).

God intends for believers to grow spiritually throughout their lives. He does not wait until Christ's return to perfect them. His work is expressed by the word *epiteleo*, meaning "to fully finish, bring to completion." Salvation is more than birth "from above" (John 3:3); it means growing and maturing now. The context shows that this is a process that anticipates a future evaluation. The apostle also challenged the Galatians that "Having begun by the Spirit, are you now being perfected by the flesh?" (Gal. 3:3 NASB).

> So that you may approve the things that are excellent, in
> order to be sincere and blameless until the day of Christ.
> (Phil. 1:10 NASB)

The use of "in order to" affirms a causal relationship between authentic Christian living and the day of Christ. This kind of life requires the discerning of spiritual values, "approving the things that are excellent." God enables believers to test their motives, actions, decisions, and plans and to select the best, the outcomes of which will have value when Christ returns. In this verse Paul also notes two characteristics of the Victorious Christian Life: "sincere," probably derived from "to judge by sunlight," and "blameless," from a word that means "not stumbling against." As we look for our Lord's return, we grow in transparency and genuineness of character and in concern for how we affect others.

> Work out your salvation with fear and trembling; for it is
> God who is at work in you, both to will and to work for
> His good pleasure. (Phil. 2:12–13 NASB)

Who is responsible for this perfecting, God or me? Paul's reference to the "good work" begun by God in the believer (v. 6) anticipates his linking this concept ("for it is God who is at work in you") with the believer's personal responsibility ("work out your own salvation with fear and trembling") in Philippians 2:12–13. The Victorious Christian Life is not solely the work of God or solely the effort of the believer. It is a life driven by the dynamic of a Father who wills His child to consistently overcome the gravitational pull of the enemy and thus to grow in grace. It also requires the enthusiastic commitment of the child to achieve that victory. The Father not only begins this "good work," He persists in motivating and empowering the believer to achieve its goal. To "work out your own salvation" is our mandated responsibility, not an option to be treated casually. We must pursue this goal in "fear and trembling," conscious that today may be the "day of Christ."

> So then, my beloved, just as you have always obeyed, not as in my presence only, but now much more in my absence, work out your salvation with fear and trembling. . . . So that in the day of Christ I may have cause to glory. (Phil. 2:12, 16 NASB)

Paul frequently uses the word *parousia* ("presence") to refer to Christ's coming and to His subsequent presence with believers. In this passage he uses the term to describe his own absence (*apousia*) and His anticipated coming (*parousia*) to Philippi. In effect, Paul's message to the Philippian believers that they should live and work well in his absence parallels his exhortations concerning Christian living in Christ's absence and His anticipated presence at any moment. In addition, the purpose of Paul's command, "that in the day of Christ I may have cause to glory" (v. 16), reflects the motivation for our living victoriously, that we might bring glory to Christ when He appears.

2. Colossians 3:1–4

> If then you have been raised up with Christ, keep seeking the things above, where Christ is, seated at the right hand of God. Set your mind on the things above, not on the things that are on earth. For you have died and your life is hidden with Christ in God. When Christ, who is our life, is revealed, then you also will be revealed with Him in glory. (NASB)

Seeking things of eternal value prepares us for the coming of the One who is now seated above and for our residing with Him there for eternity. It is what Vance Havner called "living in kingdom come." "Seek first His kingdom" (Matt. 6:33 NASB) describes the heart of authentic Christian living. It is a life controlled by the conviction that Christ is coming and that He will transfer us instantly into His physical presence. Anticipating that moment, eternal realities become the focus of our aspirations and the plumb line of our values. Because Jesus may return at any moment unannounced ("just like a thief in the night"), we are challenged to daily adjust our lives to the ethos of heaven. To the extent we experience the Victorious Christian Life now, we will minimize cross-cultural shock when we are suddenly extracted from this earthbound environment and inserted into the environment of Christ's presence.

We are not only to seek the things above, we must set our minds on them. The apostle Paul often emphasized the right mind-set as a basic requirement for biblical Christian living. For instance, in Philippians 2:1–5 he uses the word *think (phroneo)* three times. He challenged the Philippian believers to be of the same mind, to have humility of mind, and to have the mind of Christ Jesus. Because we will "be revealed with Him in glory" we have a strong motivation to align our attitudes and values to His, to think as Christ thinks in preparation for meeting Him and living with Him when He is revealed.

3. 1 Thessalonians 3:12–13

And may the Lord cause you to increase and abound in
love for one another, and for all men . . . so that He may
establish your hearts unblamable in holiness before our
God and Father at the coming of our Lord Jesus with all
His saints. (NASB)

The Victorious Christian Life is not self-centered. That
would be contrary to the character of Christ. An authentic
vertical relationship with God is always reflected in loving
horizontal relationships with other believers and a concern for
the lost. The "love one another" exhortations in the New
Testament testify to God's purpose that we should reveal Him
as a God of love for His children and for those still outside His
family (Rom. 13:8; 1 Thess. 4:9; 1 Peter 1:22; 1 John 3:11, 23).
In the Upper Room Jesus Himself established the model, the
motive, and the mandate for Victorious Christian Life relationships. He commanded His disciples to wash one another's
feet and to love one another (John 13:14, 34–35), and to love
one another as the Father had loved Him and He had loved
them (John 15:9, 12).

Our motivation to "increase and abound in love" is to be
found in hearts that are established unblamable in holiness
when Jesus returns. The apostle Paul often links these
dimensions of the Victorious Christian Life, "unblamable"
(*apemptous*) and holiness (*hagiosune*), to the presence/coming
(*parousia*) of Christ. That in the presence of a holy God, our
hearts would be established holy and unblamable should be
the highest possible motivation for living the Victorious
Christian Life.

4. 1 Thessalonians 5:2, 23

For you yourselves know full well that the day of the
Lord will come just like a thief in the night. . . . Now may
the God of peace Himself sanctify you entirely; and may
your spirit and soul and body be preserved complete,

without blame at the coming of our Lord Jesus Christ.
(NASB)

The "day of the Lord" refers to that period when God will intervene directly in human history to fulfill His prophetic commitments to judge evil and to establish His kingdom. Since the time of this event cannot be predicted, Paul emphasizes constant readiness. In effect, he defines this readiness in terms of victorious Christian living. His exhortations not to sleep, to be alert and sober, and to put on spiritual armor (vv. 5–9) reflect a posture of anticipation. Pursuing the horizontal dimension of the Victorious Christian Life, we are to "encourage one another and build up one another" (v. 11).

Authentic Christian living does not compartmentalize our lives. For instance, it is characterized by sexual purity (4:3–8), brotherly love (4:9–10), personal responsibility (4:11–12), respect for leaders, consideration for other people, rejoicing, prayer, thankfulness, and a concern for excellence (5:12–22). The apostle further focuses his definition as he prays that God would "sanctify you entirely." The victorious Christian is one who is "cleansed and reserved clean for the exclusive use of the Master." The words "spirit and soul and body" and "preserved complete" remind us that there is an integrated wholeness, a unified realness in everyday living that characterizes the life of victory. The result, that we would be found "without blame" at Christ's coming, links this goal directly with His return.

5. Titus 2:11–13

> For the grace of God has appeared, bringing salvation to all men, instructing us to deny ungodliness and worldly desires and to live sensibly, righteously and godly in the present age, looking for the blessed hope and the appearing of the glory of our great God and Savior, Christ Jesus. (NASB)

Beginning with the appearance (*epiphane*) of Christ to provide salvation and concluding with His return (*epiphaneian*) in glory for His own, these verses directly connect our conduct in the present age to His return. Based on what He accomplished for us on the cross, the instruction in verse 12 captures the essence of the Victorious Christian Life. It says no to living as though God didn't exist ("denying ungodliness") and resists the gravitational pull of a world system under Satan's control ("worldly desires"). Positively, it begins with a mind that is balanced and disciplined. To "live sensibly" translates a root word that also occurs in verses 2, 4, 5, and 6. It is a mind that is liberated by the power of Christ and motivated by the joyful expectation of His appearing.

Christ's return is a "blessed hope"; it should not be a fearful dread. The certainty of the event should be a strong motivating factor. It gives meaning and incentive to godly living, providing focus for the direction and destiny of our lives.

6. Hebrews 10:23–25

> Let us hold fast the confession of our hope without wavering, for He who promised is faithful; and let us consider how to stimulate one another to love and good deeds, not forsaking our own assembling together, as is the habit of some, but encouraging one another; and all the more, as you see the day drawing near. (NASB)

"Hold fast the confession of our hope without wavering." People who hope are people who are prepared to conform their lives to be prepared for the realization of that for which they hope. If we are really convinced that He will return ("our confession"), this event will determine the way we live. Our unwavering hope is the firm conviction that Christ will return, ("the day" of verse 25). We can fully trust Him to keep His promise in the Upper Room, "I will come again, and receive you to Myself" (John 14:3 NASB). We can also fully trust Him to empower us to live in victory over sin until that day. Certainly this is one of the "greater works" (John 14:12)

Christ will perform through the Holy Spirit in His own absence.

As in the churches in Philippi (1:10) and in Corinth (3:13), "the day" (of Christ's return) became the controlling motivation for authentic Christian living. The focus of this Hebrews passage is on interpersonal relationships within the church. Not only does this hope affect our own lives, it also determines the way we relate to other people. The Victorious Christian Life is not an end in itself; it "frees" God to use us in the lives of others, both in evangelism of the lost and in edification of the saved. Following "Let us draw near" and "Let us hold fast the confession," the third exhortation in the passage, "Let us consider," challenged that second generation of believers to a mutual ministry of "stimulation to good deeds." The word translated "to stimulate" is actually a noun, *paroxysmos,* which usually means "irritation" or "exasperation." The Lord's return is so important that believers are exhorted in these strong terms to become involved in the lives of other believers, to encourage them to produce spiritual fruit. Better to be irritated into action now than to be ashamed when Christ appears! The focus of this ministry of stimulation and encouragement is the local assembly of believers. Mutual ministry requires regular contact with other believers. The urgency of the need for this ministry increases the closer we come to His return, thus forging another link between this event and authentic Christian living.

7. James 5:7

> Be patient, therefore, brethren, until the coming of the Lord. Behold, the farmer waits for the precious produce of the soil, being patient about it, until it gets the early and late rains. (NASB)

Although we can appreciate the high level of expectation of Christ's immediate return among first-century Christians, it needed to be tempered with the realities that Jesus had intentionally not revealed the time of this event and that He had given specific assignments, both in maturing and in ministry until He returns. Realizing that impatience can affect negatively the believer's preparation for Christ's coming, James cited the kind of patience illustrated by the farmer. As there is a sequence in the germination, growth, and harvesting of a crop, so there is an orderly process in the fulfillment of Christ's prediction that He will build His Church. Without the coming of the early rains in October and November in Israel and the latter rains in March, there is no harvest. Although the time frame of this age is not defined precisely as it is in agriculture, it is evident that the sowing and reaping of the gospel worldwide require time. One day the Lord of the Harvest will come, and He will interrupt forever the metaphor of the agricultural sequence (John 4:35–38).

James's exhortation not only emphasizes the need for us to be patient (literally "long-suffering") but also the importance of our activity while we wait. As the farmer must sow and reap, so we must "sow and reap." Our expectation of the return of Christ should motivate that dimension of our Victorious Christian Life that results in "bearing much fruit." And that fruit is only borne by one who "abides in Him," the one who lives in daily submission to His lordship (John 15:4–8).

8. 1 Peter 1:7

> That the proof of your faith, being more precious than gold which is perishable, even though tested by fire, may be found to result in praise and glory and honor at the revelation of Jesus Christ. (NASB)

"Trust and obey," are the foundation stones of the Victorious Christian Life. Remembering his intimate contact with Jesus, Peter emphasized this trust (*pistis* = "trust" or "faith") as he encouraged later generations of believers with the words, "And though you have not seen Him, you love Him, and though you do not see Him now, but believe in Him, you greatly rejoice with joy inexpressible and full of glory" (v. 8 NASB). It is this conviction that Jesus lives and will return that Peter so confidently proclaims. It is this faith in the person of Jesus Christ, though tested like gold refined by fire, that characterizes the life of the Christian controlled by the Holy Spirit. He resists temptation and lives in anticipation of seeing, at any moment, the Savior he has trusted for so long. Faith involves the conviction of fact that cannot be verified by the senses (Heb. 11:1–2). The great dynamic of the Victorious Christian Life is our unshakable conviction that one day we will see the same Jesus we have read about in our Bibles, talked to in prayer, and proclaimed in witness.

9. 2 Peter 3:10–14

> But the day of the Lord will come like a thief. . . . Since all these things are to be destroyed in this way, what sort of people ought you to be in holy conduct and godliness, looking for and hastening the coming of the day of God. . . . Therefore, beloved, since you look for these things, be diligent to be found by Him in peace, spotless and blameless. (NASB)

Peter cites the awesomeness of coming judgment on the heavens and the earth as a strong reason for our need to be ready to meet Christ. Believers should realize that the God who has the power to melt the elements with fervent heat is the One to whom they are personally responsible. Although this destruction will occur at a time when least expected, it is an event the believer should welcome. So desirous should believers be of Christ's return that, from a human perspective, they will evidence the kind of diligence and enthusiasm that would indicate they want it to happen as soon as possible (v. 12).

The apostle uses *spoudazo*, "to make an intense effort," to remind us that authentic Christian living is not automatic. It requires intentionality and commitment. The "Helper" then enables us to present ourselves "spotless and blameless."

These are words Paul often associated with Christ's return. Peter uses these words of Jesus in 1 Peter 1:19, translated there "without blemish or defect." Perhaps the fact that these terms are used both for Christ and the believer reflect John's promise that "when He appears, we shall be like Him" (1 John 3:2 NASB).

10. 1 John 2:28–3:3

> And now, little children, abide in Him, so that when He appears, we may have confidence and not shrink away from Him in shame at His coming. . . . Beloved, now we are children of God, and it has not appeared as yet what we shall be. We know that, when He appears, we shall be like Him, because we shall see Him just as He is. And everyone who has this hope fixed on Him purifies himself, just as He is pure. (NASB)

In this classic passage the aged apostle deftly demonstrates the direct linkage between the return of Christ and the Victorious Christian Life. He draws us back into the Upper Room, where Jesus promised that although He was about to go to the Father, He would return. Written a half-century later, this passage brings us back full circle to Jesus' teaching at that last Passover meal. His purpose was to prepare His disciples to reveal Him through their lives after He departed. This is authentic Christian living, Christ so completely controlling us as we "abide in Him" that, as Paul expressed it, "it is no longer I who live, but Christ lives in me" (Gal. 2:20 NASB). His "abide in Him" (*meno*) in verse 28 recalls Jesus' "Abide in Me" (John 15:4 NASB).

John addressed his readers here as Jesus had done that night, as *teknia*, "little children" (John 13:33), a term of endearment emphasizing birth into the family. Using a related word, he exhorts the "little children" to purify themselves, to become like the One who is pure. Jesus had made the same point in His prayer, asking the Father to "Sanctify them in the truth" (John 17:17 NASB).

When He appears, we will be like Him, instantly, without any sin in thought, motive, or action. Is this what our hearts desire? Is our hope fixed on this kind of Person and on our being like Him? If so, the anticipation of His appearing will motivate us to continually purify ourselves, to live in victory over sin. Impossible? Just as it has not yet appeared what we shall be like when He comes, so, for many we have yet to see how much He can transform our lives now to "be conformed to His image." The power is His, the choice is ours. The results are as awesome as they are different: confidence or shrinking away from Him in shame! What greater motivation for victorious living than our anticipation of meeting our victorious Lord? (Rom. 8:37).

Our Motivation: How Then Should We Live?

To be "ready for His coming" does not mean to live in terror of being found misbehaving at that critical moment or to expect His commendation for our conforming to self- or community-imposed standards. Readiness for Christ's return is not achieved by living in fear, nor should it be motivated by a desire to "earn an A on the final exam." In reality, we face a "final exam" every day, for each day could be the last day of the "course."

It is tempting to evaluate our attitudes and actions by asking ourselves if we would want Jesus to find us in a certain questionable activity or place when He returns. This is a reasonable check, but the issue is much larger than how we are behaving at that instant when He interrupts our lives unannounced. Our rewards and commendations from Christ are not determined by our status at the moment of our death or of His return. When we stand before Him at the judgment seat to "be recompensed for [our] deeds in the body, according to what [we] have done, whether good or bad" (2 Cor. 5:10 NASB), He will consider the whole pattern of our lives from the time we entered His family. He will take note of the trajectory of our lives, the pattern of downward or upward trends.

This long-term perspective directly relates His return (or our death) to our pattern of not practicing sin and to our growth in grace, to His "perfecting" that which He began at our spiritual birth. At that moment His Holy Spirit came to reside in us, our bodies became His "holy of holies" where He presences himself (1 Cor. 3:16). He has provided the resources and incentives needed for us to live in victory over sin (2 Peter 1:4), to be salt in a rotting world and lights in dark places (Matt. 5:13–16), and above all, to "live Christ" (Phil. 1:21). We became stewards of these resources, not just to preserve them but to produce, to "bear fruit that remains" (John 15:16).

Robert C. McQuilkin leaves us with two classic challenges:

> If the coming of the Lord is in God's Word linked so vitally with a life of personal holiness, it is essential that Christians should understand what the Spirit has revealed to us concerning the truth of his coming. . . . It is not an accident that most of those who are rejoicing in the Victorious Life are, or are becoming, deeply interested in the truths of the Word concerning Christ's coming.
> Are we rejoicing in the "present tense of salvation," victory by grace through faith? Are we surrounded by his own light in these dark days because we know that the world's problem is to be solved by grace, by God himself, so that we live "soberly, righteously, and godly in this present age: looking for the blessed hope, and the glorious appearing of the great God and our Savior Jesus Christ?"[4]

The linkage between our readiness for our Lord's return and victorious Christian living is "loving His appearing" (2 Tim. 4:8) because we love Him. And because we love Him, we keep His commandments (John 14:15). Keeping His commandments is abiding in Him, and the one who abides in

Him does not practice sin (1 John 3:6). This is living victoriously, to "have confidence at His appearing."

Notes

1. The Southern Bible Institute, precourser of Columbia Bible College, was founded by a group of young women who "prayed the School" into existence.
2. Robert C. McQuilkin, *Victorious Life Studies* (Philadelphia: Christian Life Literature Fund, 1918), 65.
3. Ibid., 64.
4. Ibid., 65.